Dear Poppa

TO: Major Reuben Berman
O 29755 6
1st C.C.R.C. group
APO 639, NYC

(CENSOR'S STAMP)   SEE INSTRUCTION NO. 2

FROM SA
3528
(Sender's

Dear Poppa

THE WORLD WAR II
BERMAN FAMILY LETTERS

Compiled by Ruth Berman
Edited by Judy Barrett Litoff

MINNESOTA HISTORICAL SOCIETY PRESS
St. Paul

Cover and frontispiece: Drawing by Sammy Berman, August 24, 1944.
Sammy drew a picture of his family—mother, brother, and two sisters—
and the family car. The sun is crying because Poppa is missing.

Minnesota Historical Society Press
St. Paul 55102

❧ The paper used in this publication meets the minimum requirements of the American
National Standard for Information Sciences—Permanence for Printed Library Materials,
ANSI Z39.48-1984.

Manufactured in the United States of America
10 9 8 7 6 5 4 3 2 1

International Standard Book Number 0-87351-357-6 (cloth)
0-87351-358-4 (paper)

Library of Congress Cataloging-in-Publication Data

Dear poppa : the World War II Berman family letters / compiled by Ruth Berman ;
edited by Judy Barrett Litoff.
p. cm.
ISBN 0-87351-357-6. — ISBN 0-87351-358-4 (pbk.)
1. World War, 1939-1945—Children—United States—Correspondence. 2. Youth—United
States—Correspondence. 3. United States—Social life and customs—1918-1945.
4. Berman, Reuben—Correspondence. 5. Berman family—Correspondence.
6. Children and war—United States. 7. Youth—United States—Correspondence.
I. Berman, Ruth, 1942- . II. Litoff, Judy Barrett.
D810.C4D347 1997
940.53'161'092273—dc21
[B] 97-6447

All photographs are from the collection of the compiler.
Photographers are Arnold Rosten, p. 3 (all), 18, 19 (both), 93, 133, 156, 218,
233, 282; Gene Garrett, p. 43, 96, 196, 305.

Dedicated by all of us
with love
to the memory of
Isabel Esther Rosenstein Berman
1909–1989

Contents

Introduction

America's Children at War

JUDY BARRETT LITOFF

∽

I wish you would come back because I want to see you.
I wish you would come back right now. Are you going to
come back some day, Poppa, are you, are you?

This innocent plea appeared in a letter dictated in May 1943 by four-year-old Sammy Berman, shortly after his "Poppa" departed for overseas duty in Europe (p. 11). It captures the anxiety and longing that children throughout the United States experienced when their fathers left for war. Family separations and dislocations were commonplace during the 1940s, with just over 18 percent of America's families contributing fathers, sons, and brothers to the armed services during World War II.[1]

Samuel (Sammy) Berman, along with his nine-year-old brother, David, and six-year-old sister, Elizabeth (Betsy), composed hundreds of unabashedly honest letters to their father, Reuben, an army physician stationed in Europe from June 1943 until September 1945. Although the Berman children occasionally penned handwritten letters, most of their correspondence was dictated to their mother, Isabel, who, with minimal interjections, typed exactly what the children told her. The publication of this unique collection of letters from the Berman children, along with selected correspondence about family life from their parents, offers us the first significant opportunity to incorporate the actual wartime voices of America's children into accounts of the Second World War.[2]

The letters are reprinted exactly as they were dictated or written, without spelling or grammatical corrections. Parentheses denote when Isabel interjected her own comments into the children's letters. Only about one-third of the letters that the Berman family wrote during World War II appears in this volume. In fact, the extensive wartime correspondence of Isabel and Reuben that focuses on topics other than the children could form a book all of its own.[3]

Throughout the wartime years, mail was universally recognized to be the number one morale builder for service personnel overseas as well as their loved ones stationed at home. The arrival of the mailman, the bugle call to mail distribution, or the opening of the mail deposit box in the local post office were precious times in everyone's life.[4] Writing to his daughter Betsy on June 19, 1944, Reuben underscored the importance of the mail when he commented: "Do you know what I like most of all? It's letters from home. From you and the boys and Momma" (p. 136).

America's children, like their adult friends and family members, could hardly have failed to understand the significance of letter writing in wartime. Magazine covers featured children, mothers, and war brides writing letters and receiving mail from loved ones in the military service. Advertisers were quick to use "mail call" to promote their products. Government posters, with messages such as "Be with him at *every* mail call," lined the walls of local post offices and public buildings.[5] Schoolteachers organized letter-writing campaigns and contests for their students. In Atlanta, Georgia, for example, Rusha Wesley, principal of Lee Street Elementary School, located the names and addresses of more than three hundred graduates of the school who served in the military. She and her students sent hundreds of handmade cards and letters to Lee Street graduates stationed at "far-flung fronts."[6] Schoolchildren from Warwick, Rhode Island, wrote to schoolchildren in Warwick, England.[7] Children wrote to General Douglas MacArthur to tell him about their war work and wish him speedy victory in the Pacific.[8] Even preschool children, such as Sammy Berman, quickly learned the significance of writing to "Poppa" and hearing from him.

As the war expanded, the volume of mail rose enormously. Following British precedent, the United States government began to experiment in 1942 with reducing mail to microfilm size for shipping and then enlarging the photographs for distribution to addressees. Victory Mail, or V-mail as the procedure was more commonly called, saved much-needed space in scarce wartime transport. Letters with a bulk weight of 2,575 pounds could be reduced to a mere 45 pounds when processed in this manner. V-mail letters were written on specially designed 8½-by-11-inch stationery, available at all post offices. Each piece contained space for about seven hundred typewritten words. After shipment, the letter was delivered to the recipient in the form of a 4-by-5½-inch photograph. Isabel observed in December 1943 that V-mail from Reuben took no longer to arrive than a conventional air-mail letter (p. 62).[9]

Although many wartime letter writers were reluctant to use V-mail because the letters were often difficult to read and seemed incomplete, like receiving a postcard, the Berman family corresponded mainly by V-mail. In a September 1943 letter to her husband, Isabel explained why she preferred V-mail to regular letters. Discounting Reuben's argument that V-mail contributed to the illegibility of his handwriting, she replied:

> Reuben, my darling, the trouble is with you. Your writing is practically illegible to most people irregodless. Please use V mail. I have a filing system. I put all your V mail letters on a safety pin. When people come over and say, "What do you hear from Reuben?" I just hand them the file and they read to their heart's content. The hand written letters don't fit into the filing system (p. 38).

Isabel Berman, like war wives throughout the United States, composed "miles of sentences" during the more than two years that she and her husband were separated.[10] She wrote about coping with inadequate gas rations, searching for new overshoes for the children, and tending to childhood illnesses, such as measles, chicken pox, tonsillitis, and ear infections. Other topics included the cantankerous coal furnace, their diminished income, the turkey shortage during the Thanksgiving of 1944, and, of course, the myriad activities of the children. She bemoaned the fact that she did not write Reuben every day because "sometimes it gets so late at night before I am through the work that I let it go" (p. 23). But Reuben understood, reminding her that "you have a big job on your hands taking care of four little ones" (p. 204).

In contrast to most other war wives, Isabel also took time out from her busy schedule as a "single mother" to type letters dictated to her by the children. Determined to maintain a close family circle, despite the wartime exigencies that separated them, Isabel devoted many hours to these dictating sessions. Acknowledging the difficulty of this task, Reuben wrote in June 1944: "Momma must get typewriter's cramp some evenings what with three dictators around" (p. 136). In addition, she supplemented the children's letters by sending drawings, photographs, and occasional "home" recordings and movies to Reuben.

When Reuben was drafted in July 1941, the Bermans, who were Jewish, had been married for a decade. Theirs was a strong and secure marriage based on love, trust, and respect. In a July 1944 letter written in honor of their thirteenth wedding anniversary, Reuben remarked, "We have had a very happy married life. I think we have solved the important secrets of how to be happy 'though married'" (p. 147). Two months later he wrote: "The beautiful part of our marriage is our complete trust and understanding" (p. 204).

Although the popular and scholarly press devoted a great deal of attention to the pros and cons of "war marriages," the impact of the Second World War on mature "depression marriages" was rarely the subject of discussion.[11] Despite the difficult economic times of the 1930s Depression and the pervasive anti-Semitism of that era, the Bermans managed fairly well. Reuben established a successful medical practice in Minneapolis while Isabel worked on her doctoral degree in psychology at the University of Minnesota. David, Betsy, and Sammy were born during this decade. A fourth child, Ruth, was born in November 1942, the same year that Isabel received her Ph.D.

Following Reuben's induction into the army, the Berman family packed up their furniture, rented out their Minneapolis house, and became "camp followers."[12] Throughout the wartime years, millions of people were on the move in the United States as one of the major demographic shifts in the history of the nation took place. The Census Bureau estimated that 15.3 million civilians moved during the war years, over half of them across state lines. Another 16 million men and women were in the armed forces, some 12 million of whom were stationed overseas. With almost 20 percent of the population on the move within a four-year period, this was a mass migration that surpassed even the westward movement of the nineteenth century. People hurried to new jobs opening up in shipyards and war plants. Families, like the Bermans, crisscrossed the nation as they sought out the precious times they could steal together "for the duration" or for as long as would be granted them at the military bases where their husbands and fathers were stationed.[13]

Within less than a two-year time span, the Bermans lived in three different states. From August 1941 until June 1942, they lived in San Antonio, Texas, where Reuben directed a medical processing unit for Army Air Corps cadets at nearby Kelly Field, and Isabel worked as a statistician at Randolph Field. Their next move took them to Fort Knox and Louisville, Kentucky. Early in 1943, Reuben received his third and last stateside station, MacDill Field near St. Petersburg, Florida. Once again, he was joined by his family.

Reuben's overseas assignment, which eventually encompassed work with an intelligence unit that investigated Luftwaffe medical research installations, came in late May 1943. As he headed to Fort Dix, New Jersey, to await shipment to England, Isabel remained in St. Petersburg where she began the demanding preparations for moving a family of five, including a six-month-old infant, back to Minneapolis. Isabel's early letters to Reuben contain information about the difficulty of securing train reservations, the complicated logistics of packing up their belongings, and the problems she encountered as she attempted to arrange for temporary rental housing in Minneapolis while waiting for their own home to be vacated by their tenant. On June 3, she wrote:

I am afraid I haven't handled this moving business any too well. . . . Today was one of those days when everything goes wrong. The disposable diapers and the car seat failed to appear in the order from Sears. The laundry did not come back and I had to go after it. . . . My wrist watch is not ready yet. I have no reservation of any kind from Chicago to Mpls and I do not know where I shall stay in Minneapolis. Matters of small concern when there is a war going on (p. 15).

War wives like Isabel Berman could find a great deal of advice in the press and even in books on how to ease the difficulties of traveling in wartime. Wives were told what to pack and "how to live in a trunk." Magazine articles discussed the special hazards of traveling on crowded trains with young children, exhorting mothers to take extra precautions and carefully prepare for the trip. Mothers were advised to avoid the logistical problems associated with carrying too much luggage and, at the same time, to bring sufficient diapers, bottles, baby food, and other necessities. The title of a wartime publication on this topic, issued by the federal government, *If Your Baby MUST Travel in Wartime,* emphasized the difficulties. Yet for many women, such as Isabel Berman, traveling with young children simply could not be avoided.[14]

By the time the Bermans arrived in Minneapolis in early June, Isabel had already begun the practice of having the three older children dictate letters to their father. Almost every letter that the children "wrote" included a direct reference to the war. Indeed, it is not too much to say that the Second World War became part of their *weltanschauung*.

The letters of the Berman children contain numerous descriptions about their favorite war toys. Commentary about battleships, airplanes, tanks, and jeeps were interspersed throughout the letters of David and Sammy. Both boys also talked about how they built military models out of cardboard and wood. War toys were always among the gifts that they received on their birthdays and for Chanukah. Emphasizing the commonly accepted gender differences of the 1940s, Betsy wrote that she had "stand up paper dolls" (p. 25) that were WACs and nurses, and she expressed particular pleasure upon receiving a nurse outfit from Gramma Sarah for Chanukah (p. 60).

For entertainment, the children went to the movies, and their letters tell of seeing war films, such as *Memphis Belle, Guadalcanal Diary, Destination Tokyo,* and *Thirty Seconds Over Tokyo.* They listened to Hop Harrigan, "America's Ace of the Airways," on the radio as he successfully dodged enemy bullets. Annual trips to the Minnesota State Fair in late summer included further reminders that a war was raging. The children wrote about viewing American and German military equipment on display, visiting exhibit booths representing the

United Nations, and enjoying the "General Vitamin" food exhibit of the 4-H Club with its "armies" of fruits and vegetables divided into "companies" of vitamins A, B, and C. A special treat for Betsy was the purchase of a pin called Tanya in support of Russian War Relief.

Music and art played an integral role in the lives of the Berman family. Reuben was an accomplished clarinet player, and Isabel enrolled the three older children in clarinet, piano, flute, and eurhythmic lessons. Trips to hear the symphony orchestra were frequent, where, on one occasion, they observed the orchestra making records to send to servicemen. Art lessons and visits to art museums were also commonplace. While visiting the Walker Art Center, they viewed an exhibit of the drawings by Russian children. Moreover, many of the letters that the children sent their father included drawings with wartime themes. In November 1944, Reuben told Sammy that "you must be a very busy boy to turn out so much art work. . . . Sometimes I pass around the pictures of airplanes you send me and all the pilots here think that you draw a Flying Fortress very well for a six year old boy" (p. 219).

At school, the children participated in paper drives for the war effort, shared their father's letters and war souvenirs, including a prized Nazi pin, with their classmates, played war games at recess, and prepared reports on the war. In addition, they saved their money for the purchase of war stamps and bonds, helped their mother with rationing, and supported the wartime admonition to "use it up, wear it out, make it do, or go without." When Isabel purchased a dozen dinner plates, David cautioned his mother: "'Now, Momma, we didn't really need these plates. You know, you are supposed to wear it out or make it do'" (p. 259).

The children's letters offer clear evidence that they understood that the consequences of war included widespread death and destruction. Sammy, in particular, was concerned with the harsh realities of war. In November 1943, he informed his father that "when the war is over I want you to show me the houses that have been bombed and exploded and the bombed cannons" (p. 48). In another letter, he blurted out: "Why don't you go and kill a German? Don't you use anti aircraft guns? . . . Where do you keep your pistol?" (p. 72). Even impending surgery did not mute Sammy's fascination with the war. While in the hospital waiting for his tonsils to be "tooken out," he described a rocket as "a great big bullet with a machine in it and if it hits you you'll die" (p. 149).

So extensive was the children's involvement and interest in the war that they even had dreams about the conflict. Sammy, for example, wrote about a "very good dream" in which his father was back in Minneapolis. But, in this same letter, he also reported that he had dreamed that he had "made a Japanese airplane crash" and heard the pilot say to the copilot, "I bet he doesn't know that we've got swords" (p. 95).

David, who was well aware of the importance of increasing the nation's vital food supply, joined a junior gardeners' organization and planted a Victory garden in a nearby vacant lot. In late June 1945, he proudly informed his father, "My garden is coming along. . . . The weeds are under control. I cleared away some more space and planted four rows of beans. My radishes are almost ready to eat" (p. 290).

The three older children carefully followed their father's frequent admonitions to "keep yourself posted about this war" (p. 44). They listened to news reports on the radio, watched newsreels at the movies, and read newspaper and magazine accounts of the war. For his part, David lined his room with world maps so that he could mark the advance of the Allied Forces.

Well informed about the significance of the massive D-Day landing of June 6, 1944, both Sammy and David included thoughtful comments about the Allied invasion of France and the harm that might come to their father who, although they did not know it at the time, was still stationed in England. Writing on June 7, 1944, Sammy pondered whether his father might be killed or wounded: "I hope you're not shot because if you're shot I'll feel very bad because I would like to have a poppa, you same poppa, that same poppa" (p. 124).

As the oldest of the children, David's comments were usually more informed and sophisticated than those of his siblings. In fact, Reuben once remarked in a letter to Isabel: "David is so mature. I love the way he is always remarking on affairs" (p. 129). On several occasions, David expressed dismay that his father had not been promoted to lieutenant colonel. In January 1945, he protested: "I have a new complaint to make to General Of The Army Isenhower. You've been a Major for 3½ years. It's about time you get to be promoted to a Lieutenant Colnel and a week after that Colnel" (p. 246). On April 14, 1945, two days after the death of President Franklin D. Roosevelt, David told his father that he felt "horrible" about the president's death (p. 270). Isabel reported that David endorsed the establishment of "a league of nations with police power" as the best way to achieve a "new world" (p. 128). But perhaps David's most astute comments came with the end of the war in Europe when, on May 6, 1945, he told his father:

> At long last we have had victory over the would be destroyers of mankind. For 6 years the Nazis oppressed humanity in ways which have never been exceeded in the history of the earth. But now I want to get to the point. I believe that now that we have won victory over the Nazis, you and other men should be allowed to come back home again. . . . Have you seen any of the prison camps? Please for God's sake Don't (p. 273–74).

Of course, many of the letters of the children were filled with declarations of love, longing, and concern for the safety of their father. Less than a month after Reuben's departure, David abruptly wrote: "I hope you are not dead already" (p. 20). In September 1944, Betsy remarked: "If i had wings like a angel I would take some bombs and fli over to germany and japen and bom them. then you could come home sooner. I want you most if all" (p. 201). Referring to the fact that his father had not had a leave in eighteen months, David announced in November 1944 that "if something doesn't happen pretty soon I'm going to write to General Isenhower" (p. 229).

Sammy, who was not quite five when his father left, seemed to have the most difficulty in understanding his "Poppa's" absence. In December 1943, a perplexed Sammy mused: "I wish you were back this day. Once in a show well I saw some soldiers coming back. Why don't you come back?" (p. 56). Like many wartime children, he sought the attention of a surrogate father, turning to Isabel's cousin Sam Rush for this purpose. As Sammy's memories of "Poppa" were blurred by time and distance, his father began to take on a larger-than-life quality. In several letters, Sammy compared Reuben to Abraham Lincoln. On June 20, 1944, he remarked: "You aren't like Abraham Lincoln but you're almost like Abraham Lincoln. There's only one thing that's not like Abraham Lincoln. It's to spank. But if

Abraham Lincoln spanked I would say you were *just* like Abraham Lincoln, just exactly" (p. 138–39).

As they grappled with the meaning of the war, the Berman children struggled to distinguish between the atrocities masterminded by the Axis leaders and the conduct of the ordinary people of Germany and Japan. When Sammy told his father, "I don't want you to be kind to the Germans or Japanese because they're mean," Betsy quickly interjected, "Don't you want him to be nice to the Japanese babies and the Japanese mommas and the Japanese daddies who are not in the army." Having listened to his older sister's comments, Sammy continued, "I'll let you like the German babies and the German people who are not in the army," but then he also added, "Hitler . . . is a very wicked man." In this same letter, he recited a poem that emphasized his dislike of the Japanese emperor: "Hirohito, I hope you choke when Tokyo goes up in smoke" (p. 124). On May 2, 1945, shortly after Reuben arrived in Germany, David asked his father: "How is Germany? How do the German civilians feel about the war? How do the German prisoners act?" (p. 271). Three weeks later, with the war in Europe now over, he pondered: "Have you seen any German youth? If so what is their attitude to you? What is the attitude of all the German people?" (p. 280).

In his letters home, Reuben did not unduly shield his family from the horrors of war. Even with wartime censorship regulations in effect, he composed letters that carefully balanced accounts of his daily routine with sensitive commentary on the ravages of war. He wrote about life in wartime England, with its petroleum, food, clothing, and fuel shortages, and he noted that "an English family spends a lot of time together in one room where the fire is" (p. 97). In September 1944, he described the "terrible and wonderful sight" of V-1 buzz bombs and the destruction that they caused (p. 202). Yet he also included detailed descriptions of his visits with the Maurice Edelman family, and, at his urging, David and Betsy began corresponding with the two Edelman children. Other letters told of the antics of a stray dog, Rafni, that he adopted. He explained how Rafni had learned to ride on the handlebars of his bicycle, and he even included a stamp of Rafni's footprints at the bottom of one letter.

In an August 1944 letter to "Dear Children," Reuben described a picture in a newspaper of a French child, a "little wan creature with legs wasted and belly swollen from starvation," and reminded them that "it is nothing more than an accident of geography that the struggles of the world have overflowed elsewhere and haven't engulfed our home" (p. 165). Shortly after his arrival in France in March 1945, he wrote to Betsy about seeing "a little boy of nine hopping about on one leg. The other was machine gunned off by a German who was having some fun with French civilians coming out of a church one Sunday morning." He continued: "I am telling you that because I saw the boy myself. I want you to know what is going on over here" (p. 265).

Throughout his absence, Reuben worried that the children might forget him. At the same time, he marveled at how they had grown and matured. In an effort to reach out to David, he wrote a long letter in September 1944 in which he told him "stories about what I did when I was ten. Your age" (p. 188). A letter to Betsy included a philosophical paragraph about his "simple ideas about bringing up children" (p. 192). Occasionally, he wrote to Ruth, including a birthday letter in which he observed that this is "the second one that I'm not home to give you two kisses for it" (p. 216). He delighted in the news that Ruth picked out a picture of him and called it "Poppa." Of course, he received comfort and reassurance from the children's letters, remarking to David in December 1944, "It makes it a lot easier to stand this separation to know that all of you at home remember me. . . . your letters convinced me that as far down as Sammy I am still a real poppa" (p. 237).

Even as the war was raging, the Bermans began to discuss their postwar plans. During the summer of 1944, Reuben wrote to Isabel and suggested that they move to California and establish a medical practice in Sacramento at the end of the war, as he believed that more opportunities awaited him on the West Coast. Although Isabel disagreed, she went ahead with his request to make application for his California medical license. When the children heard this news, they also entered into the discussions. Taking the democratic values of the war years quite literally, they did not hesitate to tell their father that they did not want to move to California. Betsy was adamant on this matter, informing her father, "I don't want you to practice in Sacramento. . . . When the war is over, we are going to get a little house and a big garden and a cow and an apple tree out at the lake [Lake Minnetonka]" (p. 155). David was just as unyielding: "Now you look here if you dare go to Sacramento you can go by yourself because I'm not going to that horrible place with no lake. I'm going to Hudson Bay. Put that in your pipe and smoke it. I'm sorry" (p. 158). In a later letter, however, he partially recanted, saying that he was "very sorry I got mad at you but Sacramento is strictly no good. If you really want to go some place let's go to Alaska and have some fun" (p. 171). Given this outburst of opposition, Reuben decided that they would defer any final decision on the matter until his return.

By the late spring and summer of 1945, with the war in Europe finally over, Reuben became "very restless." He groused about the point system of demobilization and redeployment, arguing that "the point system entitles us to three children only but I can't pick out the extra one so we'll have to keep all four" (p. 281). He began his July 4 letter to Isabel: "Waw! Waw! I'm crying to go home." For Reuben, as well as for most American troops stationed in Europe, the uncertainty shrouding their return to the United States resulted in the "most trying" of times, for "we think our job is all but done and we want to go home" (p. 292–93). Further complicating the situation was the possibility that the troops might be shipped to the Pacific to fight the war that was still raging there.

Only with the final surrender of Japan in August did Reuben's spirits begin to rise. The dropping of the atomic bombs at Hiroshima and Nagasaki ended the war much sooner than he and others had expected, but he still worried about the ultimate meaning of this new and powerful weapon. Writing to Isabel two days after the August 6 bombing of Hiroshima, Reuben commented: "Everybody is buzzing about the new atomic bomb. . . . It doesn't take much foresight now to predict that if we have another war every major city of both sides will be destroyed. . . . All in all if we are not to see the complete annihilation of modern civilization we must prevent further warfare" (p. 302).

These last days of separation were equally difficult for Isabel and the children. In her last letter to Reuben, she emphasized that "it is a little hard to write when I have no letter to answer." Sammy, moreover, was no longer comforted by the solace of his surrogate father, Sam Rush. Isabel reported an incident in which a frustrated Sammy declared to Sam Rush: "I hate you. I do not want to see you again. I am lonesome for my poppa, not for you" (p. 303–4).

Finally, on September 17, 1945, Reuben wrote the letter that Isabel and the children had "been waiting for," telling them that he had received his orders for the States. Although he did not anticipate arriving in New York until October 8, he was still happy because he was "going home." Following twenty-eight months of separation, he simply concluded, "I love you. Reuben" (p. 304–5).

Thankfully, the letters of the Berman children survived the war and the postwar years. Their letters are honest, unassuming accounts written "at the scene" for an absent father and with little idea that historians would one day be interested in their content. They represent the complexity of the experience of war for many of America's children. Better than any available source, they exemplify the many important ways that children throughout the United States actively engaged in the extraordinary events of that era. They provide new meaning to the idea that World War II was "everybody's war"—including that of America's children.

Notes

I would like to offer my deepest appreciation to my dear friend and colleague, David C. Smith. Although his name does not appear on the title page, *Dear Poppa* is unmistakably a product of our collaborative project, The World War II Letters of United States Women.

1. William M. Tuttle, Jr., *"Daddy's Gone to War": The Second World War in the Lives of America's Children* (New York: Oxford University Press, 1993), 31.

2. The most comprehensive work on United States children and World War II is William M. Tuttle, Jr.'s, pioneering study, *"Daddy's Gone to War."* In the early 1990s, in an effort to include first-person testimony in his work on America's home-front children, Tuttle solicited letters from Americans, now in their late fifties and sixties, about their childhood experiences during World War II. Eventually, more than twenty-five hundred individuals wrote to him. Despite the richness of the information contained in these letters, Tuttle had tapped into people's memories—memories that had been tempered by a half century of successive events. He did not, however, make extensive use of the actual wartime letters of America's children because he was unable to locate such correspondence; see Tuttle, *"Daddy's Gone to War,"* x–xi. Over the past decade, David C. Smith and I have conducted an exhaustive search for the World War II letters of United States women. This search has resulted in the identification of occasional letters by chil-

dren. A few of these children's letters appear in Judy Barrett Litoff and David C. Smith, *Since You Went Away: World War II Letters from American Women on the Home Front* (New York: Oxford University Press, 1991). For letters of British children evacuated to the United States during World War II, see Jocelyn Statler, comp., *Special Relations: Transatlantic Letters Linking Three English Evacuees and Their Families, 1940–45* (London: Imperial War Museum, 1990).

3. Bracketed material within a letter is in roman type if it is needed for sense and in italic type if it adds information. The entire collection of Berman family letters from World War II is archived at the Minnesota Historical Society and is available to researchers.

4. For an analysis of the relationship between mail and morale during World War II, see Judy Barrett Litoff and David C. Smith, "'Will He Get My Letter?': Popular Portrayals of Mail and Morale During World War II," *Journal of Popular Culture* 23 (Spring 1990): 21–44.

5. Litoff and Smith, "'Will He Get My Letter?'" 24–28.

6. Lee Street School Papers, Atlanta Historical Society, Atlanta, Georgia.

7. Letter of Ida Cayouette to the author, June 11, 1996. Ida Cayouette has approximately twenty letters that children from Warwick, England, wrote to her and her sister, both of whom lived in Warwick, Rhode Island, during World War II.

8. Record Group 3: Southwest Pacific Area, Commander-in-Chief Correspondence, MacArthur Memorial Archives and Library, Norfolk, Virginia.

9. Litoff and Smith, "'Will He Get My Letter?'" 22–23.

10. On this topic, see Litoff and Smith, *Since You Went Away,* 23 (quote).

11. For a discussion of the contemporary debate on "war marriages," see Judy Barrett Litoff and David C. Smith, *Miss You: The World War II Letters of Barbara Wooddall Taylor and Charles E. Taylor* (Athens: University of Georgia Press, 1990), 11–12.

12. See, for example, Barbara Klaw, *Camp Follower: The Story of a Soldier's Wife* (New York: Random House, 1943).

13. Litoff and Smith, *Miss You,* 68; Tuttle, *"Daddy's Gone to War,"* 51.

14. *If Your Baby MUST Travel in Wartime,* Children in Wartime No. 6, United States Department of Labor, Children's Publication No. 307 (Washington, D.C.: Government Printing Office, [n.d.]). For a discussion of the difficulties of traveling in wartime, see Litoff and Smith, *Miss You,* 70–74.

Prelude

The Berman Family at War

RUTH BERMAN

〜

My earliest memory is of seeing a uniformed stranger walk into the house. I thought to myself, "Who's that strange man?" The memory cuts off there. I don't remember being told the stranger was my father. He had vanished overseas two and a half years before when I was six months old.

When Hitler invaded Czechoslovakia in 1938, the United States delayed taking action. The country had not fully recovered from the Great Depression, and Hitler's menace seemed far away. But it was soon obvious that the threat was too great to avoid. The nation as a whole did not go to war until after Japan attacked Pearl Harbor on December 7, 1941. But in the summer of 1940 my father, Reuben Berman, started spending his weekends (and occasionally whole weeks) working for the army, examining National Guardsmen. A Minneapolis physician specializing in cardiology, he was asked to examine draftees in towns in Minnesota and the Dakotas. The boys who passed would mostly be sent to Bataan in the Philippines.

His own draft notice arrived July 1, 1941.

During the year that followed, he was an Army Air Corps examiner at Kelly Field in San Antonio. His wife, Isabel, and their three children went with him, renting out their house in Minneapolis.

In June 1942, he was transferred to a unit that was being prepared to go overseas, first at Fort Knox near Louisville, and then at MacDill Field in Tampa. In late May 1943, his unit was sent to Fort Dix in New Jersey to await transport, and around the beginning of June they sailed to England, arriving in Liverpool June 23. Isabel and the now four children (I was born in Louisville on November 15, 1942) returned to Minneapolis and rented a cottage at nearby Lake Minnetonka for a few weeks until they could move back into their home.

Reuben and Isabel had been married twelve years, since July 26, 1931, and this was the first time they had been apart for more than a few weeks. Most of those rare separations had been in 1933. Jobs were scarce during the Great Depression for doctors just finishing their internships and especially scarce for Jewish doctors in Minneapolis. Medicine all over the country still had enough anti-Semitism to impose quotas on the numbers of Jews who would be allowed into medical schools, into internships, and onto the staffs of hospitals. Minneapolis was labeled the capital of anti-Semitism in 1946.[*] The shock of the war and aggressive action at the state and local levels led to the end of this unenviable distinction.

My father's first job after internship was as the physician for a Civilian Conservation Corps camp near Orr in northern Minnesota. The CCC camps gave employment in the depths of the Great Depression to many young workers—and the occasional doctor. My mother was doing graduate work in psychology at the University of Minnesota and came up to the CCC camp every other weekend. Their first child, David, was born April 10, 1934, in International Falls, which had the closest hospital.

After his year with the CCC, Reuben entered private practice in Minneapolis, as Moses Barron's partner. Isabel continued her graduate work, receiving her Ph.D. in 1942, just a few months before I was born. Between David and me, Elizabeth (February 27, 1937) and Samuel (July 17, 1938) were born. Elizabeth was and is usually called Betsy. Sam's childhood name was more complicated because my mother had wanted to call him Peter and went right on calling him Peter in spite of the birth certificate that made him a namesake of his great grandfather Samuel Berman.

---

[*]See Carey McWilliams, "Minneapolis: The Curious Twin," *Common Ground,* Autumn 1946, p. 61–65, for a discussion of this topic.

David, cutting willow boughs, about 1939

Betsy, 1939

Sammy on the dining-room table, 1940

During the war, Peter was lonesome for his father, incomprehensibly far away. Both grandfather Alexander Berman and grandfather David Rosenstein had died in 1931. Peter looked to Isabel's cousin Sam Rush for an adult male friend. Soon he decided that Sammy was a better name than Peter. Thus in the letters he used the name "Sammy" but occasionally was referred to as "Peter."

Sam and Anna Rush were both Isabel's cousins (Anna was Sam's and Isabel's first cousin once removed; see Genealogy, p. 315), and as their house was only a few blocks away from the Bermans' home in Minneapolis, the two families were much together. Two-year-old Betsy was the flower girl when the Rushes' daughter, Rosalind, married Second Lieutenant Lincoln Simon in 1939.

Isabel and Reuben had a "mixed" marriage: his parents were "Litvak" Jews, Alexander Berman from Kroz and Sarah Cohen from Calvaria in Lithuania; Isabel's parents were "Romanische" Jews, David Rosenstein from Kishinev, Bessarabia, and Gertrude Spiegel from Ramnicu Sarat, Romania. The Bermans belonged to the Conservative Beth-El Synagogue, which they helped to found; Isabel's family belonged to the Reform Temple Israel.

Reuben and Isabel maintained a double membership in Temple Israel and the Conservative Adath Jeshurun Synagogue, which was closer to their Calhoun neighborhood home than Beth-El on the North Side. But the double cost was a burden, and the less ritualistic practice of Reform appealed to both of them. Isabel dropped their Adath membership during the war. The children's letters reflect some of this tug-of-war between sects.

The two families, in spite of these differences, had many similarities. Both grandfathers were businessmen. Alexander and his two brothers went into a fur-and-hide business as Berman Brothers, the forerunner of Berman Buckskin. David Rosenstein had the Town Market, a furniture store. Each family had four children; Reuben was the youngest, following Rose, Bill, and Ted, and Isabel the oldest, followed by Arnold, Sylvia, and Jack. Both families valued formal education and learning of all kinds.

In both families, many members wound up serving in the war. Isabel's brother Arnold Roston (the family shortened their name during the 1930s) went into the navy, and Jack served with the American

Red Cross. Reuben's cousins E. B. (Buddy) Cohen, Abe Berman, and Iz Goldberg were called up to serve as armed forces physicians.

Isabel and Reuben, an ocean between them, began writing back and forth to each other, sometimes almost daily. In this, they were like many others separated by war. Isabel, however, did something unusual. Every few days she called the three older children together around the typewriter and asked them, "What do you want to tell Poppa?" She then typed to their dictation.

Freed from the mechanical difficulties of putting words on paper, they were able to say what they wished, in spite of being so young— nine, six, and not quite five in June 1943. Dictation made it possible for them to express themselves with a length and complexity young children cannot normally manage—and, as children, they opened their hearts as adults rarely do. (My favorite is David's explanation, June 24, 1943, of why he hit Sammy on the head with a croquet mallet: "After all, you know, Poppa, I'd rather hit Sammy than have Sammy hit me.")

Isabel did not censor them but simply put down whatever they wanted to say. Occasionally, however, she interjected a comment of her own in parentheses. The earlier letters, especially Sammy's start-and-stop letters, suggest that she would sometimes prompt the children to keep going by asking, "Don't you want to tell about . . . ?" The children soon learned to enjoy telling about their doings. In addition, David and Betsy handwrote some of their later letters.

Dictating sessions must have taken an hour, or two hours, at a time. It was a heavy investment of time for a "single" mother with four small children to take care of. But she wanted Reuben and the children to feel that they were not completely estranged. Somehow she found the energy.

Occasionally she went to stores that made "home" records to have the children play music they were studying or tell stories or recite or sing for their father. When David sang in the Sabbath service at Adath Jeshurun Synagogue, Isabel splurged and spent $13.50: five unbreakable 10-inch records at $2.00 apiece, two of David's Sabbath singing and three of all the children, plus two breakable records at $1.75 apiece of David's singing as a present for David's grandmother Sarah Berman, recorded in two sessions, one at the store and one as a house call (letters of December 29, 1944, January 6, 9, 18, 1945). Once in a while, when cousin Nathan Berman could get film for his movie camera, she would ask him to make movies to send Reuben. Stationed in the British Isles until March 1945, he could arrange access to a phonograph or a projector and screen. Sadly the films and records have not survived. (Reuben does not remember if they were lost in being sent home or if they were lost later.)

The children's letters, and Isabel's letters about them, give a detailed portrait of what it was like to be growing up in wartime Minnesota. It was a slower time, when people were more dependent on the immediate family, the extended family, and nearby friends for companionship and amusement. Computer games did not exist. Television did not arrive in the Twin Cities until KSTP-TV (Channel 5) began broadcasting in 1948. A second station, WTCN-TV (Channel 4), went on the air a year later.

Along with clothes, camera film, sugar, and many other supplies considered essential, gasoline was rationed. Car trips had to be planned and limited carefully. Buses and streetcars were the primary means of transport. The amusement park at Excelsior on the shore of Lake Minnetonka loomed even larger in children's lives than the vast amusement parks in the area now—Valleyfair in Shakopee and the Mall of America's Camp Snoopy in Bloomington. The annual Minnesota State Fair had the impact of a visit now to Disneyland or Disney World.

The children made much of their own amusement. For instance, Betsy and Sammy created cardboard pioneers (April 25, 1944) to fight off cardboard bandits armed with bows (cardboard and rubber bands) and arrows (toothpicks). The children also performed a play (August 19, 1944) about Sir Richard and the Dragon (evidently composed by Betsy).

The extremes of summer and winter weather were felt more keenly. Air conditioning was rare in homes. Part of the popularity of movies was that the movie houses were air conditioned. A coal-burning furnace would keep the house warm in winter quite effectively, but a family had to consider carefully how many tons of coal they could afford to buy and how many would be available under rationing. Once they had their coal, they had to keep the furnace stoked. The

Berman house had an Iron Fireman, a mechanical stoker, but at intervals it broke down, scattering hot coals and threatening to set the house afire.

Childhood illnesses were more extreme, too. Penicillin, only just discovered, was not yet available to the civilian population. Scarlet or rheumatic fever, ear abcesses, measles, German measles, mumps, and assorted influenzas had to run their course.

Isabel soon realized that the correspondence was something special. The earliest letters Reuben sent home are lost—probably because so many friends and relatives wanted to borrow the letters to read. But she had her side of the correspondence; Reuben would pack up the home letters to return each time he ran out of space to keep them. Beginning in September 1943, she began saving all the V-mail correspondence systematically, bundling packets together. Even so, some letters were lost, especially ones sent to Reuben on the front in France and Germany. Some did not reach him, and some went astray in being sent home.

Isabel did not try to save the much smaller number of letters they exchanged by regular mail, although one "regular" letter is included in this collection: the one of December 23, 1943, written "on the back of Peter's drawing."

This collection contains about a third of the letters. The letters from home focus on those by and about the children. The home letters are by Isabel and the children, except for two by other relatives about the children, one by Reuben's cousin Buddy Cohen (April 7, 1944) and one by Reuben's mother, Sarah (May 16, 1944).

Reuben, on his side, could not give a comparably detailed portrait of the war. Regulations forbade him to say much about what he was doing. As David said (December 9, 1943), "everything is a military secret over in England except the trees and houses." During the time when he was in Britain, Reuben was assigned to an intelligence unit. He spoke German, and his job was going to be investigating Luftwaffe medical research installations, but he could not actually carry out his assignment until German territory began to fall to the Allies, which was well after D-Day.

Much of his resulting free time he spent getting to know people, especially his second cousins, the Naftalins, and also writer-politician

Maurice Edelman and his family. The Edelmans (no relation to his Minneapolis friend Hyman "Chimes" Edelman) lived in Chesham Bois in Buckinghamshire, just outside London, near Bovington Airfield, where Reuben was then stationed. The Naftalins he knew through their mutual cousins, the Minneapolis Naftalins (including Arthur Naftalin, who became mayor of Minneapolis). He was related to them through his grandmother, Chieh Naftalin Berman. Most of the Naftalins lived in Glasgow, and Reuben visited them on holidays, but one branch—Dr. Joe Naftalin, his wife, Leonore, and their son, Adrian—lived in London, and they became close friends.

When Reuben was sent first into France and then into Germany, he became much more directly active in the war, and his letters (in spite of censorship restrictions) told much of what he was doing. His letters are supplemented by an Epilogue (p. 309) with the account of his war activities he wrote for the fiftieth anniversary of D-Day.

In a May 17, 1944, letter to Reuben, Isabel suggested, "Maybe sometime we can take your letters and ours and write a book, 'Letters from a wife and four children to a husband overseas.'" Mama, here it is.

The Letters

The Berman Children at War

Departure: 1943

~

May 20, 1943

870 26th Ave. N., St. Petersburg, Fla.
to Major Reuben Berman 0-297556
HQ 14th Bomb Wing, APO 3683 NYC

Dear Poppa:

I wish you would come back because I want to see you. I wish you would come back right now. Are you going to come back some day, Poppa, are you, are you? I wish you would come back. Should I talk on the telephone to you? You come back and then you could see the baby some more. You would see what the baby is doing. Then I would be glad to see you. I would like you and I would show you what I get. I will type you a letter but you won't come back any days, Poppa. If you come back any days tell me when you do. If you come back any days I'll like you.

Peter

Dear Poppa:

We chased a mouse over to Mr. Sprinkel's, and we told Mr. Sprinkel There was a mouse or a rat and Mr. Sprinkel stepped on it. He killed the rat. Dear Poppa: Turtle got lost and I wished you would find him. I put my finger in the turtle's mouth and he bit me. That's all I want to say.

Sammy

Reuben and Isabel, about 1943

⤲

May 25, 1943

Dearest Reuben:

Yesterday we received two letters from you, one dated the 19th and one the 21st. I was especially touched by your letter of the nineteenth. Yes, we have had twelve happy years together, but let us hope that this separation will not be long and we will be together for many years more. I wish you had taken the little radio. If you want to leave something else behind to make room for a radio I will be glad to send it to you. Yesterday we went swimming at the municipal beach. The children love to be in the water. All three of them go out as far as they can and wave about with the tide. Peter was a regular angel yesterday afternoon to make up for being too difficult in the morning. He started out with "Why didn't you take me to Minneapolis last year? Why didn't you, Momma? You took Betsy and you didn't take me. The next time you must take me and leave Betsy here. Talk to me. Why don't you talk to me, Momma?" "Why didn't you dress me first? Betsy and David got dressed before me. You'll have to take off their clothes and put mine on." "Why didn't you wait for me to ring the bell on the street car? Why didn't you Momma? You're a mean Momma. You'll be an old lady. You won't be a young lady anymore. I don't like you, Momma. Why don't you talk to me?" This last accompanied by hitting, scratching and pinching. But in the afternoon the halo was on.

Love, Isabel

‚

May 27, 1943

Dearest Reuben:

Today we received no letters from you. It is now past ten o'clock and I have just got the last child to bed. That was Ruth Amelia. I don't know whether it was the bananas she had for supper, a possible tooth coming in, the heat or fatigue that got her down but she surely cried. Both David and Betsy had to tell me momma da baby is crying. Why don't you do something. The combination of water, orange juice, aspirin, bath, rest in front of fan, finally wore her down and she is asleep now.

This afternoon Mrs. Townsend and Rippy [*a neighbor in St. Petersburg and her son*] came over. We were carrying on polite conversation in which David joined. I was telling how Etta [*Swenson, who worked for the Bermans as a maid in the mid-1930s*] used to think I did not know how to bring up children because I never spanked them but I thought I did fairly well. David said, "I have travelled around the country a good deal and I have noticed that mean parents have mean children."

The last word, secured by the payment of $166.14 in cash is that all four children and I are going on the train [to Minnesota].

{ 13 }

I had to make two trips downtown today because I did not have enough money for the ticket on the first. Over the phone they had quoted first class fare to Chicago and coach to Minneapolis but they are extremely reluctant to mix their passages like that.

David had a bad tooth ache and had his tooth taken out the other day, cost one dollar. Now mine is starting to ache. But I would like to wait till I get to Mpls.

Love, Isabel

↩

May 28, 1943

Dear Poppa:

How do you like it in New York? Did you see the Statue of Liberty and the Empire State Building? After you get overseas please send us a post card telling us. Do not tell us before you go because enemy agents might have their ears open.

We go swimming every day. Mostly at the municipal beach and the officers club. Last time we went to Passo Grillo, the waves were higher than I was and I could only go about ten feet into the water. When a big wave came along I would have to climb up it like a glass mountain. If I would not reach the top on time the wave would hit me smack in the face and knock me over. I hope you are having a nice time in New York or overseas. If you are in England when there is an air raid be sure to get in the bomb shelter or no more you.

Yours truly, David Berman

Dear Poppy:

If you are in England could you send me a present? I do not care what it is. If you do I will send you a present. It might be some cigars, and I bet that you will like that. Ruth Amelia can get in the position to crawl.

Love, Betsy

Dear Poppa:

I wish you would come back. That's all I want to say.

Malcolm

[*Sammy—he did not explain why he preferred that name that day.*]

〜

June 3, 1943

Dearest Reuben:

I am afraid I haven't handled this moving business any too well. I should have taken your advice and not tried to make any rental for June and July till I arrived in Minneapolis.* I have wasted a lot of time in futile correspondence, shed a few tears and lost a lot of sleep. I am no better off than when I started. I wrote you how I got the telegram from Morry [Schanfield] saying, can find no house, OK make your own deal. Then I got the letter from your mother saying the Cohen cottage was available till July 4. I sent her a check for one hundred dollars instructing her to reply collect. I sent the letter air mail last Monday. This is Thursday and no reply. Meanwhile I can make no other reservation. Today was one of those days when everything goes wrong. The disposable diapers and the car seat failed to appear in the order from Sears. The laundry did not come back and I had to go after it. Eloise [*a St. Petersburg neighbor who babysat for the family*] came in the morning instead of the afternoon. My wrist watch is not ready yet. I have no reservation of any kind from Chicago to Mpls and I do not know where I shall stay in Minneapolis. Matters of small concern when there is a war going on. Now this afternoon, the laundry is all done. We are all fixed for clothes, anyhow.

Last night Betsy, Peter and I went to dinner at the Wilners'. David begged off to go to a carnival at Webb's with Oliver and Mrs. Horn.** Betsy carried on a conversation that had us nearly doubled up with more or less silent laughter. "Rabbi Wilner, you should not keep your elbows on the table. Mrs. Wilner, where is the baby? But I thought that was your baby at the beach the other day. (Embarrassing since the

---

*The family had to rent a place temporarily because their own home had been rented out, and the tenant, Miss Schmidt, needed some time to relocate.

**The Wilners, Webbs, and Horns were St. Petersburg neighbors.

Wilners had a still birth a few months ago.) Is water very expensive here? Do you mind if I don't finish this water? Do you mind if I don't eat the crusts? When I grow up I am going to have three children. Why not four? Because my mother has four and she has all kinds of trouble. The baby cries, David hits, Sammy yells and sometimes I scream. Other people don't know I can be bad because I am always good when we go out or when we have company. This is a Jewish picture. This is a Jewish Easter bunny."

Love, Isabel

↩

June 3, 1943

Dear Poppa:

We get our report cards Friday. I am pretty sure I will pass into fifth for a girl named Freda and Jack and I are the smartest children in the room. The baby is learning to crawl very rapidly.

Your son, David Berman

↩

June 9, 1943

Hotel Del Otero
Spring Park, Minn.

Dearest Reuben:

I haven't heard from you for so long that I got out of the habit of writing every day. Besides I have been busy, as you can imagine.

Just before we left I worked night and day. I packed bedding rolls in the trunk and assorted junk in the back seat of the car. I packed three suit cases, basket, thermos jug and small case to take with me. I packed trunk, boxes, etc. to check through. I got professional movers to take the bicycles, trunk, and boxes to the depot. I was glad I did too. They charged only three dollars and undid the crib and secured the trunk and other boxes with rope. When I got on the train I was all in. Oh, yes, we might well have missed the train but for the fact that the Stuckerts [*the family's landlords in St. Petersburg*] came over and helped with last minute details and took us to the station. We all enjoyed the comfortable pullman sleeping accommodations and the excellent meals on the diner. The air conditioning did not work for the first twenty-four hours of the trip, but being used to the tropical heat of St. Petersburg, a little thing like lack of air conditioning did not bother us. In Illinois it started to get cool. The north has been having unseasonable cold and excessive rain. Buddy* met us in Chicago. He helped us change stations. My ticket read for the Burlington. We got in on the Illinois central at 8:40, as per schedule, but were unable to make the 9:00 Zephyr which left at another station. Buddy got the tickets changed so they were good on the Hiawatha. He stayed with us till the Hiawatha left, at 10:30. He is the flight surgeon for the army air force technical training command at Chicago [*Madison*]. He has known for some time that you have gone and approximately where because he tried to reach you by phone at Maccensored Field [*MacDill Field, Florida*] and was told that the umpty-umph wing had moved and would not be back for a long time. Arnold and Ethel [*Roston, Isabel's brother and sister-in-law*], your mother, Teddy [*Reuben's brother*] and the Rushes [*Isabel's cousins Sam and Anna*] met us in Minneapolis. I had a reservation at the Curtis [Hotel] but had to cancel it because I could see that Arnold and Ethel would be insulted if we did not stay there. Stepha [*Mrs. Myron Berman*] also wanted us. Tuesday we drove out here to the Del Otero [hotel and cottages on Lake Minnetonka]. The cottage costs as I wrote before plenty but it has many advantages. We have discussed before the fact that a large hotel offers services at a price that one sometimes is glad to take advantage of. Anyhow, it isn't for long. I simply was not in a position to go hunting for lake cottages. If I had, I know I could have gotten more for less. But here we are. The view is beautiful. The grounds are well kept. The beds are comfortable. We had lunch at the hotel today. I plan to eat lunch there a few times a week. Teddy has been a real help. More later.

Love, Isabel

*Buddy Cohen, Reuben's cousin, came from Truax Field in Madison, Wisconsin, where he was then stationed.

David with a sailboat, about 1939

⌐

June 10, 1943

Dear Poppa:
I wish you would come back.

Sammy

Betsy and Sammy, standing outside the house, 1941

Dear Poppa:

We arrived in Minneapolis safely. We are staying at some cottages near Lake Minnetonka. If Uncle Teddy comes over we are going to go fishing. I saw a baby bass and a couple of sunfish down by the lake. I threw some stones at them. Some of them came very close. The porters on the train are very nice. They make up our beds. It is funny to see the way the seats come up into beds and the ceiling goes down to make the upper berth. I hope you are not dead already.

Yours truly, David Berman

Dear Poppa:
I found a dime under the table today. Mommy was supposed to give me a dime too but instead of that she gave me five pennies. On Saturday I am going to get a dime. That will be twenty-five cents. I'll save up to one dollar. When we went to Minneapolis Mommy bought me some toys for the trip. Half of the way we were [in] a drawing room. Mommy bought me a doll house too. Right now I have almost built it up but Sammy finished building it. We are in Minnesota now.

Love truly, Betsy
P.S. for David. We stayed overnight at Arnold's house and we ate on the diner.
P.S. for Betsy. We went through three tunnels and we passed a flood. I saw Roger [Jackson] and Peter Edelman too. Peter Edelman was standing (in front of his house) and waiting for me. He said, "I've been waiting so long for you." And then I said, [*but she stopped there.*]

Dearest Reuben:
Now that I have found a place for most of our things I can see that we will like it here. Being here puts me back about twenty-five years. You know I went to school right here in Spring Park [*town on Lake Minnetonka*]. I know every tree for miles around.

Love, IRB

⏋

June 17, 1943

Dearest Reuben:
This morning I went over to look at the Mack cottages across the street. Now I am satisfied with this cottage. You know at first I

thought I was paying too much for it. The Mack cottages have a chemical toilet, no bath tub, and sink on the back porch—all of which make for onerous housekeeping. They rent for twenty to thirty dollars a week. They do have the advantage of being right on the lake shore. Rabbi Aronson is taking one of the Mack cottages in July.

Right now the lake seems deserted except for year round inhabitants. Many of them are old settlers who remember me when I was as big as Betsy. I went to Mound [*town on Lake Minnetonka*] the other day. It has a fine grocery store and meat market. It surely is a pleasure to shop here after St. Petersburg. Round steak is thirty-five cents a pound. Sirloin is forty-two cents a pound. Milk is twelve cents a quart and of delicious flavor. Maple Plain brick ice cream is thirty-five cents a quart and extra delicious.

Love, IRB

⌣

June 24, 1943

Dear Poppa:

I wish you would come back. That's all I want to say. Sammy. Dear Poppa: We went to the fun house. We went through a long tunnel that went round and round. We went on a deep slide and he told me to hold on tight because that thing went so darn fast I could slide off. I steered it good. The man closed up one door. Then David stepped and the man letted David out. Dear Poppa: Do you know how I stirred the fudge, Poppa? I stirred it like this and I burnt myself. That's all I want to say. Sammy.
(Burn not serious. Sorry it happened. IRB)

Dear Poppa:

Momma bought me a croquet set. If it hadn't been for the little devil everything would be OK. Once he threw one of the black croquet balls at Betsy and made her lip bleed. Another time he was pulling up the hoops and when I told him not to and got mad at him he picked up one of the mallets and was going to hit me but I picked up another mallet and hit him. After all, you know, Poppa, I'd rather hit Sammy than have Sammy hit me. The baby is acting as good as gold. The baby can crawl sort of flop up and flop down and she knows how to do it. No one can read a magazine or a comic book when she is around. When the baby sees me reading a comic book her face lights up like a candle and she starts to come toward me. In a couple of minutes no more comic book. Once I was showing a friend of mine how the baby can crawl. At first she did not see the comic book but when she saw it she really put on a big smile and started toward it full speed.

(Peter says, I wish you would come back because I have a bad burn on my stummick and on my wrist. Momma, I wish you would buy some wings and a propeller and make an airplane out of our car.)

Me and Sammy had a sword fight today. First of all we knocked each others' head off the croquet sticks. Then I started waving my stick in the air hitting Sammy's stick. As the battle grew in fury Sammy started to cry a bit and I put the head on my stick and gave Sammy a gentle tap on the head but the weight sort of put a little extra weight on the thing and Sammy burst into tears, the poor little thing. I hope you are having a nice time in England. We are all lonesome for you.

Love, David

Dear Poppa:

I hope you are having a nice time. Would you send me some English money? I went to Excelsior [amusement park on Lake Minnetonka] on Tuesday. I went in the fun house. It is awfully fun. I went in a barrel that went round and round. It was slippery. I did not know where I would come out but finally I came out at the other end. I know how to tie my shoes now. We have a nice cottage at the lake. We have a friend who lives in the third cottage. I like her very much and she likes me very much. Her name is Suzan.

Love, Betsy

Dear Poppa:

Remember the last time we went to Excelsior? When we went to the fun house I was afraid to go down the big slide. It still looks scary but I went down it once. Betsy went down once and Sammy three times. I had the hardest time getting through the tunnel.

Love, David

⤳

June 26, 1943

Dear Poppy:

Did you ever examine a pilot? I have colored in a whole coloring book and two whole pages in one of these coloring books you sent me. Would you ask the man that's been bossing you if you could come see me? We are in Minnesota, Minnetonka.

Love, Betsy

⤳

July 4, 1943

Dearest Reuben:

Today is the quietest July fourth I can remember. Not one fire cracker! Fortunately for the hotel business it has been clear and hot. Sarah [Berman] came out and assisted with the children so David, Peter and I were out on the lake for over three hours. I should write to you every day but sometimes it gets so late at night before I am through the work that I let it go. Now I am writing to the tune of a croquet game outside and Ruth Amelia's bedtime protests inside.

Miss Schmidt [*the tenant who had rented the family's house*] is moving out August 1 or 2. She can't move any sooner because her new place will not be ready. Dayton's, that wonderful store, has purchased for you and sent overseas, twelve packages of gum, one box of Muriel's, and two officers' shirts. They were unable to find the expert's medal.* Seems to me I heard that medals are not sold off of PX's any more. I may write to Ft. San Antonio for it.

Love, Isabel

↩

July 5, 1943

Dear Poppa:
   David lost my toad. I wish you would come home. Dear Poppa: David lost my toad and I want you to find me another. Dear Poppa: I wonder if you got any money because one time I saw a big street car boat and I wanta ride on it to Excelsior. Mommy write. Dear Poppy: We went on a boat and we didn't catch any fish but we saw a lot of speedboats. That's all I want to say.

Sammy

↩

July 6, 1943

Dear Poppa:
   I believe I should've stayed in Minneapolis because the people are talking to me like when I was five years old. They are babying me around too much and I don't like it. I want people to think I am a nine year old, not a two year old.
   I built a boat out of wood, a battleship. Me and Sammy are collecting lady bugs for the crew. Already there is a captain and two gunners. I want some signal men, a couple more gunners and a first mate, and a petty officer. One gunner mans the lower guns while the other mans the upper guns. The captain walks around giving orders. I have them tied up to a dock across the street. Me and Sammy made a sort of diving board for them. There is so much wood work to do around the ship that there is not much time to play on it.

---

*The reference is confusing as Reuben had with him the medal for expert pistol shooting he had earned in San Antonio. Apparently it was thought to be lost, and Isabel was trying to get a replacement.

I build many things out of wood we get at Streeter Lumber Company, such as two chairs, no three chairs and two tables, and four shelves to keep things in. Also there is some wood cut to make wonderful blocks. Sammy is playing with them right now making railroad tracks and other things. Everything would be all right if you were here with us.

Love, David

P.S. When I write letters in my own handwriting they are too messy and I always make mistakes and waste a whole sheet. Anyhow I am going to learn how to write a typewriter fairly well and I might write you letters on the typewriter myself.

D.

Dear Poppa:

I have some stand up paper dolls. Some of them are nurses and some of them are waacs. I am working on a nurse now.

Love, Betsy

July 7, 1943

Dear Poppa:

I went to Excelsior and here is what I rode on. I rode on the caterpillar and the airplane. That's all I want to say.

Sammy

Dear Poppa:

Momma bought the baby some new dresses, colored dresses too. I wear them on fairy sweet.* On July 17, that day, I wore one of the baby's white dresses on fairy sweet.

*Betsy does not remember what this intriguing phrase meant.

We go to Excelsior, not often times. In July 17, I rode on the cater-pillar, and David and Sammy went there too. Me and David went in the Laff House. And we all went on the airplanes. The caterpillar was the most fun. The man squirted air in our seats too. We got a map of Minnetonka free at the hotel. We found Christmas Lake and Silver Lake. I saw Christmas Lake and Silver Lake. Silver Lake is shaped like a spoon. And Christmas Lake wasn't.

For Sammy's birthday Mommy gave him a dollar. Sammy bought a flashlight with it. Sammy wanted a flashlight because sometimes at night we have to go to the bathroom and if we cannot find our way we can certainly do it with a flashlight.

Love, Betsy

July 8, 1943

Dear Poppa:

I am happy to tell you that last night when I tried fish I liked them. So that from now on I can bring home four sunfish a day. I got a map of Lake Minnetonka from the hotel. Everyone said it was free for me and Betsy. I marked it with ink where Mound, Excelsior and Spring Park was. Those are the three cities we go to the oftenest. In Mommy's letter she should really write [the return address] Hotel Del Otero, 109 Cabin, Minnesota, because the hotel Del Otero is out of Spring Park and by itself although it is very close to it. We are all wishing that you will be sent back soon.

Love, David

July 10, 1943

Dear Poppa:

I built a little raft. Gramma Sarah already told you in the letter you sent to us that Gramma Sarah wrote. I take it and paddle out to a div-

ing raft that is too far out for me to swim to. I probably could do it if I had to. In a cartoon there was a censor and he had cut out all the writing of a letter and was looking through the hole that he had made. I can imagine how the people who got that letter felt when they got it and there was no writing. Here is what he probably said, "Dear so and so. We are going to attack at France at nine o'clock. There will be a formation of twenty-five B17's with the escort of thirty fighters." The censor didn't like the looks of it so he cut it out. I would like to cut the cartoon out and paste it on a V mail letter and send it to you but you are not allowed to paste on a V mail letter. A regular letter would take a month to arrive.
(After conversation with me.)
I will send it to you by regular mail.

[David]

Conversation in car.
Peter: When is Poppa coming back?
Isabel: Next summer.
David: Maybe Poppa will never come back. What would you do if Poppa died, Sammy?
Peter (after long thought): I'd ask Momma to marry another man.

⌣

July 19, 1943

Dear Poppa:
Yesterday was Sammy's birthday. We had lots of fun. Practically the whole Berman family was there and we had some extras too. Sam Rush [*who had a printing business*] brought a whole big box of paper for all of us because it was too much for Sammy. There is a great big roll of huge sheets of sticky paper. Sammy got three puzzles, not made of wood. They are made out of sheets of cardboard glued together and the pieces are held together by little strings kind of like cardboard. If you take out one of the pieces by pulling out the string you can just take out the rest of the pieces by pushing under them. Sammy also got a wooden tank and a wooden jeep. Sammy also got an animal bingo

set. It is just like real bingo except there is a big wheel with animals all around it. They are separated by a spoke on each side from the other. You twirl it and the animal that the rubber stops on you call out. You look on your card if you have that animal. If you do you put a red marker on it. The first one to get a full line says animal bingo. He also got some red slippers. He was mad because they weren't toys and he threw them in the wastebasket. But he will want to wear them when the cold weather comes along. I got a shirt and a share in a toy farm set. Every once in a while we see a pheasant out here. I go fishing every day. Yesterday I caught my limit. I do not mean the real sunfish limit which is thirty but I mean our limit which is four. I cannot think of much more to say so will close.

Love, David

~

July 23, 1943 [*handwritten*]

Dear Papa,

Momma hired a girl about 13 she helps quite a bit.

We went fishing yesterday with frogs but we didn't catch anything. I catch lots of sunfish off a friend of mine's dock. They are nice sized ones too.

I have decided to go to Hebrew School because I would like to learn Hebrew so that it can't be said that I am a Non Jew.

Love, David

~

August 8, 1943

3528 Holmes Ave. S.
Minneapolis, Minn.

Dearest Reuben:

I am finally getting some semblance of order out of all this mess. Things were put away in bad shape, packed nicely, mistreated on the train, stored well and unpacked well. The wash machine is broken but can be repaired. The refrigerator is all broken and cannot be repaired. We are getting a brand new one, mostly at our expense. Ruth Amelia pushed over our fan at the lake and broke it. My high school girl dropped the radio phonograph and broke it. Your mother has fixed a beautiful new cover for the carriage but two wheels are broken. I have not tried the sewing machine or the mixer but have no pleasant anticipations. Some chairs are also broken.

Love, Isabel

⌐⌐

August 10, 1943

Dear Pop,

I think that pop is better than dad because I've never called you dad before and I have called you poppa, and just to make it shorter is easier than to change it.

We got a new General Electric refrigerator the day before yesterday except it has rubber freezing trays compartments.

We have three gold fish. One of them died. And one is not anyplace in the pool. We looked all around but he might be hiding in the rocks. The other is safe and sound.

Gerald [Jackson] and I cleaned out the pool a couple days ago. When we came the pool had mud and rocks and leaves at the bottom. Gerald and I took a shovel and swept most of it up. The little that was left was mostly muddy water and it did not make much difference. So I put water in the pool.

Mommy made a chocolate cake minus the frosting on account of Sammy because he would just eat the frosting and not the cake. It certainly is nice to be back in our own home again and have furniture that is our own. Betsy and I have seven dollars and twenty cents saved up. We want money to take us downtown so we can buy things with our money. We have decided to get a good dog as cheap as we can and if he does not cost much half of what is left will go for defense stamps and half for toys. If he costs a lot all of what is left will go for defence stamps. I hope I can get a collie like Friskie. But no

The Berman house at 3528 Holmes Avenue South, about 1943

matter what I get it will be a puppy because puppies are cheaper and if you get a puppy and keep him till he dies he will get to know you very well but if you get an old dog that will only last about two more years you will make friends with him but he will not mind you and that is the kind of a dog I don't like.

Coming in from Spring Park, I saw a place where all kinds of dogs were for sale. That will be the first place I go when I go dog hunting.

Love, David

～

August 16, 1943

Dearest Reuben:

I can imagine how pleased you must have been to receive twenty-five letters in one day and how neglected you felt until those letters came.

Today I took all four children downtown on the bus to the home trade shoe store. For $14.50 and three coupons I purchased four pairs of shoes. Your mother wanted to know if the people at the store did not seem surprised to see so many children at once and I said no they were used to it. Then she said that she used to take you there and I recall all four Rosenstein bratlets going there too. Ruth Amelia takes a size three. It is the smallest shoe I have ever seen.

Yesterday I walked down to the lake with the baby in the carriage and Betsy and Peter walking along beside. We saw Penny Norseen and her mother and father. Betsy had forgotten Penny but Penny still remembered that she had wanted baby Betsy to stay and be her little sister. It was chilly at the lake and it has been around sixty all day here.

Love, Isabel

⌣

August 18, 1943

Dearest Reuben:

We now begin to feel settled. I bought 100 pounds of potatoes for two dollars, also two dozen ears of corn for twenty-five cents and about ten pounds of duchess apples for fifty cents. Then I decided to go to the A and P. I bought twenty-five pounds of flour and a crate of apricots, also other things. Then I left the fan to be fixed and came on home. I still have enough gas left to go to Sears and pick up the radio phonograph when it is ready. But that is all.

I sent an air mail letter to the war ration board at Fort Knox asking for another A book. They say they sent it to me at the hotel but I did not receive it and the hotel has not received it since I left.

Last night I put up five quarts of apricots. I did it mostly for Peter. That child has the most peculiar taste in foods. The other day David came in crying, "Momma, Sammy is going to die. He is eating acorns." I went outside. Sure enough, Peter was sorting out the best acorns, cracking them with a stone and eating them. He claimed they tasted good.

Love, Isabel

~

August 20, 1943

Dearest Reuben:

The other day Mr. Gustafson [*Axel Gustafson, a cabinetmaker*] came out with the what nots. I was glad to have them back. They are very pretty even if they are not very useful. Mr. G. estimated the repairs to be paid by the RR [*railroad*] at 31.00. Of course, some items like the base of one of the oak sectional bases, and a kitchen chair and our bedroom mirror will not be repaired. Mr. G. recalled the fire at the old town market [*the furniture store that had belonged to Isabel's father*]. He said that shortly before the fire he had dickered with my father about some pieces but my father was not anxious to sell. He lost them all in the fire. Peter's special chair went in for glueing and recovering glueing at the expense of the RR, recovering at our expense. I also sent in the magazine rack for repair and the spool end table for refinishing. Gustafson-Wesson keep the same workmen and charge the same prices they always did.

I have taken Ruth Amelia off the bottle and give her cold milk from a glass. At first I had to hold her over the sink because she spilled so much, but she will learn. I did not ask Dr. Seham's advice because he would say to keep her on the bottle for a few months longer and I don't want to do that.

Love, IRB

~

August 31, 1943

Dear Poppy:

We got a new ice box and it has ice cubes and it is a beautifuller ice box than the other one and we got a new one and it is so beautiful and it has a light and you never saw it and it is so beautiful and every once in a while Mommy would clean it up. No, I would clean the ice box up. Our car is so dirty I think you had better save up another

Betsy, August 24, 1943

seven thousand dollars and buy a launch. (How much do cars cost?) And Poppy I want you to get a car for a thousand dollars. I want it to be a Plymouth because I like it to be a Plymouth and our car is so dirty I want you to get a car and another car and then you'll have two cars but not that old dirty one. Then you'll have two cars and Mommy'll have a car and you'll have a car, see? I don't wanna say no more.

Peter

P.S. Dear Poppy: I want you to buy a pump and a bus.

Dear Poppa:

We got the sand for our sand box yesterday but we did not get enough. I told her to get three bags and she got only two. I think four would be enough. Betsy is kind of crabby because you are not here, same with Sammy.

Mommy won't let me get a dog even if I buy it with my own money. (What do you think I've been saving up for. I didn't save for some measly old games.) You write a letter to Mommy and get real mad and say, Isabel, you buy David a dog. I will go down on my bike to the butcher shop and get dog food for it and I will teach it how to do tricks. The Jacksons are going to move down to Irving Avenue near the school. He [*Gerald*] will be in walking distance from our house but I will go down there on the bike when I want him to come over. Then Gerald will buck me or I will buck Gerald.* We can both buck each other but Gerald has not tried to buck me yet.

I'd like to go to England but only for two or three months because I do not like unamerican accents.

We all have tinker toy sets except Betsy and Ruth Amelia. I made Betsy and Sammy a wheel that turns around and is on a stand. I hope you are having a nice time in England or did I say that before in another letter.

Love, David

⌐

September 2, 1943

Dearest Reuben:

We have received mail from you this week that more than makes up for the lack of it last week. The pictures of you and the others are just grand. You look wonderful. But trust Reuben to be sitting next to the one WAC. You should have put her in the center of the group. If it were not for the four children I should love to be a statistician for the eighth air force. I enjoyed my work at Randolph and the people I worked with.

Yesterday I took the children to see Max [*Goldberg, cousin and dentist*]. Max asked Peter [*Sammy*] if he brushed his teeth every day. I sure do, he said—some of the time. David is to get orthodontia starting Sept. 4. Typewriter ribbon doesn't jump up when keys are struck. I see I struck stencil bar by mistake.

Love, Isabel

*"Buck" is a Minnesota regionalism, meaning to carry someone on a bike or the ride so given.

[September 4?, 1943]

Dear Poppy:

   We are going to have another picnic. That's all I want to say. One time I went to Rush's for dinner. I said to Sam Rush, "Let's go for a horse back ride."

Love, Sammy

Dear Poppa:

   I am taking clarinet, piano, art and Hebrew lessons. I am going to get my music book for the clarinet pretty soon. I am using your black clarinet not the silver one. I take piano lessons from Martha Baker at the MacPhail school of music. I can already play a lot of pieces that are in the book. I take art lessons at the Walker gallery and my teacher is Mrs. LeSeur [*Le Sueur*].

   Do you remember Albert Kapstrom? He came over to my house for a little while. Sammy does not walk to school with me.

   I don't exactly agree with you about the dog. I would like to have a dog now. I would buy the dog food because there is a store right near Ben's drugstore that has all different kinds of dog food and I would read the directions and mix it myself. So far we only had a dog make push once, maybe twice.

   I am going to go to the children's symphony and the University plays at school.

David Berman

September 4, 1943

Dear Poppa:

   It took us a long time to get to the fair on the street car. And the other thing, I couldn't ride on the airplane. It went round and round.

I couldn't ride on it because I already rode on some cars.

We saw thousands of fish and one of them were as big as David and the rest of them were bigger than the baby, so big. They were all bigger than the baby except the one smaller. The bullhead was smaller than the baby.

We went to a picture show and the picture show was all about Minnesota. And when we went to the state fair we went right over the Ohio [*Mississippi*] river.

We saw German equipment and we saw an American trailer and an American truck and we saw an American jeep.

Dear Poppy: I ate so much caramel apple and today I don't feel very good and neither does Betsy so I wish you would come back today. Betsy is sick and I feel better than Betsy but still I don't feel very good so you should come back and do something about it. That's all I want to say.

Poppy, the baby crawls better than she used to crawl. She can stand up by herself. She has to hold on something and I got a new book about a lazy automobile. Betsy has got a book about a dog. That is all I want to say.

Sammy

Dear Poppy:

Ruth Amelia stands up to go to the toilet sometimes.

We went to the lake one day and on the way back David stepped into some push. In the car there was an awfully bad smell and pretty soon I noticed that it was push on David's foot and I told everyone that it was push and he got out and scraped it on the sidewalk.

I had a great big glass of root beer at the fair. I had more things than David and Sammy.

One day I bought a book about a dog at the dime store and I bought a great big comic book about Andy Panda. It had a great big cover on and it was like a book and it was skinny for a comic book.

I have a tooth. I went to cousin Max. And it's real loose. And cousin Max found I had a loose tooth. It was my biggest tooth.

Love, Betsy

September 8, 1943

Dear Poppy:

I am the president in school. David is the secretary in his class. I went to class with Roger [Jackson] but Roger was not there that day because the teacher told him to go on home. I was there that day though. We didn't have nothing but fun. We didn't have no work just played with puzzles. When I came back I told Mommy that I was not in Miss De Smidt's room. So she gave me a note that said she would like me to be in Miss De Smidt's room. So I was put in Miss De Smidt's room. At recess I always hunt for Roger. I find him and then we play tag. Today we played tag and airplanes. Everyday after recess we take a rest. I did some work all straight and better than the work I did before on it. Tomorrow we are going to do Dick and Jane and not Mother and Father. I think some day we are going to do Puff and Spot. Tim is the teddy bear. And there is baby too. Tim and baby have no partners so they are partners themselves. Someday we will have them.

I got some paper from Anna Rush. It is very big sheets of paper. It is not really paper it is light weight cardboard. Mommy is making a cover out of it for my pages.

Grandma Sarah made me a new dress. It is a corduroy skirt, purple and a white and blue blouse to go with it. The white and blue blouses are made of silk and designs and she made a jacket to the dress. The dress is a jumper. Grandma Sarah put a rose on the corner of the jacket. It is awfully pretty. It is a yellow rose. The dress has one pocket which every day I bring a handkerchief in. The teacher wants us to bring handkerchiefs. She does not want us to talk all at once.

Love, Betsy

Dear Poppa:

I have a problem that I would like you to answer in your next letter if you can. I have two bikes as you know. But it is against the law to buck. So far we have walked to school but when I get a license for my bikes I may as well use them but if I cannot buck how in the world will Betsy and Sammy get to school on time. They are pokey when they go by themselves but when we go along with them they go fast.

We have a sand box now.

Arnold fixed the stoker the day before yesterday because it was getting quite cold and so we wouldn't have to run the stove and keep the oven open.

I have not heard you answer about the dog so would you please put your answer in the next letter too.

We have been trying to get film for my camera but we cannot find it anyplace and I am getting mad because I want to take pictures.

Love, David

David, September 8, 1943

September 11, 1943

Dearest Reuben:

Today I received two letters from you, one dated the third and one the fourth of September. That is pretty good service. I love your comment on the effect of V mail on the legibility of your letters. Reuben, my darling, the trouble is with you. Your writing is practically illegible to most people irregodless. Please use V mail. I have a filing system. I put all your V mail letters on a safety pin. When people come over and say, "What do you hear from Reuben?" I just hand them the file and they read to their heart's content. The hand written letters don't fit into the filing system.

David has been working hard for the school paper sale. He says he is doing it for the school and for the war. David was afraid to ask the lady next door because she has lectured the children so many times about noise. David calls her Mrs. Turkey because she looks like one. But Betsy went right over and asked her if she had any papers for the school and for the war. She said there were so many that David should come over. Now David no longer calls her Mrs. Turkey but Mrs. Mark, which is her name. Yesterday, Betsy as class president called for news and then volunteered this. When the officers who are in Europe now have beaten Germany they will come back here and those who are here now will go and beat Japan. Peter saw Diane [McFarlane] in the drug store the other day. He went up to her and said seriously, "Diane, I am *not* your boy friend. I am Roger's boy friend."

Love, Isabel

⤛

September 15, 1943

Dearest Reuben:

Betsy pulled a fast one in school. The first few grades are out of school fifteen minutes before the higher grades. Betsy wants to wait for David. So one day she waited. Miss De Smidt came out and told Betsy to go home. So Betsy hid beside the wall. Then she came out and waited on the steps. Then Miss De Smidt came out and told her to go home. But Miss De Smidt told Betsy she could wait if her momma wanted her to. So the next day Betsy said I wanted her to wait. Then she came home and told me what she had done adding, "You don't want to make a liar out of me, do you?" I suppose I should write a note to Miss DeS. saying that Betsy has a good imagination and I want no special favors for her. David's mind does not go into such devious channels.

L. I.

↜

September 19, 1943

Dearest Reuben:

Thursday I got Hortense to stay with the baby while I took the children down to the MacPhail [School of Music]. Martha [Baker] gave Betsy and David a [piano] lesson together. But we agreed that hereafter the lessons will be separate. David reads letters and Betsy does not read much. Betsy is too impatient to play on the wood while David plays the piano. David will go once a week and Betsy twice. Betsy will have one individual lesson and one class lesson. The class lesson will be in eurhythmics. Peter is to take eurhythmics also. This will all cost $3.50 a week, not counting bus fares and nursemaid pay.

You would have been thrilled if you could have been here late Friday afternoon. David had taken a clarinet lesson and he was tootling away. Betsy was picking out tunes on the piano. David takes clarinet at school from a Mr. Weinberg, or maybe Weinstein, who says he taught you flute lessons. The clarinet lesson comes Friday noon and Friday after school.

Friday afternoon I packed Ruth Amelia and Peter in the car and drove down into the Young and Quinlan [*Young-Quinlan department store*] to pick up my suit. It surely looks elegant. Even so, Peter claimed that even when I wore the new suit and hat, I still looked older than poppa. I finally realized that to Peter, poppa is perfect, and everybody is older, meaner, and generally not as nice as poppa. Saturday, I started the children in with art lessons at Walker, but more of that on another letter.

Love, Isabel

↜

Betsy, September 19, 1943

September 21, 1943

Dear Poppy:

I am taking piano lessons and art. So far every picture I made in school is excellent. I made a pretty design. For the pictures I make I have a booklet. The design is a very pretty one. There is a big sunflower and cute little things in the corners and some little round things like I always make grass but much smaller. On the side of it I have two hearts and flowers sticking up. The teacher has gave us the most scrap crayons. Today I went around collecting the scrap crayons. The teacher gave us some real good crayons. I straightened the shelf real neat. While one group is working the other group comes up and reads. I have a lot of children in my group. And then there is Diane's group but not the Diane who is next door but another Diane. Then there is Peter. Diane comes next of all and Peter last.

The teacher has gave us books. My group has finished the red books and now we are starting on our yellow books. First day we got finished with them in the afternoon my group got to take them home. We are starting on yellow books now. As soon as we finish the yellow books we can take them home.

Roger has moved since we've came back. I've lost my six teeth. I told Mommy that I would like to send you the baby.

Love, Betsy

Dear Poppy:
When we were living in Spring Park Mommy would take me to Excelsior. When we came we came on a beautiful train. This train was such a beautiful train. It had a little drawing room. This drawing room had a upstairs berth and a downstairs berth. The downstairs berth would fold into two chairs and the upstairs would fold around. It had a little bathroom with a toilet and a sink and an air conditioner. It had a davenport. When we came in we missed the Bowlington [*Burlington*] Zephyr so we took the Hiawatha and it went just about as fast as the Bowlington Zephyr. That's all I want to say.

Love,

Dear Poppy: My name is George Henry Smiggles.

[Sammy]

⤸

September 21, 1943

2d Bombardment Division, APO 634 NYC

Dear David,
If it is against the law for you to buck Betsy, that does make a problem about getting everybody to school on time. I think it would be very nice of you to walk with Sammy and Betsy to school in the morning. I'm just the least bit afraid of such small children walking across streets alone.

I have written to Isabel about the dog. I think you should have it and that is what I said. But I am afraid you will have to wait until I get home to buy it for you. The way the Russians are rushing through the Ukraine and we are pushing the Germans in Italy, perhaps you won't have too long to wait for your dog.

Major Reuben Berman, about 1945

You must keep yourself posted about this war by reading the news-papers. When you are grown up you may be in a position to help pre-vent another war.

Love, Poppa

⌐

October 12, 1943

Dear Poppy:

I go to Calhoun school and sometimes I put a piece of paper in the typewriter and make the thing move and then I take the piece of paper out and walk away. Dear poppy: I go to school and write an apple tree. That's all I want to say.

Dear poppy: I went to the liberry and bought a book of a train and the other thing is I went to eurhythmics class.

Dear poppy: I play with Diane. That's all I want to say.

Peter

Dear poppy: I want you to send me some pictures of you holding a baby.

Sammy

Dearest Reuben:

I understand why we haven't heard from you recently. Your outfit has been busy. Denise hasn't heard from Ted either.*

Did your momma write how Betsy put me on the spot? I rushed out of the car into the house, leaving Sarah and Ruth Amelia to fol-low. I explained to Betsy who followed me, "Gramma Sarah will have a fit if she sees how upset the house is." When Sarah came in Betsy said, "I don't see you having any fit, Gramma Sarah."

Ruth Amelia is too busy crawling around investigating things to

*Denise Stafne McFarlane and her daughter, Diane, had moved in with Denise's par-ents, Albert and Alice Stafne, next door to the Bermans, while her husband, Ted, was overseas.

bother using her toilet seat. So she often fills her panties. Yesterday some spilled out and got on one of the blocks and Peter sat on some. Peter went over to Diane's house and said, "Guess what, I sat in the baby's push. Let's play here. Don't come over to our house. It stinks."

I went to market today and paid fifty cents for fifty pieces of okra. Peter must have his okra.

Love, Isabel

⌐

October 23, 1943

Dearest Reuben:

Last night I had about twenty people over. It was almost like the parties we used to have. The only person missing was you. Miriam and Chimes [Edelman] were here. Chimes said he would write to you soon. Lou Sperling and Ruth stopped in for a little while. I almost hugged Lou because he was dressed like you. Officers blouse, pinks, maple leaves, army service command on the shoulder. I know you don't wear that army service insignia any more but you used to. Lou took your address. He expects to get in touch with you before so very long. Stepha and Myron [Berman] were here and also Barney and Clare [Berman]. Barney and Myron stood in the kitchen and talked shop. Myron is a big shot in the place where Barney works. When it came to the serving, Evelyn Frisch, your momma and Anna Rush pitched in and did practically the whole thing. As usual I was busy with the children. By the time I got Betsy and Peter to bed, David had to come down and see who was there. When David was asleep, Ruth Amelia woke and was determined to stay up and enjoy the party. The party was lovely, with very few mistakes. One mistake was that I put salt instead of sugar on the crust of one of the apple pies. Every one ate his pie, though, and thought the salt was intentional. Another mistake was that I forgot to offer second helpings of pie. The party was fine, though. Every one talked busily. There was no need to show movies or haul out the bridge table. I had bought two decks of cards in case they might be needed. But I purposely did not invite Ruby and Leon [Klugman] because I didn't want a bridge party.

This morning your momma took David to a Frisch Bar Mitzvah at the Adath. David thought it was wonderful. Such a layout of food, and all free. Oh yes, there was a speech too. Mr. Kahz called me about sending David to S. S. Talmud Torah. David seems to want to go. I shall have to make some adjustments for his music lesson.

We have been having more trouble with Peter's teeth. When you come back, you can see to it that he drinks milk, eats vegetables, and brushes his teeth. I try to take good care of him.

Love, Isabel

⤺

October 25, 1943

Dear Poppy:

I am getting along in school fine. We have finished our sixth book and now we are on our seventh book. We have already had the teachers over, for dinner. Sammy is not in my room in school. I used to be not getting 100 but now I am getting 100's just fine. I like school.

Arnold took just David on a weiner roast. I told Arnold that when the war is over, well we will like the Americans a little bit better than the Germans but that won't mean that we won't have to give them a cigarette when we visit them and they ask for it or a match. So he said, "Well, I guess that's right." He said next Sunday I should come over.

Gramma Sarah is making me a plaid dress. She is making a hat that matches it.

Love, Elizabeth

Dear Poppa:

I do my best to find my teacher. I go to school in the afternoon. Sometimes I play a record and that's what I did today. We went to a show and the other thing is that we got new storm windows put on.

Dear Poppy: When we moved our piano was all shut up tight so we couldn't play it. Now the piano is open and we can play it and we're settled. And when you close it you can open it up again.

Dear Poppy: I haven't got nothing else to say. Yours truly across the sea exploding be.

Sammy Hirsch Peter Berman

Dear Poppy: Today we took out a clinker and the clinker was burning and when we put it in a can I saw fire creeping out.

Yours truly, S.H.P.B.

Dear Poppa:

Every month we elect a new president and a new vice-president and a new secretary and a new treasurer. And I was elected president. Albert Kapstrom nominated me. From now on I am going to clean out my clarinet. I wish you were here to help me because I do not do well in my clarinet lessons because Mr. Weinberg wants the poppas to help us. To help me out I am going to take private clarinet lessons. Do you know Mr. Weinberg? I think he has you mixed up with Teddy because he says that poppa plays the flute but you play the clarinet. But he might have helped you on the clarinet.

When do you think you can get leave to come home? Do you know how we are going to go to England after the war? On a China clipper. Or does a China clipper only go to China?

With all my love, David

Dear Poppy:

When we were at the lake, three times I rode on a speed boat. The speed boat went so fast it turned around. Pretty soon it ran into its own waves and went—(gestures).

Yours truly, S.H.P.B.

November 2, 1943

Dear Poppa:

I would rather have you come home to the United States than to see our cousins in Glasgow. If you do come, it will be quite a chance to see the bright lights. Of course, the army camp you are at may not be near a town.

I go to Hebrew School. The teacher is Mr. Kahz. I already know keesay which means chair and dallas which means door and yeled which means boy and kum which means stand up for a boy and kum-mee which means stand up for a girl and shave means sit down for a boy and shavee means sit down for a girl. I know that shoo means return.

I have braces and pretty soon my teeth will be nice and straight. We have learned in our geography that Greenwich, a little town in England, is the place where the meridians start.

Mr. Weinberg gave me a cloth that was really meant for cleaning the clarinet and also a kind of a wax which you use to make the clarinet slip together easier. I do not do so well so I am taking private lessons as well as the ones I have in school. The reason I do not do so well is that you are not here and Mr. Weinberg expects the father or the one who plays the instrument or knows about it to help you on it.

I joined the cub scouts at the Adath Jeshuran. The cub leader is a man named Abe Green. I am going into a den with Albert Kapstrom.

Yours truly, David

Dear poppy:

I think that when the war is over I want you to show me the houses that have been bombed and exploded and the bombed cannons.

I can see Betsy making a real pretty colored thing out of blocks. I went to two Hallowe'en party and I didn't feel good on the next one so Sam Rush carried me in. I talked to cousin Sam on the telephone. And cousin Sam said that he was too busy cutting paper. And I am going to Cousin Sam's paper store and watch him cut the paper.

Your truly, Sammy

Dear poppy:

On one day I was invited to two parties and two lessons. I will say them in order. The first one is rhythmics; the second one is art class; the first party was Mildred Pass and the second was Louis Green's. At Mildred's house I had a loose tooth. And it was so loose that a little boy named Harold hitted me and it fell out. One night we had a ceremony because David started Talmud Torah.

Love, Betsy

⌒

November 5, 1943

Dearest Reuben:

I have spent the evening preparing a financial report for September. It came out too good to be true. The bank balance checked with the expenditures to a dollar. Anyhow here goes.

Item	
Groceries	67.70
Baker	5.16
Milkman	10.00
meals out	5.24
Total food	88.10
Moving expense	5.00
Gas, phone, coal	7.45
Insurance, house	47.51
Home equip., repairs	30.15
Busfare	4.00

Clothing	54.88
Laundry	13.41
Nursemaid, day help	27.80
Ashes	2.50
Total operating	259.61
Music and art	11.00
Auto expenses	6.50
Moviefilm	2.00
Churches, charities	28.25
Dental care	10.00
Drug supplies	6.54
Newspapers, toys, mag.	12.95
Gifts, incl. Gertie	41.16
Stamps	1.64
Total Advanc, recrea	120.04
Total expenses	479.95

Income

Balance Sept NW	350.79
Balance Sept Ft. S.	378.33
Estate	125.00
Allotment	250.00
Refund on insurance	6.48
Total income	1110.60
Balance Oct NW	454.40
Balance Oct Ft. S.	265.15
Total balance	719.55
Total expenditures	479.99

To check with total income above:
1109.50

Please understand I did not use a calculator on this. I think there are a number of errors, but they cancel each other. The one hundred dollar draft came through to the bank OK. I am leaving it in the checking account and will reimburse the savings acct when the allotment comes through.

11/6/43

I knew there was something wrong. Add to income: debt paid, 30.00; office 9.00. Add to expenditures: unrecorded, 39.00

Love, Isabel

⤸

November 7, 1943

Dearest Reuben:

Fall has been unusually mild until now. Today it has been snowing and blowing. The snow was wet and ploppy. By afternoon it turned to rain. Diapers put out to freeze and dry had to be taken in after dark dripping wet. The children were thrilled with the snow. David made a very wet snowman. Peter decorated the snow man with pieces of coal. Later David changed the snow man into a fort.

I have been putting off the purchase of overshoes in the hope that you might come back and we would go someplace where overshoes are not needed. No such luck. Yesterday I had to take all four children down town and buy four pairs of overshoes. I was lucky to get them too. I also got shoes for the older three children.

Love, Isabel

⤸

November 9, 1943

Dear poppa:

When you come will you bring the pictures that I sent you.

We changed my music lesson. From now on it is on Saturday instead of Thursday.

The snow is deep. Yesterday it was so stormy that there was no school in the afternoon so momma could not come to see how Sammy worked.

There is a little girl across the street from me. Her name is Marlys. I play with her often.

We had open house today and the mothers came.

We are on our eleventh reader.

I brought a coloring book to school.

A little boy named Ernest on the way home took my ballet slippers.

Love, Elizabeth Berman

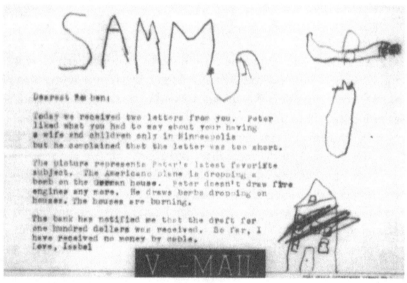

Sammy, November 9, 1943

November 13, 1943

Dearest Reuben:

I am afraid that two years in the south have dulled my enthusiasm for Minnesota winters. Prospects of mountains of coal to shovel, walks to clean, car battery run down, slippery ice to drive on, overshoes, snow suits, runny noses do not fill me with delight. But the children love it. Peter practically lives in the snow. He loves his overshoes and ski pants. David loves it too. One day he explained to me that Betsy should be dressed warmer than he because Betsy had not lived through as many cold winters as he had.

I have about decided to stop Betsy's piano and eurhythmics lessons. I am inclined to agree with Dr. Seham in his no lessons till nine edict. Betsy does not make good progress with her piano for two reasons. One, she plays the pieces by ear and sees no reason for bothering to read notes. The other, I simply do not have the time to sit down and practice with her. David does not practice either, but he makes good progress. About January first the art term is over. We shall not continue the art lessons then but may perhaps resume the eurhythmics for Betsy.

Love, Isabel

⤶

November 19, 1943

Dear Poppa:

Yesterday night Arnold called me up and said he wanted me to come and see him and the bus goes every twenty minutes at 3:14 and 3:34

Dear Poppa: I went to the symphony concert at the Cyrus auditorium [*Cyrus Northrop Auditorium at the University of Minnesota*]. There was mostly violins but I believe I saw a clarinet. It had a famous pianist, named Casadesus. He played gardens in the rain. Hurry up and get leave so you can help me on my clarinet. I do not do very well because you are not here and Mommy does not know anything about the clarinet and Mr. Weinberg gives you a lot of homework and expects you to get help on it. He teaches instruments. There are four children in our clarinet group. Albert Kapstrom plays the coronet. Another boy in our room plays the French horn. I am not sure it is the French horn but I think that is what it is.

Your loving son, David

Dear Poppa:
　　The teacher likes me and I am a good boy at home. I like you and think you are the best man in the whole world.
Dear Poppy: The baby has her birthday she is one year old. I would like to go to Ireland and see you but I can't cause the army won't let me. All I have to say is that there's books in the book case. That's all I have to say.

Love, Sammy

Dear Poppy:
　　I hope you are having a nice time. We are on two books. One in the morning and one in the afternoon. The one in the morning is green. The one in the afternoon is blue. The blue book has a *hard* cover. It is a great big fat one.
　　(Betsy will type you a story.)
　　where is baby
　　mother said where is baby. Dick said where is baby.
　　jane said where is baby where is baby baby is not jere not h

[Betsy]

⏡

November 29, 1943

Dearest Reuben:
　　Did your mother write you about Peter, the little devil. Last night he came in from the show with your mother. Sylvia was here. Auntie Sylvia smells, he announced. And he held his nose. He held his nose

while he ate supper, sang a song, went to the toilet, undressed and read a book in bed. He kept holding his nose after Sylvia left. When I explained that that showed it wasn't Auntie Sylvia that smelled he said that he did not know she left, that was why he kept holding his nose. This morning I explained to him that he had hurt Auntie Sylvia's feelings. He said the next time she came over he would go outside.

Today Peter is sick, not very sick but sick enough to stay in bed and get waited on. He came home from school and went to bed. His temperature was 102. With aspirin and staying in bed his temperature stays down. He talks like this, "Betsy, are you going to see Marlys? Tell her I am sick. Momma, call up Miss Seidlitz and tell her I am sick. David, will you do me a favor tomorrow? Go see Miss Seidlitz and tell her I'm sick. Momma, if Diane comes to play with me tell her I'm sick. I'll be careful not to die. Write to Poppa and tell him to come home because I'm sick."

Love, Isabel

⌣

November 29, 1943

Dearest Reuben:

Betsy brought home a most wonderful report card. I quote Miss De Smidt, "Elizabeth is a friendly, happy child and she is usually cooperative. She has a very good vocabulary and a store of general information of interest to other children. She has an eager interest in learning that I hope she will never lose.

"Elizabeth does superior work in reading. She learns words easily and usually retains them. She reads well independently as well as with the group. While reading Elizabeth speaks clearly but when giving news at news time it is often hard to understand her because she does not speak clearly.

"She has an unusually sweet, true singing voice and is one of our pupil teachers. Elizabeth is always eager for story time and gives good attention."

You would surely have been amused to see Betsy try her pupil teacher technique on me. She finally got me to sing the scale, but not to get single notes right.

Love, Isabel

⌒

December 2, 1943

Dear Poppy:

I wish you were back this day. Once in a show well I saw some soldiers coming back. Why don't you come back?

When I am sick I don't feel good and I am sick so I don't feel good. I wish you would come back.

I have a lot of toys and books. I have got a couple of crayons too.

Dear Poppy:

I would like you to write a letter to Dr. Ershaler [*spelled to reflect Sammy's pronunciation of Dr. Irving Ershler's name*] and also I would like you to come back.

There is snow falling outside but when winter wasn't beginning it was a blizzard. The snow went up high. But sometimes it goes up so high that it buries people.

There is a volcano in Mexico. Volcanoes are mountains that blow up. Come back is come back and go away is go away but I want you to come back not go away.

My mother gives me aspirin. She takes my temperature. We have got some Gross Brothers paper. All the time I get some Gross Brothers paper to draw on. I have a fire engine and it has firemen but two of them are lost. My fire engine is a toy fire engine. It is right on the floor.

What do you do in Ireland? Do you ever fly over England in a plane?

My mommy gives me aspirin all the time. I am not very sick.

Sammy

⌒

December 2, 1943 [*handwritten*]

Dear Papa,

 Mamma was sitting on a little chair holding the baby and she faint-ed.* The baby was not hurt very badly but she cried a little. The reason Mamma fainted is because she works too hard. I should not have wrote this letter but I thought you should know about it.

Love, David

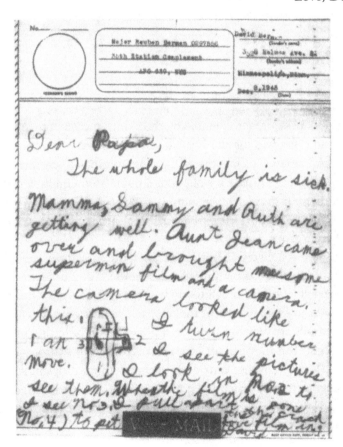

David, December 8, 1943

*Probably the first sign of the meningioma that was not diagnosed and operated on until forty years later; see Postlude, below.

December 9[?], 1943

Dear Poppy:

On Chanukah I got a tank and from Arnold I got two packages of gum and a box of candy. Do you know how long Chanukah lasts? It lasts eight days.

Dear Poppy: For my presents Mommy got me a soap circus and I don't know what to say more so I better stop dictating.

Love, Sammy

Dear Poppa:

I got six presents for Chanukah last night. One was a basket making set and that was for all of us. So was a set of Peter Rabbit puzzles and a soap circus. For just myself I got an automatic pencil, a world map puzzle, a tie, three cans of paint, a book from Gramma Gertie, three tops, and some defense stamps, and skates. Excuse me, I did not figure right. I did not get six presents; I got nine. I did not count the Bird Letter game.

Your letters are getting boring. Please write something more interesting. Please write something like the mouse. I do not blame you for not being able to find much to say because everything is a military secret over in England except the trees and houses.

My pupils are very big and I do not like them for letting in so much light. But they cannot help it on account of the drops put in. But Dr. Virgil Schwartz can't do anything without drops in the eyes. I can't play bird lotto or work the map puzzle or do hardly anything without a magnifying glass. And a magnifying glass is very boring to have around your neck.

Love, David

Sammy, December 10, 1943

December 11, 1943

Dearest Reuben:

I think that Ruth Amelia has had a sinus infection with recurrent fever for the past month. On Monday, Nov. 29, she was fussy and Peter came home from school and went to sleep. I found he had a fever. I talked to Dr. Seham who advised one aspirin every three hours and to keep in touch with him. Peter continued to have a fever going up to 102 or a little more and coming down with aspirin till Saturday, Dec. 4. Then Dr. S. came out to see him. Peter looked terribly sick. You know how small and pale he is anyhow. Dr. S. prescribed sulfadiazine (I think) and promised to come back the next day. For Ruth

Amelia he recommended aspirating the nose and feeding aspirin for the fever. I also ordered cheracol in case of need. Dec. 5, Dr. S. found Peter practically well but recommended continued rest to prevent recurrence of the infection.

Meanwhile, I had already alarmed David, Betsy and your momma who heard of it late by collapsing on the floor in a faint Friday morning, Dec. 3. Dec. 4 and Dec. 5 your momma was here. I must have had a fever because I was bundled up in slacks, flannel shirt and sweater with the house at 70. I had a sore throat and extreme drowsiness and fatigue. Dec. 4 David got a fever and a sore throat. Dec. 6 Betsy got a fever and a sore throat.

At the present date, Ruth Amelia seems to have no fever. Peter seems to be fully recovered but tonight he had a temperature of 100. I feel pretty good, my appetite is much better, my sore throat is gone, but my nose is stuffy and I feel a little tired. David and Betsy have normal temps most of the time but just when I feel that I can sigh with relief because they are well I find a temperature of close to 101. All the children have been coughing some.

With the help situation what it is I was lucky to have your mother come two days and Aunt Jean one day. Since then, Hortense Wyman has been coming in for a few hours a day.

Love, Isabel

~

December 15[?], 1943

Dear Poppa:

I hope you are having a very very good time in Ireland. When will you come home? That is what I would like to know.

I will tell you what I got for Chanukah last night. I got a nurse outfit which I wanted very much from Gramma Sarah. And I got a red pencil with the eraser on it. It was the automatic pencil. From Arnold. I got a pinafore from Gramma Sarah. Gramma Sarah made the pinafore.

Today I had to go to a party at Martha Baker's. I wore the pinafore.

I played "Indian Wigwam" at the party. At the end of the party, the people came around offering people cookies. But they let me have three. I didn't win a prize but two children gave me and Sammy a prize. Sammy was not invited to the party.

This night I had two games of Bird Lotto with David. I won the first game. David won the second game.

Mr. Weinberg taught me how to play some chords. They sound like chords in the song but I made them so they sound a little better.

This night I get to light three candles for Chanukah.

Love, Betsy

⌇

December 18, 1943

35 Station Complement
APO 639 NYC

Dear Son Sammy,

I was sorry to hear from Momma and you that you have been in bed sick. It is too bad we doctors haven't found out yet how to keep children well all the time. My little dog, Rafni,* has been sick too. She throws up. I know you would like her very much. She follows me wherever I go. When she runs she is so eager to get there she runs faster than her front legs can go so she has a tendency to ground loop. I haven't taken her flying yet. I'm afraid about the throwing up. Maybe the war will be over soon and I can come home to you, Ruth, Betsy, David, and your momma, who is my wife.

Love, Poppa

⌇

December 22, 1943

Dearest Isabel,

The dog has turned out to be a perfect companion. Her disposition is like Poochie's. It's easier for me to call her Poochie rather than

*He found and adopted Rafni while visiting the Royal Air Force in Northern Ireland.

{ 61 }

Reuben with Rafni in Northern Ireland, 1943

Rafni. Right now she is rolling about on the rug in my office wrestling with the new dog tag on her collar. She is mostly white so she'll be bathed once a week or oftener. Her wt is half a stone—7 lbs to you.

Love, Reuben

⌐

December 23, 1943

Dearest Reuben:

I received two letters from you today, one dated December 3 and one dated December 6. One of them had been sent airmail. It looks as if in winter air mail is no faster than V mail and both are slow.

I am writing on the back of Peter's drawing that looks as though it might be an illustration for Myron's phrase, "Ich kach auf dir." It repre-

Sammy, December 23, 1943

sents Peter sitting on the toilet and David in it. Actually Peter is sitting on top with the sole purpose of preventing David from getting out.

David's music teacher gave me an admit two ticket to the military ball of the Minnesota State Guard Dec. 27 at the armory. I thought about whom to ask. I finally decided to ask Al Gottlieb. He is divorced now. He is my cousin and likes me in a brotherly sort of way. I called him up. He was astonished to hear my voice after so many years. He said he did not want to go but he would. So I am going on a date. I told Anna Rush about it and I could tell from the dull tone of her voice that she had discovered that her idol (me) had feet of clay. But I assure you that everything will be overboard and that one evening of listening to talk of you and the children will be enough for Al.

I just spent eight dollars on the piano. Most of that was for regluing the action. The glue had been melted by the same Texas sun that blistered the table. I also spent thirteen fifty for a classy storm door for the maid's room. I got the storm door on just on time because we have had two cold spells since. The wind used to whistle through the little room but now the little room is nice and warm.

Love, Isabel

⌐

December 26, 1943

Dear Poppa:

We had a party at Sunday School this morning. I got a comic book and a box of chocolates. Then this afternoon there was another party. There were fish pools and people who guessed your weight and pin the tail on the elephant. You always get prizes because the man who guessed your weight he would guess it wrong on purpose. For instance, for Betsy he said a hundred something. In pin the tail on the elephant even if you pinned it in the wrong place you get a prize. And in the fishing pool you had to get something. There was another place that all I did was go in and the man said what do you want and I took it.

I got for twenty-five cents for the tickets a cardboard anti-aircraft gun, a tuck with a gun on it, a baseball game, and a popcorn ball. Sammy got crackerjacks. Oh, yes, I got a horn. Sammy got cracker-jacks and a holder. Oh gosh, and I got a key holder too. Sammy got a blackboard set too. Betsy got a plane that you blow off a stick, a horn, a blackboard set, a cheerio and a popcorn ball.

Love, David

⌐

December 30, 1943

Dear Children,

Happy new year to all of you. I hope it will be a better year than 43. And I hope your father comes home. How did you like the pictures of me and the dog? She is a good dog and you will like her I'm sure. Someday she will come flying home. Sammy sent me a nice pic-

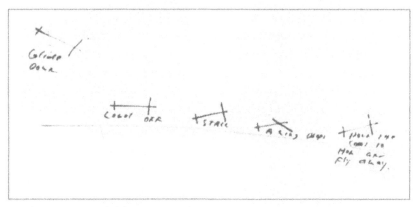

Reuben to Dear Children, December 30, 1943

ture of a paratroop attack. Here is a picture of a poor landing one of
your relatives made.
Glide down
    level off
        stall
            a wing drops
                pour the coal to her and fly away
But you learn from mistakes.
    You won't hear from me until I get back from Belfast at the end of
next week. I love you all.

Poppa

December 30, 1943

Dearest Reuben:
    Here is some more about Ruth Amelia. David has a map of the
world tacked above his bed. She climbs over to that end of the bed
and reaches up to tear the map, meantime looking very sweet and
mischievous. There was a piece of wall paper in our room a little
loose. She had to tear it more. When she is in the bathroom, which is
often, she gripes and squirms and makes angry and demanding noises

till she gets all the toothbrushes. She also likes to pull the toilet paper off the roll. On occasion she also pulls books out of shelves and destroys the continuity of games of cards or Chinese checkers. I made the mistake of giving her some chocolate marshmallow cookies. Now when she is in the kitchen she leans toward the cookie box and yells for chocolate cookies. Her nose runs all the time. Just the same we love her. She pats us all on the head and murmurs indistinctly, "Love, love, love, I love you." To which one of [us] always answers, "I love you too."

Love, Isabel

⌐

December 31, 1943

Dearest Reuben:

As the old year winds to a close we see that the slogan Victory in 43 was a snare and a delusion. Let us hope that Eisenhower's prediction of victory in 44 will come true.

Peter is going through another attack of illness. He has been sick off and on for about a month. I hope this letter reaches you before the one I wrote a couple nights ago. Right now, Peter is doing pretty well. I took him to Dr. Seham's office this morning. Dr. S. found that the entire drum was thickened, that the ear was draining nicely, and that nothing else was the matter. He advises continuing the sulfadiazine for another couple days and keeping in touch with him. Today Peter's temperature has not gone over 100, as far as I know.

The other day Betsy and David were having a tussle and Betsy was giving David a good fight. David said admiringly, "My, but she can fight well." Betsy remarked to me, "Some little girls are pretty and they can sing good but they're tough." Betsy was very cross the other day when I got David a new suit and no new clothes for her or Peter. David wanted a real suit. So I took him to Rothschild's and for $16.50 purchased a jacket and two pairs of knickers in a rather light blue all wool.

Ruth Amelia is very cute, but, in case you have forgotten, I will tell you what a year old baby will do.

Love, Isabel

The Long Away: 1944

〜

January 2, 1944

Dear Betsy,

My first letter of the new year goes to you because the first letter to reach me in 1944 was yours. I am very glad to hear from you and David and Sammy. You tell me things that Momma doesn't and they are things I want to hear, for instance about Ruth sucking her thumb. I don't want my children to be sucking their thumbs. I got a letter from Momma with my pictures in it. You must tell her I say thanks. I am going to Belfast for the week so I probably won't write again for a while. Will you do something for me? Kiss Momma, and David, and Sammy, and Ruth for me for Happy New Year. Soon I will have more pictures to send you. I love you all very much, especially my wife and children.

Love, Poppa

〜

January 18, 1944

Dear Poppy:

I am tired of having you to be overseas. I hope it is not a long time for the war to be over. I don't like to wait this long. I wish you were back in a minute. You are the nicest man in the whole world. When I was sick a girl who was called Happy she sent me some slotties.*

Dear Poppy: I want you to send me some cars.

---

*"Slotties" were a series of books with slotted, die-cut pieces at the back that could be removed and assembled to make three-dimensional figures.

Dear Poppy: We have got a fluorescent light in the kitchen. The (old) fixture we are going to give to Stafne's.

I love you very much and I hope the war will be over soon and you back with me.

Dear Poppy: I go back to school now and I had a test (Stanford Binet). I don't have to go to school till next Monday.

Dear Poppy: We went to dinner at Harry's cafe. We had roast beef, and apple pie, mashed potatoes and gravy, salad. Momma had two cups of coffee.

Dear Poppy: When I was coming home from the school the other day the baker saw me and he gave me a ride.

Love, Sammy

Dear Poppy:

I've got the letter that you wrote me. When I went to school this afternoon the nurse gave me a handkerchief and tomorrow morning when I go to school momma has to wash it real good and I'll take it back because it is the school's hanky.

When will you come home? When will you send me a present too? Gramma Sarah is going to make me a skirt out of the material that you sent me and momma. There was a magician show this afternoon. They are selling war bonds and stamps at school. They will give you the stamp book free. But I didn't go to the magician show on account of my nose is plugged up and I was coughing.

Happy sent me five paper doll books and I like them very much. Once in Sunday School well we went down in a room. There was a magician show there. The magician took an egg and cracked it in a bird cage and a canary came out. There was a man who guessed how much you weighed. Then you went fishing and you would get a prize. You would have to give him a ticket. I went fishing and got one of those airplanes that you blow. I got a whistle too. Sammy got a whistle and David got a whistle. It was very fun there and the next Sunday there was no Sunday school.

Love, Betsy

January 23, 1944 [*handwritten*]

Dear Papa,

Mr. Altrowitz took our den (I belong to the cubs you know) to see the Tribune and Star Journal [*Minneapolis newspapers*] being made. We saw the engraving dept and rows and rows of metal print. We also saw the machines that made the metal print. I got a lot of souvenirs. I got some metal print and some pieces of mats witch [*which*] are put under the metal print when they go under the rollers.

(Take this seriously) Arnold wants you to chip in on building a cabin on the point of Camp Arrowhead he did not sell.

Love, David

January 25, 1944

Dearest Reuben:

On Jan. 18 I took Betsy, David and Peter and three other children to the University to hear the second Children's concert with Serkin the soloist on the piano. David has already written to you about it. Peter drew airplanes and fire engines again. Betsy was somewhat tired but perked up when Serkin played the Mendelssohn concerto. That concerto was played beautifully by soloist and orchestra with no rehearsal.

Before the concert we had lunch at the Rainbow. David's friend Stephen Diamond ate there too. Betsy likes to tease him. When Mrs. Diamond came in she said to her, "I tell Stephen that when he grows up I'm going to marry him, but he doesn't like it." Mrs. D. said, "What, a nice little girl like you. I should think he'd be glad. I tell you what, I'll put in a good word for you." "Oh, don't do that," said Betsy. "I don't really mean it. I just tease him."

After the concert, thousands of little boys could not resist the temptation to throw snow balls.

Love, IRB

January 27, 1944

Dearest Reuben:

David has almost 18.75 saved up in his bank account. He wanted to buy a bond. I gave him a check. He is supposed to pay me back out of his savings account. Actually, he can have both. He did not want to put the bond in the name of David Berman and Isabel R. Berman. He made me the beneficiary. He said the bond was all his, and any explanations on my part about probate court only evoked from him the remark that he was going to live a long time. Betsy will get a bond next. They sell war saving stamps at school. With four dollars from Rose and Dave and about fifty cents a week at school it won't be long before Betsy can have a bond. And then will come Sammy.

Love, Isabel

January 27, 1944

Dear David,

Rafni is all mine but I don't know for how long. She has distemper and small dogs often die with it. I'll keep you posted on how she goes along. That was a very fine letter you wrote me about the hunting and fishing trip. And I promise you that we will go on a fishing trip the first summer I get home. I'm not so sure about the grizzly bear hunting. Maybe we should go after elephants and tigers.

Love, Poppa

February 2, 1944

Dearest Reuben:

Tonight Mr. Weinberg brought over a Conn soprano b flat curved saxophone. It has just been overhauled at a cost of $18.80. The dealers want fifty dollars for it. The sax is small enough for Betsy to handle. Would you be interested in buying it and having Betsy take lessons on it? I said I would write to you. My own inclination is to say no. Betsy looks awfully cute with the little saxophone slung on her neck. But I think you want her to play a more classical instrument. Besides, unless someone has time to help her with her practicing I think she should not take lessons now. Just the same, let me know what you think. Betsy is too small now, and probably will always be too small, to handle a cello. So that is out.

I will tell you about my dinner for Sam and your momma. I had vegetable soup, steak, baked potatoes, broccoli, mixed greens salad, cookies and tea. All trafe [*treyf, not kosher*], but your mother ate it anyhow. The soup had ox tails, steak trimmings Scott's tomato soup, celery, onions, carrots, parsnip, hot pepper, garlic, thyme, rice and barley and sugar and salt in it. The broccoli had steak fat, garlic and hot pepper. The cookies were a recipe I made up. I'll give it to you. Maybe you can use it in the army. Beat three eggs and one cup of sugar till light. Add one and one-fourth cups of flour and two tsp of baking powder sifted together, also a pinch of salt, add one cup of raisins that have been put through the grinder and the peeling of one orange that has also been put through the grinder. Bake in a rather flat pan at 360 degrees for about forty-five minutes. When not quite cold cut with a knife.

Your momma is so fond of pretty things that, tired as I am and unnecessary as it is, I have to doll the children up. Ruth Amelia has a fancy hair cut that makes her hair curl all over her head. Peter is going to get a hollywood suit. That has a jacket like a Florida sport jacket and a plain pair of pants. Ruth Amelia should also get a coat and hat and legging set.

Would you be interested in letting Maurice Goldberg have a fourth of the camera? The arrangement now is very convenient because Nathan, Arnold and I all live close together.

I bought some wieners at Abrams the other day. The Abrams work too hard. A customer came in and said, "I want some corn beef. It should be juicy and lean." Mrs. Abrams snapped, "How can it be both—What are you laughing for? The difference between you and me is I consider the guy behind the counter."

Love, Isabel

⌐

February 4, 1944

Dear Poppa:

You need a cat. The cat will find the mice. And when the cat finds the mice the cat will eat the mice. That's why you should have a cat. And you should have a dog for a pet. Why don't you go and kill a German? Don't you use anti aircraft guns?

I eat a lot. I do eat everything. I am going to be like you. I am getting fat. I hope you come back very soon.

Dear Poppy: I got a new suit today. We went there on the bus. We got it at Rothschild's. Dear Poppy: It's a light brown suit with long trousers.

Dear Poppy: Where do you keep your pistol?

Dear Poppy: Mommy is getting tired of you to be overseas. But there is some good use of you to go overseas. If you didn't go overseas we would not win the war.

Dear Poppy: The baby walks very fine. Momma knows how to run the movie projector.

Love, Sammy

Dear Poppa:

I was over at Arnold's house Sunday. Ethel gave me all different kinds of clothes and some overshoes too. I will tell you what they are. A plaid skirt, a velvet dress, a summer coat, three pairs of stockings, three pairs of pajamas.

I am a brownie scout and I got my pin too. The more you wear it the shinier it gets so it is a lucky pin. Penny is in it and we have a penny box. We bring pennies for the treats we get but so far no one has brought a penny and we are lucky that we have a girl named Penny.

Last Monday we didn't get any treats because we'd used them up the Monday before that.

You ought to send me a present today because my birthday is very near now. The month is February. On Christmas vacation we got some popcorn balls. Once in Sunday school well we got a box of candy free and in the afternoon we got to see a magician show and we got to see this man and he gave us some toys. I got a whistle. By the time Sammy came to him he was out of whistles but he went to another man and he got a whistle.

Goodbye, Betsy

⌐

February 7, 1944

Dearest Reuben:

Betsy was talking to Judy Beddor on the phone tonight. It seems they belong to different brownie scout organizations. Judy must have asked Betsy why she couldn't join the troop at [their] church. Betsy answered, "I don't go to your church. In fact, I am a Jew." Peter gave Ruth Amelia a pot of pee to drink yesterday. Fortunately, she spilled it on the floor. When he is feeling better, Peter thinks up mischief.

Love, Isabel

⌐

February 11, 1944

Dear Papa,

Ever since Arnold took those pictures of me playing the clarinet I have not puffed out my cheeks.

Mr. William Weinberg (you might know him) is my clarinet teacher. A boy in Wind Beginners class does not play so well so Mr. Weinberg told me to give him some help. He is going to come over every Friday. I am going to use the book I use for my private lessons.

Be careful about Rafni. I want you to bring home a live dog not a dead one.

Love, David

❧

February 13, 1944

Dearest Reuben:

Your mother has said that Rosie was afraid of the job of moving. Since the move is from one house to another in the same city with a lot of assistance from a well trained husband, she doesn't get much sympathy from me.

Yesterday I put Betsy on the bus and let her go down to the MacPhail by her self. My she was thrilled. Another time she took Peter to school on the bus. She said to him in a lofty way, "You don't need to pay any fare. You're too small."

Love, Isabel

❧

February 16, 1944

Dearest Reuben:

We have been having another session of sickness, nothing to compare with what we had in November and December, but enough to short me on sleep. First I got a bad cold in the head, one hundred per cent obstruction. Then Ruth Amelia got a cold and David a cough. Betsy and Peter are OK so far. I got some more of Dr. Seham's medicine. It is some sort of expensive nose drops with sulfa in it. It worked fine for me and for the baby. In a burst of enthusiasm I tried it on David. He swallowed a little and said it made him sick. That was about nine at night. At two AM he woke up with the symptoms of food poisoning. He had no fever. He kept throwing up. He stayed in bed a day, up and around a day and then back to school. Of course, it may have been the mucous from his nose that made him throw up.

Ruth Amelia has had an upper respiratory infection with nose running more than usual. Her fever has been up to 103.2 by tail. I give her aspirin. I have not called Dr. S., but may do so if she is not over it in a day or so.

I am sure you are not worried by this. It is just routine winter illness in Minnesota.

Peter was talking to Mr. Weinberg this evening in this way. "I am going to take our toboggan and a propeller and an engine and wings. Then I'll have a plane. Poppa will be the pilot. Betsy will be the belly gunner. Ruth Amelia will be the tail gunner. David will be the nose gunner. I will be the navigator. Momma? Oh, she'll be dead by the time we're grown up."

Mr. Kahz always calls up when David is absent from Hebrew school. This time he told me, "Ach, such a lovely boy, Davie. If only all the people in the world were like that what a wonderful world it would be. Such an understanding boy. Such judgment. Such perception!"

David is getting a fine clarinet tone.

Love, Isabel

⌣

February 18, 1944

Dearest Reuben:

On Feb. 16 we received your air mail letter dated Feb. 7, with check for Betsy enclosed. That is the best mail service since you left 634 [*the APO number*]. Betsy was suitably impressed to get a check for her to spend. She wants to go to Dayton's and buy a book.

David, Betsy, Sammy, Isabel, and Ruth in the living room, about 1943

It is easy for me to send you a package if it is for one thing. Then I make the arrangements by telephone and mail and some one else does the mailing. In such a manner I am having sent to you a two-pound box of FF [*Fanny Farmer*] candy and four and a half pounds of Feinberg's kosher sausage. It may be that getting the sausage just off the line and having it packed professionally will decrease the amount of green mold. All to the good now that penicillin is known to come from mold. Of course it may be a different mold.

I did not tell you all about our dinner Monday night. Your momma could not come. We had only Sam Rush. It was Valentine's day and he brought me a heart shaped box of candy. He brought candy for the children. We had gefillte fish, nice fresh people's bread, baked potatoes, salad, tea cookies and candy.

While I put Ruth Amelia to bed Sam was having the children balance on one quart mason jars. Peter had two of them. Sam told him that one was enough but Peter kept on playing with two. Finally one broke. Sam spoke just a little sharply to Peter. Peter's feelings were hurt. After a while Sam said, "You come over here and tell me you won't do that again and give me a hug and a kiss and we'll be friends." "That," said Peter, "is just what I was thinking of doing." Then Sam said, "Now you know you shouldn't have played with that jar when I told you not to." Peter answered, "Yes, it was a darn thing to do."

Betsy was talking about fractions to Osher, who is almost eleven. He was rather hazy on the definition of a fraction. "What," said Betsy, "don't you know what a fraction is? A fraction is one or more equal parts of a whole."

Peter also started to draw a boat in school, but used the mast to start him off drawing a stork. He drew the stork carrying an empty diaper. Miss Seidlitz told him to finish the picture and put in the baby. He told her that his stork was on his way home. Once Miss Seidlitz was lecturing the children because they had not paid attention to something she had said. Peter looked sad and then said softly, "I try to be good."

I went to a PTA party last nite.

Love, Isabel

⌁

February 22, 1944

Dear Poppy:

I went to the fathers and sons banquet. I did eat every thing. I ate some of my milk and David drank the rest. We saw a magician show and a moving picture show and it was really good. In the moving picture show, the teeter totter always hit the man on the head.

I got an airplane that you blow away and a whistle.

I had milk, meat loaf, green beans and potatoes. And for dessert I had vanilla ice cream with chocolate sauce.

Arnold took me.

Dear Poppy: Sam Rush was over at our house. I putted butter on his suit, just for fun. And Sam Rush threw most of the butter and it landed on the wall. And in ten hours, (ten minutes) we made friends.

Sammy Berman

Dear Poppy: I saw some little rooms at the Art Institute today. They weren't the Thorne rooms. They were the cutest rooms.

[Betsy]

⤴

February 22, 1944

Dear Poppy:

I am not teaching that boy to play the clarinet because there is another boy who is in wind advanced who can play just as good as I can and lives a little closer.

I went to a fathers and sons banquet with Arnold. They passed off [*out*] solid model airplanes and blow airplanes [that] blow off a cardboard stick. For your information I built that solid model all by myself with a little help from a friend who wasn't very good at it either. It was a Spitfire. It was built something like the F39 I got in Louisville, I think Louisville, and you built [it] while I was in Sunday school and I got mad at you.

Arnold gave me a notebook and three world maps that look the same that you can draw on with a pencil and also a world map puzzle consisting of triangles and squares.

Our class in clarinet has gotten a new book. I can play every song in it now. At the beginning there are just songs but towards the middle there begins to be trios and quartets. There are some green music books down in [the] basement which say by Lind. They are duets with part violin. I was wondering how come part violin. It should be part clarinet. I would like you to tell me what you use them for. There are quite a few.

I have a cardboard horn and guess what I did with it. I punched holes in it so now it can play four notes.

Up in my room I have four maps, no five maps. But two of them are not hung up.

When I said your letters were boring I only meant that I'd like you to talk a little more than about the countryside and things like that. I would like you to tell me a little more about Rafni and about Miss Skinner's sister.

We went two times to try and see Mrs. Thorne's miniature rooms but we have failed.* We could not go because the first time we would have to wait an hour and a half and today we would have had to wait four hours. There was a line a block and a half long. I would think that all the people in Minneapolis and three fourths of the people in St. Paul went to see them. If you don't know what the Thorne rooms are, a lady named Mrs. Thorne who lives in Chicago has a hobby of making little miniature rooms and she called upon some architects to help her and she has, I believe, thirty-six rooms from olden times like the Pilgrims to a penthouse in San Francisco. One of the rooms, Miss Skinner said, would cost three thousand dollars to copy. That is a bit out of my line, yours too.

Love, David

⌐

February 28, 1944

Dear Poppy:

I have the funniest things to tell you about Betsy and Sammy. I'll take up Sammy first. Well, one day Sammy and I were having a little quarrel so Mommy started to get mad at me so I said, "Mommy, even if you kill me I won't let Sammy play with any of my toys because he always wrecks them." (That's the truth.) Sammy said in the most angelic way, "If Momma kills you then I'll play with your toys." We all laughed very much and Sammy started to get mad because we laughed.

*Mrs. James Ward Thorne's American rooms in miniature were exhibited at the Minneapolis Institute of Arts, January 5–February 28, 1944, on loan from the Art Institute of Chicago.

The one about Betsy is not so funny but it will tell you how funny Betsy is sometimes. Well, she was inviting guests to her party and the first one that got the funny part was me. Betsy said, "I don't think I'll invite you because you didn't get me a present." To Gerald Jackson she said, "You'd better hurry up and get me a present." And she said to Osher, "I don't think I'll invite you because it's too late for you to get me a good present."

At the Temple Israel Sunday School we have a little bit of Hebrew and there was a story about a bird in our book and I took one look at it and knew it by heart so the Hebrew teacher sent me downstairs to the library to get a book and read for the last fifteen minutes while the rest of the class was studying their Hebrew.

At orchestra (you know I'm in the school orchestra) Mr. Weinberg told us that for next Thursday we would have to be able to play "Mares eat oats." I could play it by ear if I know the tune but I only know part of the tune so I can just play a little bit. I would be in quite a fix but since I take private lessons from Mr. Weinberg I can ask him where I can get the music.

I hope Rafni gets better because I got your letter that said that she wasn't feeling so good.

It is almost a year that you have been overseas. I should think that the army would give you leave to come for a while. But you must come to Minneapolis, and not to New York or San Francisco or any other place like that. Because I am not going to leave Minneapolis.

Love, David

⌐

March 1, 1944

Dear Poppa:

Thank you for the check. For my birthday I got a book. The name of it was Whitetail. Whitetail was a baby deer. He was a boy deer. I got it from Suzan, Ruby's little girl.* Peter Edelman gave me three

*Ruby Gottlieb Klugman was Isabel's cousin.

Uncle Wiggly books. And I got a petticoat and two blouses and a plaid skirt. I had a doll without no hair but Gramma Sarah made some red hair for her and she made her two beautiful dresses. They were both satin. One of them was purple with a sash and a flower on it. And she made some stockings and some shoes. And the other one was a striped dress, all different colors stripes with a bandanna to match. And I got some flowers that I could plant and directions too. I got a shovel and an axe and a rake, and flower pots and little dishes. The directions said not to keep them up in my room but to keep them down in the basement for three days.

We had two cakes. One was a chocolate cake. It was very beautiful. It had six pink candles and one blue candle. It had little designs on it. I was seven years old. For my birthday I got some stencils too. Marlys was away on Sunday so she gave me my present on Saturday. She said I could open it so I did. It was a paint book and some paints.

Love, Elizabeth

March 1, 1944

Dear Poppa:

I hope you will send me a toy. When are you going to send me a toy, on my birthday or later? I would like it to be on my birthday.

Dear Poppa: Momma makes blintzes. I love them.

Dear Poppy: I got five pennies for the prize at Betsy's birthday and with the nickel I let David carry it and he kept it in his pocket and after school we walked down to Walgreen's and I got a whistle made of chewing gum flavoring and colored. It was colored orange. And boy did it ever taste good. And when you first get it it whistles. But when it's all chewed up it won't blow.

Dear Poppy: Mommy went to the beauty parlor and I saw a little girl. She was in my room in school. Her name was Judy Segal and I played with her outdoors.

Dear Poppy: Down in the gymnasium, that's under the school in the basement we are going to have a canary show on Thursday and Friday.

Dear Poppy: There was a paper sale and Momma stayed up half of the night getting the paper fixed up. And then next morning we had so much paper and I carried some of the boxes.

Dear Poppy: Betsy didn't win the paper sale prize and I had a bigger pile than they did.

Love, Sammy Berman

⌐

March 7, 1944

39th Service Group
APO 639 NYC

Dearest Isabel,

Yesterday came the records. Playing these was like a visit home. You tell the children that I enjoyed them all, the jokes and singing, Betsy's piano playing, David's clarineting, Sammy's sweet voice, your master-of-ceremonying. It was the best package I've had since the movies. The records came all safe and sound in their paper buffing. I also got a package from Gramma Sarah, some photographs and a salami. Will you call her and tell her it arrived? I just wrote her too before the pkg. arrived. Salamis should be small and sent whole. They keep better than when cut to fit a package as Sarah did. But a little extra mold just adds to the flavor. I'll thank her myself in a few days. It's strange that with slow mail service the packages come through at all.

Love, Reuben

⌐

March 10, 1944

Dearest Reuben:

Thursday, March 2, I took David to the University band concert. I am sending the program under separate cover. He enjoyed the concert so much that I think it would be nice to take him often. March 3 was Sylvia's birthday. I had a beautiful chocolate cake from Egequist with decorations. All I gave Sylvia was a Young Quinlan hankie. She gave me a box of Abdallah's candy. Arnold gave me a box of FF candy. Ethel and Sylvia were here for dinner and Arnold in the evening.

March 4 was my birthday. David wanted to get me a North Star woolen blanket but I think the North Star is closed on Saturday afternoon. David and Peter went to Sheffield's and got me an ivy plant. They plan to work out the money shovelling snow and drying dishes. Betsy got left when they went to Sheffield's. Her feelings were very hurt. I had to give her some money and let her go to Sheffield's. She bought two small cacti.

Sunday, March 5 was Sunday school. I thought I had pulled a good psychological trick when I got Peter the new suit and told him it was a shame to have such a beautiful suit with no place to wear it. It worked once. He went to Sunday school, but this time, he went almost as far as the door and then came back to the car. He likes it better at home.

March 6. Betsy was in the eurhythmics demonstration at the college woman's club. Oh yes, Sunday, March 5, Rosie and your momma came over. Your momma brought hamantaschen. Rose played the piano and enjoyed David's clarinet and piano playing. Rose wanted to see Betsy at the college woman's club but she overslept. Betsy was just wonderful. She wore a wine color velveteen dress. She did the march march march, the step bends, the pitch pictures and the rest of eurhythmics which you may remember.

March 8 was Purim. My hamantaschen are much better than your mother's. Mine have a cookie crust and a filling of chopped prunes, raisins, pecans, honey and lemon juice. David told me that there was a Purim party at the Adath for the Hebrew School children. I took him there only to discover there was no party but just refreshments to be served after services. Even for David, I will not go to any old religious service. We walked over to Rushes'. Anna said I was intransigent.

Love, Isabel

⌇

March 12, 1944

Dear Poppa:

I hate jazz with all of my heart. For my part, it stinks. I can play the chromatic scale very well from low A which is as low as you can go to two C's above middle C. (It would be on the piano two B flats above middle B flat, of course.) Then above, I can play the chromatic scale but not very well and I have to have the notes in front of me because the notes is how you play it. I have not done any transposing in my clarinet work. As I said, I can play the clarinet about five times as better as you heard me on the record or saw me in the movies. Please do not laugh too much on that moving picture.

The children in our room at school liked your letter very much. I am going to ask Miss Skinner if the whole class can't write to you. However, it will be quite a time, if we do, before you get the letter because she insists on the letters being perfect and we have to do them over quite a few times.

A very funny thing happened today. I went into the kitchen to get a glass of water and after I came back Ruth Amelia went Uh-uh and I had to give her the water. I went back in the kitchen to get another glass of water. When I came back Ruth went uh-uh again and I had to give her that water. Finally, when she wasn't looking I got a glass of water and drank it.

I received your check for one dollar. Thanks a lot for the check. I think I am going to have Mommy get me a set of pictures at the Art Institute for three dollars. It is too bad that those pictures of planes that you got from the Coca-cola company got lost in the moving.

I am going to see the Shrine circus tomorrow. It is going to be a lot of fun. I believe the last time I went there I was only about six years old.

In Hebrew school we are learning the kiddush [*blessing over the wine*] and the maneshtonoh* in our sidurs [*prayer books*]. In one of my next letters the whole letter will be on the kiddush and then I will have a whole letter with the maneshtonoh recited.

I got some film for my camera today over at the cut rate drugs. Tomorrow I am going to take some pictures. I think I take pretty good pictures but I will have to wait before they are developed before I make sure of it because I can't remember the last time I took pictures how they came out.

How's the old chap getting along over in Ireland?

Love, David

P.S. Improve your hand writing.

⌐

March 14, 1944

Dearest Reuben:

March 11, I took the children out for dinner at the Rainbow. I started to order vanilla milk for David. "No," he said, "I will take plain milk." "It won't cost any more to have the vanilla," said the waitress. David still said he would take plain milk. After the waitress left he whispered to me that he did not want to put them to any trouble.

Do not suppose from that that he is an angel though. He will sometimes bound [out] of bed in the morning and get dressed and then taunt Peter by saying that he, David, was the first one dressed. He will tell Betsy that she stinks or that he likes Peter better. Also when Peter chants impishly "David stinks and smells, David stinks and smells," David will reply "The same to you." Of course, this last shows up Peter even more than David.

*"Ma Nishtana" (Why is this night) are the first words of the Four Questions on "Why is this night different from all other nights?" traditionally asked by the youngest child at the Seder dinner for the holiday of Passover.

Peter loves to answer the telephone. So does Betsy. I made a rule that the first time the phone rings in the morning, Peter is to answer it, then Betsy, then Peter and so on. Of course Betsy realizes that Peter is answering the phone oftener than she does by this system but she is reconciled to it. Still when the phone rings and I am upstairs, both of them will race to the phone and howl till I get down. Both your mother and David think Betsy should give in on this matter, but I hope to have them taking turns with less excitement.

Yesterday Betsy was about to start for school. I could find two overshoes for the left foot but none for the right. Betsy has two pairs, one larger and one smaller. So I said, "Betsy, this goes to show what comes of not putting your overshoes in the closet. Now you'll have to go to school without overshoes and if you get cold you'll just have to stop in at a store and warm up." Peter said nothing but after Betsy left I asked him if he knew where the overshoes were. He replied sweetly, "Yesterday I was mad at Betsy so I took her overshoes and threw them in the bushes." I looked in the bushes and sure enough there were the overshoes.

Love, Isabel

⌣

March 23, 1944

Dearest Reuben:

On March 18, I took the children, and Roger Tweed, down to the auditorium to see the Shrine Circus. They were all good except that Betsy might have been better. The tiger act was missing because the trainer got badly scratched a few days before. David wanted to wait for the trained seal act but there wasn't any. One clown piled up two tables and three barrels with a chair on the very top. He rocked precariously back and forth and finally fell off. Tonight Peter put a box on top of the table we bought from Barney and a Mexican chair on top of the box. He sat on top of the chair looking impish but, unlike the clown, he did not fall off. They sold large Mickey Mouse balloons

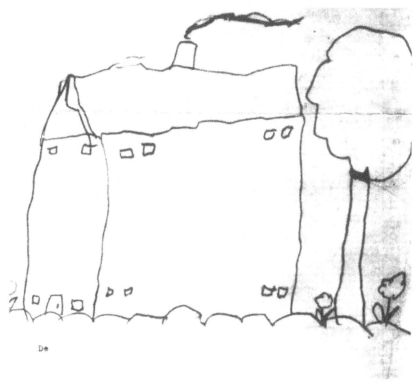

De

Betsy, August 31, 194[3]

at the circus at twenty cents apiece. Ruth Amelia got to play with the
ear of one broken balloon. It was her first experience with a balloon.
She was delighted. She said B'oom, b'oom, and bit it till it broke.
Betsy wanted a drum major's baton. She likes to strut up and down
and twirl the baton.

Sunday March 19, I took Betsy to see the Russian ballet and the
Minneapolis Symphony. It was the same ballet I saw in Louisville
with Mrs. Frittier. I mean it was the same cast. The program was
different.

Love, Isabel

March 29, 1944

Dearest Reuben:

David received a present from Jack. It was two medals "Chevalier della casa di Savoi." They are white enamel crosses with gold filigree with a gold crown on one side and a black eagle and white cross on the other. David can't go around wearing medals and I don't want to wear a cross but I could make a pretty mother and daughter set of matching chains by buying a couple of gold filled chains for the medals.

Mr. Weinberg brought over a three quarter size violin today. Betsy liked it. But it is made in Germany. It can be had for twenty-five dollars. Do you think Betsy is still too young to take lessons? Mr. Weinberg seems to think that she might as well start soon. I would not want her to start till after school is out. Please write right away what you think about this.

Love, Isabel

⌐

[April 7, 1944]

Major E. B. (Buddy) Cohen, M.C.
Artzoth Habrith, First Day of Pesach

Dear Reuben:

Well? Happy Pesach! We're truly sorry that we cannot share the sedorim [*Seders*] with you. Maybe a detailed account of the goings on at 1001 will serve as an inadequate substitute. Lil and I got 7 days off with permission to visit Canada. At the last minute we cancelled the Canadian half of the Pesach hegira, inasmuch as Barbara Sue is recovering from two weeks of another congestive but uncomplicated bronchitis. This damn machine doesn't know the difference between a comma and an asterix.

The first seder, last night, was at Jean's and Sarah's. The following were present: Marion and Israel, Mr. Grossman, Sr., Morrie and Edith, Lil and Bud, Sarah and Jean, and (now we come to the point of the communication) Isabel, Betsy and David.

Two guesses as to who were the stars of the show. Both right! Such enthusiasm! Such verve! Such pure joy in singing! Such voices! Such Hebrew! Would you part with one for a small sum? Maybe a million down and so much a week? David asked the Vier Questions in Hebrew with not so much as a moment's hesitation. Ivrith tsachoh b'fiev [*in Hebrew in a loud voice*]. And Betsy asked them in English: at least until she got to #3, at which point she got shy and sat down and buried her face in Sarah's shoulder.

The best is yet to come. In addition to taking their regular turn at the reading of the answer—Betsy's contribution being a trifle less substantial than David's because of (one) coyness and (two) age difference—your incomparable brats led the singing.

There are several ways of singing "Adir Who" and "Chad Gadyo."* But Betsy and David admit of knowing but one way. Mit *choshek* [*with vigor*]. Their sweet, clear voices sounded out over the tumult of our coarser melody like an angel's tune, and David and Betsy's "Adir Who" had something of the Last Amen.

We are shortly on our way to see the other two—forgive us if we hold off until we get to the Homestead on Holmes before we continue +++

3528 Holmes, and what a riot—of fun. Just got Betsy off my shoulders after running myself ragged playing "Silver" to her Lone ranger. David gave out all the while on his clarinet—and does he play a sweet wind? His dad never did as well at the same age. Sammy just stuck an almond in my mouth, one he had cracked with his own two hands, so I guess he's coming into his honest heritage of hospitality at a tender age. Ruth Amelia is on the floor perusing "The Ferryman" by Bishop and Wiese. David and Sammy have to their credit as shipbuilders one each aircraft carrier and destroyer; the former now sailing on the easy swells of the living room rug; the latter at anchor in the relative calm of the dining room table harbor. Sammy—a

---

*"Adir Hu" (Praise the Lord) and "Chad Gadyo" (One Kid) are traditional Passover songs.

chummy pal big of heart if ever I saw one—is sitting on my lap cracking nuts for the two of us. Which complicates the problem of taming this machine a trifle—but what a joy! Well, David shouts something to the effect that Arnie is on the phone to say hello. So I bounce Sammy off my lap. And he says "Oh nuts."

Love from Lil, B. S., Sam, David, Betsy, Ruth Amelia and Isabel and me [*Buddy Cohen*].

~

April 9, 1944

Dearest Reuben:

Well, almost a year has passed since you left me in Tampa. I thought then that you would be back in a year. Now it still seems that it will be a year before you come back.

Here is an old story about Diane. Her momma was reading a letter and weeping. Diane said, why are you crying? Denise answered, They're sending daddy overseas. Why, exclaimed Diane, the sons of bitches!

Diane also said this to her mother. Momma, do girls like me marry Jews? Denise said, well—. Diane continued, Marlys says girls like me don't marry Jews but I promised Sammy I would marry him and I have to keep my promise.

Marlys, by the way, is a dopey little girl.

Betsy took it upon herself to repeat to Marlys what I had told her about bleeding once a month. Marlys told her mother who said that it wasn't so. I have told Betsy a number of times that she should not repeat what I say, also that she should think before she speaks. Some of my advice has taken effect, because, at the seder, she was a model child.

Love, Isabel

~

April 10, 1944

Dearest Reuben:

David and I were invited to Seder April 7 at Aunt Jean's. But when Betsy told Gramma Sarah in confidence that she, Betsy, had the four questions memorized in English Sarah finagled an invitation for Betsy too. I was all set to bring some Passover dishes for a present but Sarah said not to. In the first place, she was paying for our Seder suppers. In the second, Jennie had too many household goods as it was. So I had a pretty rose plant sent out from Sheffield's.

As you might expect, Peter was very angry because he was not invited. I bought him a paper tank full of FF candy kisses, but it didn't help much. Just after we drove away your momma called up to see if we had left. Peter answered the phone. "Sob, sob. Is this Gramma Sarah? Yes, they've left. I don't like you any more. Why couldn't I come? Why wouldn't Aunt Jean let me come? Then I don't like Aunt Jean," and so on.

I wore my scotch wool suit with matching hat, red coat and black shoes. David wore his blue suit and topcoat. Betsy wore the skirt that matches my suit, white blouse, red coat and hat.

Those present at the Seder were Buddy and Lillian, Israel and Marian, Sarah, Jean, Mr. Grossman, Edith and Morris, and the three of us. Barbara Sue was asleep upstairs. Sumner and Dora [Cohen] came over later. Your momma gave David a Kiddush cup [*a wine cup to hold while saying the Kiddush*] and a blue and white silk yarmulke for his birthday. David sang the four questions like an angel. He read the responsive reading with gusto. Betsy knocked them cold with her beauty. She said one question of the four. After the supper the children sang Had Gad Yoh [*same as "Chad Gadyo"*] and Al B'nai* but I didn't hear that. David and Betsy each collected a dollar for finding the afikommen.** Your momma sent Peter a dollar too. I heard Betsy tell one of her friends that soon Momma will have false teeth because

*"El B'nai" (God of Our People) is part of "Adir Hu."

**The middle matzah, a piece of unleavened bread, of three matzoth on the Passover Seder plate is the afikomen, traditionally hidden away during the meal. The children are sent to look for it after the meal, and the finder is rewarded with a prize.

she has already lost two permanent teeth. After the Seder I had to go up to see Morris G. to have a temporary filling put in. Most of the tooth had crumbled away leaving the inlay scraping my tongue. The next day Morris tapped the inlay and it fell out.

I could tell at the Seder that your momma was not feeling too well. How? Well, Buddy was running the Seder in his smooth Cohen manner. But when he would say, "We will skip this part," your momma would say, "oh no." When Lillian said, "Let's phone Winnipeg now," your momma said, "do it later." When Buddy said, "We'll leave out the spilling the droplets of wine because it might get on the table cloth," your momma said, "If we do it this way it does not get on the table cloth." She knows better, I hope, but when she is very tired she forgets. The next night she had a gall bladder attack. David's party I shall have to leave for another letter.

Love, Isabel

⌣

April 12, 1944

Dear Poppa:

I went to the Seder at Mrs. Sarah Berman's. I asked the four questions in Hebrew, mind you. I sang them, also. For a Pesach present Gramma Sarah gave me a blue and white yarmulke. And for a birthday present she gave me a silver wine cup. She didn't give it to me at once because she wanted to get my name engraved on it. I also sang Ehod Meedayoh.* I found the afikommen and for it Mr. Grossman gave me one silver dollar. Buddy Cohen was there too.

For my birthday I had eight children and I forget how many grown ups. I got a book called Twenty Thousand Leagues Under the Sea from Adrian Pass; a globe from Arnold; two dollars and fifty cents in war stamps from Uncle Dave; a football game from Sander; a sellophone from Julian and Jeremy; an airplane game from Barney; a purse from Albert with my initials on it; a dollar and fifty cents from

*"Echod Mi Yodea" (Who Knows One) is a traditional Passover song.

David, locating his father's whereabouts on the
globe that Arnold gave him, 1944

Judy Silverman and Billy Silverman; a dollar from Anna Rush; a dollar from you; three dollars from Auntie Sylvia which I am going to
subscribe to National Geographic with. Incidentally with the three
dollars of my money I got some very very beautiful pictures of some
ships at the Art Institute. There were ten of them. And from my
beloved mother I got a fifteen dollar work bench equipped with tools.
And also from Powers Mom bought us four chairs, one for each of us
for ten dollars. Betsy painted hers red. Sammy varnished his. Myself
and Ruth Amelia are going to paint ours blue because our eyes are
blue. I hope Ruth Amelia's eyes do not change because brown is not a
beautiful color.

Do you like the picture of Momma that you got from Gene Garrett?

Arnold happens to be going into the navy today. I called him up last night to say goodbye but he wasn't at home so I left a message to call me back so he called me back today.

With forty-nine cents of my money I got a baseball. Now I play baseball almost every day with a boy named Roger Tweed and a boy named Michael Carroll. Gerald Jackson, you know, has moved to Thirty-first and Irving.

Love, David

⮑

April 14, 1944

Dear Poppa:

Remember in St. Petersburg when you were at the airfield working we found a rat hiding in the bushes when we were sitting on the steps and me and David chased him over to Mr. Sprinkel's and we called Mr. Sprinkel, "Mr. Sprinkel, here is a rat." And he came out and he stepped on the rat and he made a sore on the rat and he killed the rat. And then we went home and we buried the rat.

Dear Poppy: I told my mother to buy a box of Fanny Farmer candy to send you so when you go out you can give some people some Fanny Farmer candy. And we'll send you a Hershey bar too. And hide it so when the mouse comes in he won't get it.

Dear Poppy: You fly in a Cub but there is some airplanes that don't have any wings and they can go backwards and forwards and sidewards and they have a propeller on top.

And I drew my picture that I'm sending to you in school and I'm sure that you'll like it very very well.

What are you doing in Ireland? Do you know that I have got a new suit? And we've got some dishes and they're new and you never saw them before, you never saw them in your whole life. And they match the dishes that we got in St. Petersburg so we mix them up and have them to be a set. We have a white cup and a white pitcher and they're both little.

And I wish you were back right this minute. And one time I had a very good dream. I dreamt that you were back in Minneapolis. It's spring now in Minneapolis. I am now in Minneapolis. And don't try to say I'm not cause I am. And I wish it was really true that if you wished on a wishing bone and if you got the top half your wish would come true. I know that the war is still on. And we must win the war and that we are going to do. And last night I dreamt that I made a Japanese airplane crash and I heard them say, the pilot said to the copilot, I bet he doesn't know that we've got swords. It was good because it was only a dream.

I love you very much. And I wish that you'd get me a Hershey bar, too. I do go over to Anna Rush's and I want my momma to leave me there. And I drew a picture. Anna Rush has an infection in her knee. And Sam Rush he works. And Anna Rush has a nurse. And one time I went to Anna Rush's and I had lunch over there with the nurse. And I told the nurse that I thought it was fun to eat with the nurse. And I really haven't got a fairy. Betsy has a fairy tale. And I know you can only fly if you have wings. Birds are the only animals that can fly. And kites—they are things that can fly. Do you remember when David used to fly kites? I do love you a lot.

Sammy

April 17, 1944

Dearest Isabel,

Yesterday your long awaited picture arrived. I was thrilled with it. I think it's the best picture you've had since our wedding pictures. It looked as though caring for 4 children all by yourself isn't causing you any worry lines. I'm going to mount it in some sort of frame. There is too much coal dust about to stand it up in the folder.

My dentist is in the hospital with low back pain. I visited him yes-

Isabel Berman, March 1944. "Yesterday your long awaited picture arrived," Reuben wrote on April 17.

terday and came away with a book to read, "Capricorn"—a black and tan study on Australia.

I calibrated one ultra-violet machine yesterday. Result: my back is a blushing red and my front a bit pink. This is one way to avoid the prison pallor that I would otherwise bring home.

I have found a camera to fit Arnold's film so I shall have some larger size prints of some non-censor-able subjects to send eventually.

Love, Reuben

April 17, 1944

Dear Children,

The houses around Lake Harriet or around Fremont and 48th in
Minneapolis here would be called castles. Ordinary homes here are
mostly "semi-detached"—a euphemism for a duplex. The rooms are
mostly small. The heating system with a fireplace in each room is not
as wasteful as it sounds. There are usually only two fires going at any
one time—one in the kitchen and one in the drawing room. At meal-
time one simply shovels the fire out of the drawing room fireplace
and puts it in the dining room. Fires in bedrooms are peacetime luxu-
ries. An English family spends a lot of time together in one room
where the fire is. That is one reason many English people are good
conversationalists. They often sit about the fire talking.

Love, Poppa

When you go to a home here you must visit the whole family.
You'll find them all together. When you first come in you will be
offered the best and softest chair on which you must sit down. But
early in the evening you should find some excuse to move to the
straight back chair, so the master of the house can have his chair
which he offered and you took earlier out of politeness.

Cigarettiquette demands that you smoke an English cigarette (at
2/6=50¢ a pack) the first time they are passed around. After that you
may without offense insist on passing everyone Camels (at 3d=5¢ a
pack to us). It is wrong to judge things by wartime standards but
unfortunately those are the only standards we see.

Your loving Poppa

April 18, 1944

Dearest Reuben:

I also enjoy Sammy's drawings and scissors work. By ordinary mail I am sending you an airplane that he cut out of light weight cardboard. He wanted to play a game called Find the Airplanes. So for David's party he cut out about twenty of these little planes and hid them. He hid them so well and I keep house so poorly that I am still finding them.

David is still tactful and proper. At the Seder, Morris asked him why he didn't come to see him when he was in the neighborhood seeing Arnold. He replied that he didn't go where he wasn't invited. Betsy asked your momma to come and live with us in our spare room. David said that we would have to become civilized first. David did not invite Adrian Pass to his party till the day of the party. Edna said to David, "But, David, why didn't you call sooner?" David answered that he had tried the night before but didn't get any answer. One day Peter found some chalk and was drawing his inimitable pictures on the sidewalk. David rubbed the picture out with his heel. I thought that the motive for David's action was teasing. It was, about ninety per cent. For the rest, David said, "Momma, do you know why I rubbed out the pictures? I thought that if someone went past and saw the pictures on the sidewalk they would think we were vagabonds." Peter drew pictures on the Stafnes' sidewalk and received a talking to from Mrs. Stafne. David overstepped his authority by stepping over the chalk. I found another piece for Peter and made him use a black board in the house. He was so angry at David that the birthmark on his forehead was purple.

Love, Isabel

April 22, 1944

Dearest Reuben:

Thursday, April 20, I took Betsy down to Dr. Seham's office. Peter
went along for the ride. Ruth Amelia stayed home with Mrs. Wyman.
Ruth had a cold, a fever, and two lower molars coming in. I took
Betsy to Dr. S.'s because Betsy was going to the toilet so often in
school that Miss DeSmidt said she would write her name in a book
every time she went. I think Miss D. thought better of it later and
consulted the school nurse about Betsy's frequency. Well, we got to
Doctor S.'s office. Peter smiled brightly and announced that Betsy
was here because she went to the toilet too often. Dr. S. asked Peter if
Betsy couldn't do her own talking. Betsy is one pound above average
weight for her height and age. Dr. S. said that she has a fine physique.
He smiled appreciatively too indicating that she is a small knock out.
He examined Betsy's chest and said, "Why, this is a rash. She has the
German measles." He told me that she might have an irritable blad-
der, that I should give her lots of liquids, that if the frequency persist-
ed I should bring in a sample of her urine. Peter is underweight. He
looks anemic but his blood count is normal. His tonsils, according to
Dr. S., must come out. Do you think I should have Joe [*Dr. Joseph
Garten*] take them out early this summer?

After we got home and I had Betsy in bed, she started to cry. She
said, "When Auntie Sylvia is sick you send her flowers. Now I am
sick and you don't give me any flowers." So I got her a beautiful plant
called the Martha Washington with fuschia color flowers, blue crepe
paper, and bow of orchid ribbon. Today David got sick and I had to
get him a plant too.

Your momma invited David to have dinner at Jean's and stay over
night and go to Hillel Aronson's Bar Mitzvah. David was his usual
sweet self Friday night but Saturday morning he seemed to have a
slight cold and fever of 99.2. Your momma took him to the Bar
Mitzvah anyhow and he broke out there.

Love, Isabel

April 25, 1944

Dear Poppa:

I have had the German measles. I had some books from the library and Momma returned them and got me two books and I can read both of them.

Sammy made a covered wagon although it really wasn't covered. And we had lots of people on it. It is a play of the comic book though not exactly of the comic book. There is June and Bucky and Joe and Mary and June's little girl and Mary's little girl. And there are six bandits, who attack the covered wagon. They have a bow and toothpick arrows and that was like in the comic book. Sammy knows how to make a bow and arrow very well but it is very hard to get the materials. The materials are he cuts out a piece of cardboard like a half of a moon then he takes a rubber band and stretches it across where there is nothing and the arrows are toothpicks. Then he puts his thumb out and puts the finger next to it on that little hole and puts the finger on top and then he pushes the finger off very quickly. Meanwhile the toothpick is on top of the cardboard and between the rubber band and when you do that to it it goes away very quickly. I cannot shoot it so far but Sammy can shoot it very far. I have not once hit the bandits but Sammy has almost hit them but not quite because the bandits are lying down.

Momma got me a plant because I was sick. It was a very pretty plant. It is a Martha Washington.

Love, Betsy

Dear Poppa:

I went to the symphony orchestra last week. They were making the orchestra on records to send to the service men. You might hear it too. I went to Hillel Aronson's Bar Mitzvah. He sings very nicely.

Betsy and Sammy have been making a circus. They are going to have June and Bucky their paper dolls in it. (They got June and Bucky in the comic book.) I have heard of many silly ideas but that's the silliest.

I play base ball a lot with my friends.

I got the National Geographic today. Four magazines together! In one of them there was a map of Japan. I am now reading an article about the Gulf of Mexico.

Love, David

﹏

April 30, 1944

Dearest Reuben:

Every three weeks I buy six gallons of gasoline. Last week I managed to use up my ration for the three weeks, almost use it up that is. I took Sylvia to two shows, calling for her and returning her. I took the radio phonograph into Sears and called for it. I took Betsy to the doctor. I picked up German measly David at the Beth El. I took the riding group to Sunday school. For the past week I have limited my rides to the grocery store, the lake, and Lake Street. I had to take the little radio into Sears also. David and the radio, the baby and I made the journey by street car.

David is very thrilled with his new leather jacket. He thinks he looks like a pilot in it.

Tonight I took the children to the Rainbow for supper. As we started out, Peter was crying because Betsy got in the car first. He wanted her to get out and let him in first. She wouldn't do it. As we walked along toward the Rainbow, Betsy was expostulating to Peter about the foolishness of wanting to be first all the time. David told her to be quiet. When she kept talking he put his hand on her mouth. I made him stop. I told David to hold Betsy's hand while we crossed the street. Betsy said that a big girl aged seven did not have to have anyone hold her hand while we crossed the street. The dinner was grand. David ate one dish of split pea soup, two rolls with butter, a vegetable salad, chicken, mashed potatoes, green peas, Lady Baltimore cake. He also drank tea. The rest of us ate pretty well too. After dinner we stopped at the dime store for assorted junk. As we got out of the car at home Peter said, "To make up, I'll be the first one in the house." But Betsy and David got in the house first. I made them go out and come back in again so Peter could be in the house first. But Betsy giggled and David pushed Peter over because he thought that Peter was going to tear up David's new kite. Finally David and Betsy went outside to fly the kite and Peter sat up in bed playing with his aircraft carrier. Ruth Amelia tried to calm down Peter by making nice nice. She had stayed home with Hortense.

Love, Isabel

⌒

May 5, 1944

Dear Poppa:

I have got a snake. And the place he likes to sleep is down the basement by the furnace so I let him sleep there. For he always keeps his mouth open for flies and moths. He eats flies and moths and sand. He eats bread too. I was going to burn him up only when I found that he was nice I didn't burn him up.

Mommy is going to buy at the dime store me an American P 40 and a Jap Mitsibishi [*Mitsubishi*] Zero [*fighter airplanes*]. The Jap M. Zero goes a little slower than the American P40 but the Jap M.Z. is sure tricky. But you have to make them. They are models. And they are just like real ones only smaller. I wonder how the American P 40 will fly but Mommy is going to get that kind of plane only all made. And I'm going to fly it. You can fly it over and over again without any damage.

I think you are like Abraham Lincoln. Abraham Lincoln was so nice that he got to be the president. And one time he had three gingerbread boys. And he gave two away to a little boy and only had one for himself. Don't you think that is nice? I think it is very nice.

There is a picture of you right up on the place where Mommy keeps her good dishes. I play with them. I take them out and put them on the little children's table. I pretend like I'm washing them and then I put them away in the cupboards. I put them in three piles.

I love you very much and I'm very proud of you being a pilot. I know why the Memphis Belle [*documentary about the B-17, or Flying Fortress, of that name*] is a good show. It is about planes. Big planes have oxygen. I would love to go up in a big plane. I have seen fighting shows before. Guadalcanal Diary [*war film*]—that was very good. Salute to the Marines [*another war film*]—this one American plane shot down a lot of Jap planes. A lot of Jap planes crossing a bridge and an American blew up the bridge and the Jap tanks fell into the ocean. Destination Tokio [*Tokyo, also a war film*]—that was about an American submarine. A Jap destroyer came along and they fired torpedoes at it and sunk the Jap the destroyer. And every minute they came up to take a look. And they went through this channel and I thought there might be volcanoes there.

Once Gramma Sarah took me to see Lassie Come Home and they showed Mountain Vesuvius erupting. Mountain Vesuvius wrecked the churches; it wrecked everything. I heard on the radio about Mountain Vesuvius. That is very dangerous. Have you been in Italy where Mountain Vesuvius is? I haven't but I do think it is very very dangerous. So many people were killed by Mountain Vesuvius. It's very old. It's almost ready to stop exploding and never explode again. Paracutin is a volcano in Mexico. It hasn't stopped exploding. I think it's very dangerous to go near Paracutin in Mexico or Mountain Vesuvius.

Sammy

⌐

May 9, 1944

Dearest Reuben:

I have not made my summary out yet for this month. You know David and Betsy got the German measles and had to stay out of school for a week. Ten days from the day Betsy broke out Peter [*error for David*] had to start staying home. Two weeks after David broke out, Peter broke out. Now he has to stay home a week. The disease itself is a little nothing, but the children are on my hands all the time.

Love, Isabel

To continue about Sammy's reaction to being kept away from the other children just because he had had the German measles. I finally spanked him hard for running after the children when I had told him not to. He sat in his room and cried. Then he crawled under the bed and cried. I comforted him as best I could and let him hit me a few times. When Mrs. Wyman came to take care of him and Ruth while I went to the grocery and the court house he said, "I do not like my momma." When I came down stairs all dressed to go out I found plaster on the floor and Peter with a pocket knife. He had just carved a small hole in the wall. "I did it," he said, "because you were mean to me." I patched the hole, or rather covered it up, with matching wall paper.

The Stafne's are especially careful of Diane because they want her to be well so she can be the flower girl at Buddy's [*Stafne*] wedding. He is getting married on May 25.

May 6 I looked at Peter's neck and saw spots. I felt lumps in back. German measles. He felt fine and had no fever. Monday he went out to play. Denise told Diane not to go near Sammy because Sammy was sick. I explained that he was well. Just to be sure I called Dr. Seham and found out that Peter should not play with the other children till Thursday. Peter sat on the steps and said "I feel sad." Every time my back was turned he scooted after the children, particularly Diane. Once he threw mud at them. Once he chased them with a pen knife. More later.

Love, Isabel

May 9[?], 1944

Dear Poppy:

The comedy that I saw in Lassie Come Home was so silly. There was a man and there was a rabbit and he saw every one else's big pile and his little pile (of scrap). He saw an inner tube attached to a whole lot of things and when he got it out he had the biggest pile of all. And he tied the inner tube up on a telephone and it cracked and everything fell down. He landed right in his car and the inner tube began to go round and round. He landed right on top of the pile and the silliest part, the funniest part is that the inner tube began to wrap round and round him. I thought it was a snake. It was an orange inner tube you know those round things that are shaped like a tire. You've seen them, that the children play with at beaches, you know. And once he went up into the air and he got in his car and tried to run it but it wouldn't go not one bit. And the seat fell in.

And the real name of the boy that you saw sitting by the tree was Ronny McDowell [*Roddy McDowall*].

You're just exactly like Abraham Lincoln. You're just exactly. People don't like you, you still like them. That's how when people are mad at you you still act nice.

I think some time the war will be over. Not very long the war will be over, not very long, Poppa, not very long, not very long. Only six months.

When summer comes, you know something, school will be out. (Momma, will I be going to bed early?) It would be nicer if you never spanked. If you were me you would just get real mad. Seems like Momma's mean because Momma gets mad. Sometimes I get mad, I get real mad. Sometimes I get mad, madder than anything. I wish I was in England, where you are. And I lived right where you are. Or else, I had a stone with the inside carved out and glass on it for the windows. And when I wanted some food I would go into your house and I would have only beds in my house, only beds and chairs and books. And I would have a box and I would have a garage to keep a car. I would have a toy car, you know those cars that have pedals on them, and a toy fire engine that has pedals on it. I would keep them.

I would have two garages, one for my car and one for my fire engine. Then I would keep real house, then I would keep a glass and sometimes I would light a match and I would take the hose and turn it on and I would spill it over the fire. Or else.

At the A and P store there is some poppa size root beer, then comes momma and then junior.

Love, Sammy

↩

May 12, 1944

1st CCRC GP
APO 639 NYC

Dear Son David,

That last movie film was the best yet. Too bad it isn't with sound. I think you should make another record now, playing the clarinet. Which do you like better, the clarinet or the piano?

How did you like your trip to Omaha to Jeremy's Bar Mitzvah? I'm sure you enjoyed it. Gramma Sarah gets a big kick out of your progress in Hebrew. On the airplane trip I wrote to Sammy about was Demaree Bess, a famous newspaper man who writes now for the Saturday Evening Post. He used to work for the Minneapolis Tribune.

Momma and you must have had quite a time with the children all having German measles. I'm sure you're all well and happy again. Write often to

Your Poppa

↩

May 12, 1944

Dear Betsy,

I watched you play the piano in the movie and I could almost hear the music. Someday David and I will play a clarinet duet with piano

{ 106 }

accompaniment—you playing the piano. I enjoyed the movie a lot. I hope Momma can get Arnold to take more pictures. Momma told me what you said about a seven year old girl being able to cross the street alone. I'll bet when you're seventeen you won't be doing much street crossing alone. You'll have friends, boy friends too, who will want to take your arm to "help" you across. That's a silly notion that dates back hundreds of years when it was fashionable for women to be faint, skinny, even ill. But nowadays when people take your hand as you have to walk across the street it's a sign that they like you. Sometimes it's a sign that they like you too much. We'll discuss that later. At the present time remember that a girl's best friend is her

Father

⌐

May 12, 1944

Dear Sammy,

I want to tell you about a flight I made this morning in a B-17E, a Flying Fortress. We climbed to 10,000 feet, where the pilot said, "Pilot to crew, 10,000 feet." Then we all put on oxygen masks. We climbed up to 23,000 feet. We cruised about in the thin cold air. When we came down we were lost. We didn't know where our home field was. Finally we asked a lady in a control tower of a field command (unnamed), "Please, can you tell us which way is our field?" She could have gone outside and pointed but she gave us a compass heading instead which brought us right home. I rode all the way in the plexiglass nose. You get a fine view from the nose. But the ground comes up awfully fast when you're landing. Be a good boy and don't get mad at people, especially Momma and David and Betsy.

Love, Poppa

⌐

May 15, 1944

Dearest Isabel,

Saw the wonderful movie "Watch on the Rhine" last evening.
Lucas and Davis starred in it, performing the portrayal of the
Rhinelanders. The infant prodigy was excellent. But the parting scene
of the farmer and his 3 children was almost too much for me. It was
too close to home. I have postponed my visit to "The Lisbon Story"
to Wednesday, May 17.

David, which is bigger—one pound of ice or one pound of water?
Betsy, which is heavier—a pound of feathers or a pound of butter?
Sammy, which is longer—a thousand miles or a year in England?
Ruth Amelia, are you a good baby?

Love, Reuben

~

May 16, 1944

Dear Reubinke,

I thank you for the lovely letter you sent me for Mother's Day. Any
mother would feel amply repaid for whatever hardship raising her
child may have cost her. In your case there was no hardship—just
undiluted pleasure. Isabel and I spent a pleasant day last Sunday. She
took the three older children to the Temple to attend a Mother's Day
Program in which Betsy took part & I met her there. It was a very
nice program and Betsy as usual was the star of the class, reciting her
piece with her customary good expression and enunciation. Rabbi
Minda delivered a moving sermon on "Mother," and in the midst of
his talk your son Sammy was moved to express himself also. After all
he too has a specialty that is unusual and entertaining, so he walked
out in the aisle very sedately, and—stood on his head! Isabel, horri-
fied, ran out to catch him, for he was already looking speculatively at
the stage. Evidently his performance was only by way of practice for
bigger and better things in store. Rosie was here over Monday and

Gramma Sarah Berman, holding Ruth,
November 1943

Tuesday. She came to address the W. L. [*Women's League*] of the
Temple of Aaron, and last evening the Aronsons came to see her.
Rabbi Aronson had already heard down town of Sammy's escapade so
he remarked to Rabbi Minda, "I see your congregation is beginning
to use their heads." We had a nice lunch which Isabel made—very
good cheese blintzes and a superb lemon chiffon pie were the outstanding goodies. She is a very good cook. After lunch I took Ruth
Amelia and Sammy for a walk in the lovely sunshine. As we walked
other little ones joined us, and like the Pied Piper I came back with a
half dozen.

Love, Mom [*Sarah Berman*]

May 17, 1944

Dear Poppa:

Mr. Weinberg is making us have a practice record for how much we play our instruments. We get a number of points for how long we practice. This week I am going to get one point but next week I am going to get nine. If I practice 180 minutes I get one point; if I practice 270 minutes I get two points; if I practice 360 minutes (a week) I get three points. I want to make a correction. It was six points I am going to get, not nine. For each day that I practice sixty minutes I get one extra point. I can add on some points for the piano, however.

At Sunday School there was a mother's day program for the children so Mother took Sammy. Sam decided that he'd get some attention so right when the Rabbi was talking he went out in the aisle and stood on his head. Rabbi Aronson told Gramma Sarah that at last the Temple Israel people are learning how to use their heads.

Last Saturday the family went to see the show Lassie Come Home taken from the book by the late Major Eric Knight. It was so sad that Betsy cried, the poor little thing.

Captain Nagler from San Antonio came to visit us. He talked to me and showed me a picture of his little baby.

I wrote a poem to Mom and one to Gramma Sarah for mothers' day. I'll write Gramma Sarah's down and later I'll send you Mom's. "Gramma Sarah is so nice she takes me to so many places; And as for my opinion of her she's better than four aces." The one I wrote to Mom had four verses but I only had ten minutes to write Gramma Sarah's and about five days to write Mom's so you can see that Mom's would be better than Gramma Sarah's but if I had as much time on both [they'd] be the same.

I am going to Council Camp this summer for the second boys' period. It will be the first time that I have ever gone to a camp that is not a home camp so it will be quite an experience.

I have now on my wall as follows: nine maps, four pictures, two calendars, one National Geographic Society membership card, two little figures. You can hardly see any wall paper.

I can't think of much more to say so I guess the letter can end right here because this is almost the end of the paper anyhow.

Love, David Berman

⌐⌐

May 17, 1944

Dearest Reuben:

I have on hand four V mail letters dated May 4, 5, 6 and 11. As you see, the mail service from you to me is remarkably fast. Your letter of May 11 is almost impossible for even me to read. I have it practically all deciphered but I'll bet you won't be able to read it yourself. I also received a cigar box full of letters. That should be good for many hours of reading. Maybe sometime we can take your letters and ours and write a book, "Letters from a wife and four children to a husband overseas."

You ask what Sammy does besides draw. Part of the answer is in David's letter. Sammy stands on his head in Temple. He raises hell if he is not the first one dressed in the morning. He musses up David's hair if I brush David's hair first. He eats any kind of fruit but no milk or butter except what he gets in cooked foods. He eats frosting but not cake. He has just recently started to eat the crust as well as the filling of pies. He eats the pie crust that I make, but no one else's. He still gives me large kisses and small kisses. Sometimes David moans, "Why do I have to have such a little brother, what did he ever do for me." Sammy contributes sunshine as well as storms.

Love, Isabel

⌐⌐

May 18, 1944

Dear Poppy:

My snake is really a wooden snake and only a stick. And once David threw the roof [*snake?*] down from the maid's room porch roof.

The head broke off. So I didn't use him for a snake any more. I just put him in the pool. David and Mommy saw one of the gold fish but I saw two of them.

I love you very much and some day you will come back.

Betsy has a shadow picture, a silhouette. I hope that you would come back someday. Momma told me that the war would be over in six months. Four weeks and school will be out. Bingo! School's out.

Do you like the letters I sent to you? You are just like Abraham Lincoln. John killed him cause he was crazy. I thought you only flew a cub. Does the army let you fly a B-17? Did that B-17 have any ammunition or bombs?

Once I saw the Memphis Belle. It's a show and each plane had a belly full of bonds [bombs?]. There was a lot of bombs. One plane got shot in the wing only it still was on its bombing run. There were ten men in the crew, tail gunner, bombardier, pilot, nose gunner, top gunner.

One of the Jap fighter pilots bailed out in his parachute. There wasn't any cannon, there wasn't any noise on the ground, only the roaring noise of the planes. Cover Girl* I don't want to tell you, Cover Girl wasn't any good. It was just love. I did not like Cover Girl.

I'd like to have you back. I think it was nice when you were back home but now you're overseas. I hope you can bring back Rafni. I hope you can bring back Rafni [sentence repeated]. The pictures you sent me of Rafni were very cute. Rafni is a very nice dog. Lassie come Home, well, Lassie is a dog, he was so pretty. He was in a show. He went from Scotland to England. And a skinny old black was going to take Rafni's place. And there was some men that fighted, but Lassie always jumped on them. Lassie saved a man's life. But Toots, he was a little dog, he got killed. The man that liked Lassie he knocked the man right over the fire. He was sent away and travelled thousands of miles to get home to Junkville. (Correction by Betsy—Yorkville).

Love, Sammy

*This was a "backstage" movie musical starring Rita Hayworth and Gene Kelly.

Received letters from you today dated May 12.

IRB

⌐

May 20, 1944

Dearest Reuben:

I have some letters to me and to the children. Peter has already answered his. You should hear from David and Betsy soon.

Tonight I was giving Peter a talk about the need for getting along well with David. Finally he said to me, "I'll be good to David if you buy a cage." "What do you want a cage for?" I asked. "To put David in," was the softly spoken answer. For the present, though, everything is sweetness and light. I promised David a set of assorted dowel sticks and a new brace and bit, so he can make sail boats. David in turn promised Peter to make him a sail boat.

Ruth Amelia talks more every day. If you ask her what the kitty says, she answers, "Kiyyi, meeow." She can also say George, in a soft French accent, that the milkman just loves. Ruth likes Peter the best of all. When ever he is upset she rushes over to him, pats him on the head, murmurs da da for there, there, puts her cheek against his and in general loves him up.

Betsy gets more glamourous all the time. She likes pretty clothes and pretty things. She would like to have a long dress like Miss Mamie let her wear in San Antonio. About once every two weeks she gets some money from me and goes to Sheffield's to buy a plant. Yesterday I sent her there with a dollar for a box of pansies. Even Ruth likes the pansies. She says "Pittee." Today Betsy got a little blue plant for her room.

Love, Isabel

⌐

May 22, 1944

Dear Sammy,

I want to talk to you about loving your poppa and momma and taking care of the house and things like that. Do you know who owns our house? Not just Poppa and Momma but also David and Betsy and Ruthie and you, Sammy Hirsch Peter Berman. It's *our* house, all of ours. So you must take good care of your house just like you take good care of the other things you own.

Sometimes Momma will ask you to do things that you don't exactly want to do like staying away from other children when you have some measles on your lovely face. Then you do what Momma says because you love her and you want her to smile and be happy. Otherwise she may get mad and spank. Poppa does this too. And for this we apologize. Poppas and mommas are funny people. They can spank a child, and hard too, and love him at the same time, maybe a teeny bit less loving than other times.

Sammy, soon you will be six, and a six year old boy can go to school. And he's old enough to be taken on fishing trips and such things. Soon the war will be over and I'll come home.

Love, Poppa

⌒

May 22, 1944

Dearest Isabel,

By plane, taxi, and train I visited Abie Berman in the [Taunton] General Hospital. It was an epic meeting 4000 miles from home. He comments on my fat face; I don't on the gray hair at the temples. Otherwise the same Abe. His illness can be summed up as the psychological effect of shipment overseas. Anyway he is recovered and soon will be back to duty. There is nothing wrong with him that a lifetime with Pearl and Lynn wouldn't correct—but we all need treatment similar to that. We spent the day walking up the beautiful

mountainous countryside just this side of Wales; talking of Minneapolis, Sacramento, bragging of our wives and children—Abie was
considerably impressed by your savoir faire in the presence of infan-
tile pandemonium, by David's adult behavior, planning for the
future. I went to serve as a tonic for Abie but the medicine was good
for the doctor too. Both doctors. Very fine day of great benefit to
both of us. We discussed the possibility of Berman and Berman opening up in Sacramento after the war. I am not as positive in the summer of 1944 that we'll return to Minneapolis for the practice of medicine as I was in the summer of 1941.

Love, Reuben

⌣

May 23, 1944

Dear Poppy:

In the Shrine Circus there was a man with sticks and he danced on
wire with the stilts.

On the bus a lady said that her little boy was there when Mountain
Vesuvius erupted and that was today. (Mrs. Bloom was talking about
Sammy.)

A lady called up and said that there was a dog that bit a boy in
front of our house.

Me and Betsy are going to have a show. And there'll only be music
inside but when we play outside there won't be one bit of music, not
one bit, not one bit, not a single piece of bit, not even one line. It's
just going to have some talking in it.

You are going to show some movies. And there are going to be
comedies and fighting and the show will be as big as our living room.

I think you are very kind because you give candy to people and
everything. I heard you give Hershey bars to people when you
go out.

My mother bought Kellog's Pep. What is in it is a plane that you
cut out and put together. It's a Pep plane, made of cardboard. You

open up the package and there's your plane all ready to cut out and make.

I am almost six. I am going to tell you what I eat. I eat ice cream, lots of fruit, I eat chicken, orange juice, turkey, I eat potatoes, I eat chicken, and I eat egg on toast.

Sometimes my mother goes to the A and P store and I always like to carry everything, always. Only if my glider is too full, Mommy can carry it.

When will you come back? I hear the war will be over in six months. I know you must be a very nice man. Think how nice you are. Nicer than anything. I hear people get mad at you but you like them.

I love you very much and I think you are very handsome.

Rafni is a cute dog. He'll bark at me.

I wish you were back now.

Love, Sammy

꿈

May 23, 1944

Dear David,

I have heard that you had a good time in Omaha, and Poppa and your gramma Sarah were glad that you could get together with Jeremy. I gather that you had a good time and everyone was pleased with the visitor from Minneapolis. Gramma tells me how grown-up you are.

Rafni is in heat. All day the dogs chase her, bark and fight over her all night. They stay outside the door barking for her to come out and if they get a chance they slip in the door and come looking into my room where Rafni sleeps. Last night she was out until midnite. I went to bed at 10:30 and closed the door here. 4 different strange dogs walked into my room before poochie came home and then bedlam broke out. Such snarling, baring of teeth, raucous barking, and erection of hair! It's all very troublesome for me and poochie. The next dog will get a proper job of spaying and no more howling canine convention of dogs semiannually in and out. The dog was home for one day or so.

Love, Poppa

⤳

May 26, 1944

Dear Poppy:

Diane is a flower girl at a wedding. She has on a white dress with white flowers. Denise had on a yellow dress and Alice had on a pink dress.

One time I heard Hop Harrigan. In Hop Harrigan they were going to Gregor but if they didn't have a ring just like Gregor's ring Gregor would have them be shot immediately because he wouldn't know that they be Hop and Tank. So Hop Harrigan opened his dog tag up and there was not a sign of a ring.

I hope you should come back soon. You must. I wonder when you are going to come back.

Dear poppa: Diane had on white shoes. Mommy is going to get me a set of some plane and some anti-aircraft gunner and parachutes. You punch them out and start to make them.

In front of me there is a bottle. The cover is on, very tight. And in the bottle is mosquitoes. One of them is flying but I cannot see the others. There are some of them in this bottle.

And I'm very sad when you are overseas because you are such a nice man. But I know you would never be nice to the Germans or Japanese.

Hop and Tank they kicked the gray ghost and everything. The gray ghost was a master spy.

In Superman a man came in with a flashlight and gun pointed and he said one move and he'll shoot.

In Jack Armstrong there was the secret anti-infection drug, teheeli. Sun La's Indians chased Ladeno's Indians. Ladeno's Indians were going to escape but they went over a bridge and fell into a canyon.

Love, Sammy

⌒

May 27, 1944

Dear Poppa:

Diane is a flower girl. She had on a silk white slip and the dress was of real fine material like the red part on the ballet costume I used to have. And on the top of it there were red flowers and she had on white shoes. Denise had on a yellow dress and a yellow veil of the same material that Diane's dress was made out of but it was yellow. Diane had on a golden bracelet with a little blue stone on it and golden necklace with a cross in the middle. I guess it's on account of her religion. Mrs. Stafne had on a beautiful pink dress. There was a lady and I think it was Diane's aunt who went with them. She had on one of those black things that go over your face and a black hat and a black coat. Mr. Stafne had on a kind of gray suit. I think he had a rose in the corner or one of those flowers. Diane was supposed to carry roses and tulips but she told me they were at the church because that's where the wedding's going to be, at the Joyce Memorial Church. The Joyce Memorial Church is near my school and is where we have brownie scouts because I'm a brownie scout. There was a man and I think he was Diane's uncle and he had on some black pants with a black jacket but it was light weight, I think.

Today I went home from school and got a present. It was [a] small book, the poem book of the Organ Grinder's Garden and also it had some construction paper. I was going to Dawn's birthday party. Bethine had on a pretty dress kind of like silk cloth and it was white. And she had on black new shoes.

We played games. The games were spin the bottle and gray duck and who could jump rope the longest but as long as I had won the prize by then I didn't play it. We played musical chair but we did not have any chair in it except when we were out of the game. Maybe we played more games but that's all I can remember. We could have chocolate or peppermint ice cream. And chocolate cake with chocolate frosting. If we wanted we could have white cake with coconut frosting but I didn't get any and neither did anyone else, I think. My friend Marlys and a girl named Mary were the only ones left who didn't get a prize but there was only one prize so we played gray duck then. The one who did a tap dance and sing a song best would get a prize all except we didn't have to sing a song. Marlys would've got the prize but Bethine cheated.

Betsy Berman

Betsy, May 27, 1944

May 27, 1944

Dearest Reuben:

What with one thing and another I have let at least ten days go by without writing you a letter myself. I have typed out a few for the children.

David knew that the pound of ice was bigger. Betsy fell for the pound of butter. Sammy thought a thousand miles was longer. Ruth Amelia thinks she is a good baby. She says, "Ta good, ta good, ta good, ta good." If you tell her she is a bad baby she gives you a gentle snarl.

Sammy is very insulted when David hits even him, even though

David has a good deal of provocation. Peter says, "Poppa would not hit a little boy. Abraham Lincoln would not hit a little boy."

Love, Isabel

⤶

May 27, 1944

Dearest Reuben:

The other day I saw Lois Bloom's mother on the bus. I was very gratified to hear her say that Lois's children, aged two and four, were undisciplined little brats. Such epithets reflect not on the children or their parents but on the user of the epithets. I know some people who used to think, and some who still do think, our children undisciplined.

Peter released some stored up resentment at David by peeing on poor David as he sat defenseless in the bathtub.

Love, Isabel

⤶

May 30, 1944

Dear Poppa:

We are almost at the end of school term. So we had two days of vacation but it happened that the two days of vacation were supposed to be on Saturday and Sunday so instead we had four days of vacation. I didn't have to go to Sunday school because it was Schvous,* and then we had Monday and Tuesday for a vacation. Saturday we went swimming, and Sunday we went to a picnic with only people with the last name Berman. The picnic was at Maishie's house. Maishie owns lots of land and also two Billy goats. The girl is Mairzy

---

*Shavuoth is the Festival of Weeks, celebrated seven weeks after Passover.

and the boy is Doats. Monday we went swimming again. Tuesday morning we went swimming and in the afternoon Momma took Peter to a show not for any special reason but just because Ruth couldn't go and David and I didn't want to go so we stayed home. It was about training. I am writing this letter on that same Tuesday night.

Love, Betsy

↜

May 30, 1944

Dear Poppa:

I've been in swimming three times this spring. It is really a lot of fun. I swim out to the dock and play around there. The trouble is that I have trouble diving. Always when I dive I just belly flop. I'll have to take some more lessons at the Y.

My clarinet was overhauled. They shined it up and put on new pads and I think, I'm not sure, but I think they put on a few new keys and did some other work. I want to get another set of records to you as soon as you [*I*] can on my clarinet playing so that you can see how I've improved since the last time. I no longer puff out my cheeks at all except that I had a little trouble when I was playing sixteenth notes my jaw would move up and down and Mr. Weinberg had to put a review sign and write wooden Indian above the sixteenth notes so that I would keep my jaw still.

I would like to go to the instrument class at Jefferson this summer but it might interfere with Hebrew school. So we are going to call up and find out what classes I would be in and what time they would be.

I think that since you've been overseas a year you should get sent home and promoted to be a Lt. Colonel. Because you've been a major for two years, it's about time you were promoted and because you've been overseas for a year it's about time you were sent home.

Ruth Amelia is walking now and she says quite a few things. She says good girl and she growls at you if you say she's bad. She more or less understands what you say because Momma said, "I think I'll put Ruth Amelia to bed." "No, no, no," she blurted out. Ruth Amelia is six weeks older than Sander's baby brother yet she can walk around and go like a comet and he can't walk at all. She could walk when she was nine months old. Now she is eighteen months old and she can run. (Can she run!) Her favorite game is running circles around people. She is very sympathetic too. I wanted to make a test so I started to cry so she comes up and puts her arms around me and says Da da in a very sympathetic tone. There was some more stuff I wanted to say about Betsy but we are almost at the end of the page so I'll have to quit.

Love, David

⤴

May 31, 1944

Dearest Reuben:

May 27 we went swimming. May 28 we went to the picnic at Maishie's house. Sander pulled a typical big brother trick. He told Lael she could be everlasting fielder. Maishie had to intervene and explain that everyone had to have a turn as fielder, pitcher, catcher and finally batter. David had an elegant time wrestling Sander and Julian at the same time. Maishie is a thoughtful host, like you. Without being asked, he brought the toidy seat down to the laundry toilet. He made the fire, roasted the wieners, carried things, and escorted me and family out to the car when we left.

May 29 we went swimming again. Peter has been collecting cigarette butts at the beach. He goes around like a thoughtful beachcomber. About half the butts have lipstick on them. He brings them home, removes the paper and dissolves the tobacco in water, and admires the brownish liquid. That is an experiment. David nearly started a riot by throwing out a collection of butts before the experiment had got under way. Peter also collects measuring worms.

Love, Isabel

June 4, 1944

Dearest Reuben:

It seems to me that last week we received only one letter from you, and that one very short.

Thursday night I heard Baby Snooks on the radio. Daddy had mentioned going to Washington to join the army. After a usual hectic evening with Snooks he replied to one of Snooks's questions, "No, I am not going to Washington and I am not going to join the army. Any man who leaves this house to go to war is a coward."

David was in Martha Baker's piano class recital on June 3. He played a part of a long piano piece, called "The Vale of Song" with Martha. I'll send the program later. One child in the recital eclipsed all the others. He was a nine year old genius, named Buddy McKay. He played difficult numbers by Bach and Handel, as well as a modern piece by a fellow at Hamline [University] named Krendel. He played so beautifully that you forgot you were listening to a child. He was there with a father, or perhaps some other close relative. Sylvia and your mother were at the recital. Your mother presented David with a box of candy, a present from her and Aunt Jean. Peter looked very angelic in his white palm beach suit which the little imp is now wearing for the third season. David wanted white slacks, but having notified me only that morning, he did not have them.

Love, Isabel

June 7, 1944

Dear Poppy:

I hope you don't get killed in the invasion. If you come back and spank me I will have the right to make you feel badder than anything and tell you that you are not like Abraham Lincoln so you had better

{ 123 }

not come back and spank me. So that'll make you so you won't spank me and you'll always be kind and never never hurt anyone in your family. And I think you're still a very nice man and I hope you keep on being nice. And I think you're so nice.

Dear poppy: The paper sale is not to be tooken to school. It is to be put out on the boulevard and the paper is tooken away. And I hope you're nice yet. But I don't want you to be kind to the Germans or Japanese because they're mean. (Betsy says, "Don't you want him to be nice to the Japanese babies and the Japanese mommas and the Japanese daddies who are not in the army.") I'll let you like the German babies and the German people who are not in the army. Because Hitler men fight them. But the Jewish Germans are the kind Germans. And you know something, when the war is over the Germans will stop fighting us and start fighting Hitler. So there will be nothing left of Hitler, not a trace, just a dead man. And Hitler, you didn't know, but he is a very wicked man.

I've got a poem for you. "Hirohito, I hope you choke when Tokyo goes up in smoke." I hope the Germans are killed in that invasion. You might not be killed but you might be wounded. I hope you're not shot because if you're shot I'll feel very bad because I would like to have a poppa, you same poppa, that same poppa.

You know there's a girl across the street that I know and her name is Batty. And her father is a fat man. He is fatter than you. I have seen him.

I know lots of nice games in school. One is there's a stick and at the top there is a net and at the bottom there's a hole (Basketball). And the other one there is two things that I don't know what they are and if you get in one of two of those things, well you did it. And I think they're called beet bags (bean bags). And there's another one. The teacher draws a line and a big circle and then she gives you some balls and you roll them and the one that gets all of them (in the circle) wins. And sometimes you can print your name when you do it in the net with the beetball. If the boys get the ball in well they can go to the cloakroom first and if the girls get the ball in well they can go to the cloakroom and get their wraps. And sometimes we haven't got much time and sometimes we go down in the gymnasium and we get to see a movie. And one of them was about a gray squirrel and the other one was about making milk, about milking the cows. And one time we went down to the lake. It was a long walk.

Sammy

⌐

June 7, 1944

Dear Poppa:
    The invasion is as it had been thought to be. Although I read in the papers today that the first wave was mowed down by the Germans but the second wave climbed over their dead bodies and gained a foothold. I hope you do not go over there till the situation is well in hand (not for the Germans.)
    I was in a recital. I played "The Vale of Song" by Walter Rolfe. There was a genius. His name is Buddy McKay. Mr. Weinberg told Momma that Mr. McKay is one of the best trombone players in the Northwest. (Mr. Weinberg is my clarinet teacher.) Speaking of clarinets, your silver clarinet just got overhauled about two weeks ago. It is very beautiful. I think I'll take it to Council Camp with me. And I may be in the Jefferson High orchestra and band during the summer because, in the summer, children who play different instruments can go to Jefferson High. However, if it interferes with Hebrew School I shall not be able to go.
    Next year, when I am in sixth grade, another boy and I are going to run the school projector. Already I can thread it pretty good but I make a couple of mistakes.
    Last Sunday, we went swimming. After that we went over to Arnold's house because he had come home on a one day pass. Sammy had on a little sailor suit that Momma bought him at Daytons. Also I had on a khaki slack suit with *YOUR* tie and Momma is going to get a buckle for *YOUR* belt. Arnold had on *HIS* whites. Betsy should've had on her red cross suit. We would have had the whole armed forces.
    We are planting different things where there is enough sunshine to

grow. Such as in the front yard we have pansies and tomatoes. On the side of the house we have some lilies of the valley but they're not doing so wonderfully. And in the back yard we have a fern that came from the rock garden that used to be there. On the other side of the house are some tulips that the Schmidts planted. They are the people we rented our house to. By the pool Mom planted some irises. On the other side there are some tulips and a vine. Then also in the front yard Mom just bought a new little bush and we have some evergreen trees. That's not doing so bad considering that the trees make so much shade. In our pool we have some goldfish and they are really life savers. If we didn't have them we'd really have a lot of mosquitoes. We don't have any worry of the goldfish starving either because they can fill themselves up to their heart's content with mosquito larvae. Since I've told you about what is on the walls of my room I've added one more map and that is a map of Europe. Next Friday I'll have two more maps because Momma sent off to Sears for a map kit and that has two maps and some other stuff. And in the paper is an invasion map I'm pretty sure to tack up also. So far I've only seen a room with so many maps.

Love, David

⌇

June 8, 1944

Dearest Reuben:

Your letters, which doubtlessly have been delayed by the invasion, are beginning to come in. Today I received one letter dated May 22 and Peter received one dated the same day. Peter reacted to your admonitions about taking good care of the house and by your hint that under provocation you might spank by a solemn look and a remark that well, that shows, Poppa isn't like Abraham Lincoln.

Peter listens to Superman every day. He hears that if you buy a package of Kellogg's Pep you do not need to send any money or any box tops but right in the package you get a model plane. We had two packages of Kellogg's Pep in the house. The day Nagler was here, Peter held me up for two more packages when Nagler went shopping with us at the A and P store. Now I tell Peter that the store won't sell any more Kellogg's Pep to people that have four packages at home. Peter manfully eats a dish of it now and then. He urges me to try it. One day he spilled a half a package in the garbage can. Today he came in with Patty and Diane. He asked for a dish of Kellogg's Pep and offered some to Patty and Diane. They refused. "Aw shucks," he said, "I wanted to use it up so I could get some more."

Love, Isabel

⤺

June 8, 1944

Dearest Isabel,

I heard from you May 27 and a little bit, a little piece of bit, from Sammmy and Betsy's wonderful observations on the flower girl and the wedding party et al.

I met a new correspondent on the train last week, and our conversation ended in an invitation to dinner. I was there last night. They have a very fine house in the outer suburbs [*in Chesham Bois*] of London. The name is Morris [*Maurice*] Edelman. They were married by my friend Rabbi Rabinowitz. Sunday the Edelmans were here for dinner, which is just like old times.

We are amazed that the Channel was crossed and the beachheads taken with so little loss.* I hope the rest of the campaign goes as well. Being a believer of the rolling snowball effect, I think the campaign will go very well. I heard from Edith Marget as I think I told you. Someday I may get to see Arthur but I doubt it will be here. I think the army will not keep us in the same location.

Love, Reuben

*That was what they were told at the time! The truth about the casualties will never be known. Reports range from two to six thousand, but probably the actual number was much higher.

June 10, 1944

Dearest Reuben:

Today David received a letter from you dated May 23. The letter told about your troubles with Rafni in heat. I had to explain the whole proposition to David and I shall have to read him the letter. Can't you get hold of a typewriter? I can read your letters easily but most other people, including David, have trouble.

In another letter I am sending some clippings. One clipping shows a young man and a young lady in a rubber boat. I made the mistake of showing it to the children. Now they want me to send Macy's a check for seventy dollars, quickly, before the supply runs out, so we can have a rubber boat. I said that I could not spend that much money without asking you. So now you'll have to write another fatherly letter about why Momma shouldn't buy a rubber boat.

I have quite a time with David. He goes to Hebrew school four afternoons a week and absorbs a conservative attitude toward Judaism. He says he would like to belong to an orthodox synagogue, but since we live so far away from the orthodox synagogues, the Adath Jeshuran will do. He objects to the Temple because they do not wear yarmelkes when they pray and because there is not enough Hebrew in the service. Now, you may have your views and I mine, but in your absence I am in charge. Some hint to David that his parents agree on where he should go might be in order. I do not make any issue of the matter and am pretty sure that David will continue at Temple Sunday school this fall.

I got a card from Rose saying that Alexander will bring up the violin and a bow when he comes for camp.

Oh yes, another item in the clippings. It is a cartoon showing six possible stopping points on the road to a new world: which is your choice. It starts with 1, a treaty with Britain, and goes on to 5, a league of nations with police power, and finally 6, which points to world federation. David looked it over and pointed to 5. That, he said, is my choice. I made the mistake of laughing. He was quite insulted.

Love, Isabel

June 10, 1944

Dearest Isabel,

Recent letters from you and the children from 27 and 30 May are acknowledged. We must put the children's letters into a scrapbook, perhaps a separate book for each one. David is so mature. I love the way he is always remarking on affairs. Betsy's letters are so revealing: clothes, more clothes, presents, prices. And dear little Sammy, who tries so hard to remember his dear loving poppa, now blurred by time and distance into a benign shadow, Abraham Lincoln. I am sending you a batch of letters in a week or so. Also some records and movies, and a cookbook. A fish cookbook. I think you'll like it and I know I enjoyed reading the recipes.

The fighting in France must be desperate now. The Germans are great in counter attack. That has always been their tactic. We are sitting on the 50 yard line. The coast of France is visible from several points in England and easily seen from many places here from an airplane a few thousand feet up. So we feel very close to the war.

Love, Reuben

June 13, 1944

Dear David,

Gramma Sarah wrote me about your poem for her for Mother's Day, and I just received from Isabel your poem for her. That was a very wonderful poem you composed. We are a very nice family. I don't want to boast, but (then I start boasting) not every family goes along as well as we do. I mean the poppa and the momma love all the children, and the children all love their poppa and momma, and I think the children all like each other too. I remember how Betsy stuck up for you when I was bawling you out for something or other.

You would get along very well with the English people. They set great store by tactful behavior and consideration of others. Those are qualities you possess in full measure. Getting along with people is a highly developed art in this crowded land. Life is easy and pleasant for the lucky ones, like you, who naturally make people purr in their presence.

Rafni and I flew in a fortress today. She doesn't like the noise and the cold but she likes to go with

your loving, Poppa

~

June 16, 1944 [handwritten]

Dear Papa,

School let out yesterday. I'm going into room 202 (sixth grade). My teacher is Miss Cross. I don't do so very well in penmanship and art, but I do all right in all the other subjects.

David

Dearest Reuben:

David is ambitious about starting letters but not about finishing them. You can see why he does not do so well in penmanship.

The children's report cards were all wonderful. Betsy did not skip, as I had hoped she would. I shall send you the cards or copy them out soon.

The big news here is that I have a maid. I put an ad in the paper last Sunday and Monday morning and evening. I got about twelve answers, mostly fifteen year olds. I pay twelve dollars a week. I have a nice little Swedish girl from Deerwood, Minn. She is fifteen years old and goes back to Deerwood on August 15. She doesn't know much about cooking or cleaning a kitchen floor, but with proper training she could be a good maid. Unfortunately I do not give proper training. Anyhow, she helps me out a good deal. I can see that religion has its uses. She does not go to movies or dances and does not play cards or stay out late. She is a Baptist. I got her on June 5. That night I went to the Uptown with Dorothy Harris Israel and Minette Lifsen Kaufman.

We saw Up in Arms with Danny Kaye. The movie made fun of itself. For example, an oldtime sergeant was gazing in wonder upon Hollywood's idea of army nurses. He said, "We had nothing like this in the last war." A soldier replied, "We don't in this war either."

Love, Isabel

⌐

June 16, 1944

Dearest Reuben:

Our children are so popular that they went to two and three birthday parties last week. June 3 was Suzan Klugman's party. Being short on gasoline I got there by bus and cab and returned by street-car. David was not invited but he wanted to come. Ruby was glad to have him and he was a real help leading in games and watching the children. June 4 was Lael Berman's party. For this I made some mistakes. I was still short on gas. I arranged to drive to Nathan's house and have Betsy and Peter go with Nathan. Teresa said that David and I should stay there till the party was over, a matter of two hours. That would have been all right except that Teresa has been without a maid for a few weeks and is simply flying apart. I also wanted to have Nathan make some records and or take some movies. That would be all right too except that on Sunday Nathan helps take care of the children and he is simply flying apart. We had planned on making records before Lael's party. It was too cloudy for movies. But Nathan said we could make them after the party. Hilda had too much hamburger because Max had to get rid of six pounds of hamburger some one had ordered and not taken. So Hilda and Maishie had invited over a lot of relatives, besides the children, and

used up the hamburger. With all the excitement, Hilda too was flying apart. Maishie, as far as I could see, was calm as usual. So,
Teresa stayed home with the baby and I and four children went to
the party. On the way Nathan stopped for gas. The station atten-
dant looked in the car and at Nathan and said, "My, you're a young
fellow to have such a big family. You must be quite a man." Betsy
and Peter had to go see Uncle Dave [Berman]. They sang songs for
him and he, as usual, fussed over them and distributed thirty
centses to each child. We came home from the party. Nathan found
that the fellow across the street from his house had run his car up
on Nathan's grass and blocked the drive way. I explained that Ruth
Amelia was too tired and we would make the records some other
time. June 13, Peter went to Buddy Silverman's party. That is Toby's
little boy.* For all parties, we produced no gift at the party but a
lovely book arrived from Powers a few days later. Suzan got
Gulliver's Travels; Lael got a 1944 pastel illustrated book; Buddy got
the tall book of nursery tales with pictures by Rojankovsky.

Love, Isabel

⌐

June 19, 1944

Dearest Isabel,
    As I wrote recently I am thinking sufficiently seriously about prac-
ticing in California to apply for a license in that state. For the purpose I shall need some copies of diplomas. Do [you] have ready
access to
    a. My MD Diploma from the University of Minnesota
    b. My National Board Diploma?
Don't search too much because I have already arranged for duplicates.
You may receive a bill for the duplication from the National Board or
the Univ. of Minnesota that you must pay.

---

*Toby Goldstein Silverman was the sister of Rabbi David Goldstein, Reuben's brother-
in-law.

"I heard from Arnold from Chicago enclosing a picture
of David pointing to the map of Northern Ireland"
(Reuben to Isabel, June 19, 1944).

I heard from Arnold from Chicago enclosing a picture of David
pointing to the map of Northern Ireland. David has grown a lot in a
year. His letters are so mature too.

I suppose my interest in civilian practice reflects my own optimism
of an early outcome of this part of the conflict. When Germany is
defeated I'm going to volunteer to go home. I've been in the army
since before Pearl Harbor. I've had all I want of it. If there is to be
partial demobilization then I want to be demobbed.

I haven't been very regular in my letterwriting the past month. We
have been fairly busy although I can't truthfully say I've been too busy
to write home. But the days have been long and the weather pleasant
so we spend more time outside. I've managed to get in quite a bit of

flying. I've also done a bit of pistol shooting. I'm not the crack shot I was last year but I still have a fairly good squeeze on the trigger.

I wish I could have heard David in recital and Buddy McKay. I would like David to be a good musician but I don't want him ever to be professional. I would prefer that we didn't have a musical genius in the family and I guess I needn't worry—we haven't. I shall write David of my ideas on this subject. Isabel, my friend, my wife, my children's mother, yours are the most important letters I get, the first ones opened, the most read and reread. So with me it is the more the merrier.

Love, Reuben

⌐

June 19, 1944

Dear David,

I have already received letters from you and Momma and Sammy written since the invasion began. The mail service is indeed wonderful. Sammy, the little devil, says that I shouldn't get killed in the invasion but if I don't and if I do come home then I shouldn't spank him. He has a point—if I do get killed he needn't worry about spanking!

Well, David, you must be growing up when you can wear POPPA'S CLOTHES! And when you write about going to Junior High I know you are quite grown up. I would like to have you go to camp this summer. And when you get to be twelve I think you would like the boy scout camp. It's almost 25 years since I went to Tonkawa but I still remember my summers there.

David, I bought something specially for you and me last time I was in London: a trio for two clarinets and bassoon. If we can't find a bassoon player, cello can take the part. It is a group of three fugues by Bach. The music is a bit difficult for you right now but I will help you with it when I come home and we shall play it together. I wrote to Momma that I am glad you aren't a musical genius. Geniuses get more pain than pleasure out of their instruments. I want you to have fun out of the clarinet. I would like to have you play well enough to play in high school and college organizations and to play chamber music with me. And I must tell you that means quite a bit of study and practicing. You must own a sense of rhythm and you must develop your tone and technique. What is important is to spend some time every day with the clarinet. An hour a day is ideal, but if you can't give it an hour, play half an hour. But don't let the whole day go without playing because lost time can no more be made up than you can catch yesterday.

I hope you have been reading the Yank magazine* I send home to Momma. If you like it, I can send it each week. I think it is a wonderful magazine expressing exactly the feelings of the American soldiers overseas.

A lot of English people are a bit afraid of the Americans. Some of them think we eat too much, dress too much, talk too loud, and pay too much attention to their women. Every one of us is an American ambassador and we function as such every time we talk to a Britisher. I talk to everyone: on trains, trams, buses, tubes. To me British reserve is a myth. The average Englishman loves to talk and you can strike up a conversation with anyone anywhere. I think it is very important that the English and American people should understand each other. I'm thinking in terms of how to prevent another war when you and Sammy grow up. I don't mean between you and Sammy! I think the English speaking people COULD get together and prevent or indefinitely postpone the next war. I'm not saying we will.

In the meantime we are doing right well in Normandy and in Italy. I think soon Germany will be persuaded to adjourn the battling. We will persuade them by conquering the land, capturing their armies, and destroying their weapons.

I am very pleased with your progress in Hebrew School. As Gramma Sarah says, we're lucky parents to have such a son. But don't go getting a swelled head about it. Momma writes that you aren't

---

Yank was the weekly magazine put out by and for GIs during World War II.

perfect, tease Sammy, etc. (Confidentially, I wouldn't want you to be "perfect"!) Be the good boy who writes often to your dear loving

Expatriated Poppa

⌐

June 19, 1944

Dear Betsy,

Do you know what I like most of all? It's letters from home. From you and the boys and Momma. I must say you have all been good about writing. Momma must get typewriter's cramp some evenings what with three dictators around. Today I am writing to everybody. Poor Ruthie doesn't get any letters from me because I don't know her very well and she doesn't know much of anything yet. Do you like to get letters from me?

I shall tell you how the English girls dress. They have to give coupons for everything. Over here the first thought is "how many coupons". They pronounce it Koopons, swallowing the n. So they like to get durable material like heavy tweed or worsted. When you see a well dressed person, you assume

a. It's an American
b. She got it before the war
c. She's not a nice person who gets gifts from not so nice Americans

The girls use a lot of lipstick. A hell of a lot if you ask me. Most girls wear no stockings; some paint their legs with brown barnpaint to look like stockings only it doesn't. More like jaundice. The lipstick is quite sticky and comes off on cigarettes, on beerglasses, coffeecups, and the boys tell me it smears up their lips when they kiss them which they do quite often over here in England I'm told. Especially in the cities. And also in the country. Shoes are also a problem. They have a wooden soled shoe that is quite the craze here. You know what I mean when I say "quite the craze": people are crazy to wear them.

The Edelmans have two daughters—one seven and one ten. The ten year old is Sonya and she walks on the piano. The seven year old is Natasha and she plays the piano not quite as well as you do but she is very good at croquet. Both of them speak with an English accent which really isn't surprising because they live in England. Still I must admit I was surprised.

I have a big staff car all for myself but mostly I ride the bicycle. We need the petrol, that's what they call gasoline over here, we need the petrol for airplanes over Germany. Rafni has learned to ride the handlebars very well. Yesterday however she fell off and lit right on her back. Cats don't. They light on their feet. But poochie is not very smart. She is very sensitive and I mustn't talk loudly to her.

How are you coming on the piano? Don't you think it is time for another record? I have just sent the last records back to Momma.

This letter is by airmail. Does it beat the others dated the 19th?

Love, Poppa

↜

June 19, 1944

Dear Sammy,

If I seem to write to you quite often, oftener than I have things to say, it's because I love to get your letters. And one good way to get letters is to write them.

I suppose a good practical poppa whose son thought he was like Abraham Lincoln would go ahead and say "Oh no! I'm not a bit like Abraham Lincoln!" He would say "I have a lot of faults. I like to sleep in bed late Sunday mornings. I sometimes spank my children." But me, I'm not going to say those things. It makes me very proud to think that I have a boy at home in Minneapolis, a boy at home who thinks that I am like Abraham Lincoln. Time enough to disillusion him when or rather if I get home. So I'll promise you this, my own son Sammy: never again should Poppa spank you. You are now spankproof against Poppa. I will request you to do things, I will argue with you, cajole, even perhaps threaten; I will use psychological warfare. But never shall I spank. It's a promise.

Yesternight I had dinner with the Edelmans in A. I think they are rich people. They have a very fine home with a tremendous yard. And in the backyard what do you think? They have a croquet set. Not a little dinkystinky set like we have in the states. The wickets are of ½ inch steel. The mallets are beautifully finished. The set would cost about $100. They have a Poochie who is the same breed as Rafni only more of it. I forgot my pipe at the Edelmans' and when I go back after it I think I shall stay for dinner. Tilly Edelman is a very good cook. Not as good as Momma is but still a very good cook.

You know what Sammy? We'll all have to visit England after the war. I have it all figured out. I'll go to a medical convention in London. We'll fly from New York and take the whole family. The Dorchester is a very good hotel to stay at in London. We'll stay ten days here and come back and I'll bet the whole thing wouldn't cost more than two or three thousand dollars.

I'm doing everything I can to see that your poppa comes back to you after the war. The only duty I volunteer for is home service. I'm very careful to keep away from the front end of bullets. I still ride those dangerous bicycles and jeeps. Some of the obstinate and untutored infantry call them peeps.

This really isn't your birthday letter but it is getting closter and closter to your sixth. Are you glad to be six years old? Tell me Sammy are you a happy child? Are you eating well? Are you a solace and a comfort to your momma? Do you kiss Momma before you go to bed and sometimes during the day to show her that you love her? Specifically are you being a good boy?

Love, Poppa

⤸

June 20, 1944

Dear Poppy:
You aren't like Abraham Lincoln but you're almost like Abraham Lincoln. There's only one thing that's not like Abraham Lincoln. It's

to spank. But if Abraham Lincoln spanked I would say you were *just* like Abraham Lincoln, just exactly.

When I grow up I'm going to be a mechanic and I'm going to fix anything. I saw a show yesterday and it was about the invasion and chemistry. These two people, a man and a woman, were working like this. There was something that came out of the ground and it was called pitchblende. And it had something inside of it that was called ranium. Did you know we have a movie about fighting? It's a newsreel.

I'll smile when you come home and I'll give you a big kiss and a hug. I might even have a surprise for you but I don't want to ever tell you. It's something good to eat.

Yes, I'm a happy child. A very happy child.

I think you'll be coming back. When the invasion comes that's when the American soldiers beat the Germans. After the invasion of the Germans are done then will the Americans fight the Japs?, and the Russians? The Russians are very much closing in on the Germans. Whenever a German comes into Russia the Russians chase them out. The Russians use guns pointing at the Germans' backs and jeeps to run over them.

Next Saturday I am going to Excelsior. At Excelsior is lots of fun. Oh, it's lots of fun. In fact, you used to take David to Excelsior when he was a little boy. Can you remember? You can remember.

You would be as nice as Abraham Lincoln if you didn't spank. Dear poppy, if you never spanked you would be like Abraham Lincoln, if you never spanked. And also a kind doctor. And you are a good doctor too.

Yesterday I was playing with a beebee gun and I got my finger in the way and I cut myself on one of my fingers. And that wasn't funny either. Don't laugh when you get the letter. It is David's beebee gun. So today I gave it away to the ashman. Then David didn't have any beebee gun any more.

Love, Sammy

June 21, 1944

Dearest Reuben:

Today I drove 22 miles. That is my quota for a week. I bought groceries and had to go back again because they forgot to give me some. I bought gasoline. I had some inner tubes I found in the basement inspected and salvaged for swimming. I picked up Sylvia. I took our children and Mrs. Miller and Marlys to the main beach at Calhoun for a picnic and swimming lessons for children by the red cross. Ruth Amelia got no swimming lesson. Peter dropped out but may try again. The lessons are three times a week, an hour a time, for about three weeks. Then I took our children to Minnehaha Falls for the Temple picnic and a view of the Falls. The falls looked just like it did in that elaborately carved oil painting at the lake. The water rushed down with a mighty roar. The children had a grand time. Ruth got covered with fudgickle [*Fudgsicle*]. Mr. and Mrs. Newburg, a long time ago of Ada, said your poppa used to spend Sundays with them. Tonight I went to Edna's recital.

Love, Isabel

⌐

June 22, 1944

Dear Poppa:

Next year I would like to go to the Adath Jeshuran Sunday school, with your consent. Momma says no but she is not the man of the house; she is the woman of the house. All you to have to do is send me a letter and say that I can go to the Adath Jeshuran. Here is one reason why I don't want to go to the Temple Israel because at their services they don't wear yarmelkes and I don't like that. That's no good. And instead of being Bar Mitzvah which you're supposed to be they have you confirmed which is no good.

We are going to make some records for you pretty soon. I think they'll be on their way next month if Mom can get enough gas to go over to Nathan's.

I am taking swimming lessons at the main beach at Calhoun. The Red Cross is directing them free. It is for the sole purpose of lessening the drownings in Minnesota. During this year so far there have been fifty-seven people drowned in Minnesota because the heavy rains have deepened all the rivers and lakes. And so many people do not know how to swim. Although I know how to swim already I am going down there to learn how to swim much better than I do now. I am learning how to put my head under water, lift it up, take a breath, put my head under water again and so on. There are separate classes, boys class and a girls class.

Love, David

⌐

June 26, 1944

Dearest Reuben:

Ruby and [her son] Butchie [Klugman] came over this afternoon to go swimming with us. I drove to Lake Harriet. There was a nice breeze but the beach was full of seaweed, dead fish, and bad smells. There was also an amorous dog with designs on Peter. We came home and dressed and were about to leave again for a boat ride when David returned from his cub scout picnic. David looked hot so I gave him a glass of lemonade. At Harriet we saw Chimes [Edelman] and Peter E. David wanted a drink, so Chimes took him to the fountain. When he came back he told me that David had thrown up. I thought not much about it and David, Peter, Ruth, Ruby, Butchie, Peter E. and I jumped over the railing to get good seats on the boat. I had two empty paper cups from root beer in my hand. Fortunately I had the cups. David threw up all around Lake Harriet. When we got off the boat, Betsy asked in her clear voice if David was seasick. Butchie peered into the emesis cup to get a good look at the contents. I came home to a house and found that the house temperature was 82, the outdoors temperature 93. The moral is, stay home.

I am over my quota on driving the car. If I drive thirty miles a week I use about two gallons.

Be sure you write me that you approve of having Peter's tonsils out. Your momma said she never asked your father about things like that but just went ahead.

Love, Isabel

⌐

June 29[?], 1944

Dear Poppy:

At Excelsior there is a fun house. And in the fun house there is a big rolling barrel and it goes round and round. And you don't walk straight through it you go slant. I fell down and I tried to get up but I couldn't. I just stayed there rolling round and round till the barrel slowed up and then I got up and walked out. There is a slide that first goes down, then it goes straight, then it goes down, then it goes up and down, and up and down, and up and down, and then straight until finally you hit a pillow. And there is something that goes round and round and you sit on it until finally you slide off. And then there is something that is like a record only it has sides and a door on it and you go round and round. Then there is a caterpillar, it goes up, goes down, then goes round in circles, and a green cover and every time you go over something you feel air, it squirts air. Like machines.

There is a roller coaster and a ferris wheel. The roller coaster is very dangerous. The roller coaster, if you forget to hold on you fall off. The ferris wheel is so old that it breaks. But now you never see the ferris wheel because it is so old that they threw it away.

And there is something called a whip and it goes round and the seats turn every time it goes round. There is something in the middle that makes it turn.

And speed boats. When it rains they keep the speedboats in some garage.

And there's a merry go round. And there's this kind of toy cars that you ride in and they keep bumping into each other, bump, bump. You don't even know where you're going. You go bump, bump,

bump, bump and it's lots of fun. And that is all what there is at Excelsior.

At Excelsior they have a place where you get treats. And there's a place where you get your picture taken. One time I went to Excelsior and they took a picture of a dog and the dog moved and the dog looked so funny. Boy, did that dog ever look funny.

And I went to Lake Harriet today and I got an apple. You know these apples that are on a stick and they have caramel over them. And I got one. And yum, yum, they taste good.

Dear Poppa: I can swim now. The only thing is that I sink because I'm too skinny. Betsy can swim too.

And you are so nice that I can never have a nicer person than you because you are so nice, nicer than Gramma Gertie. That's what I want, a kind poppa.

Love, Sammy

July 2, 1944

Dear Poppa:

I went with Uncle Teddy to Lake Harriet park. He had a funny kind of baseball. We saw cousin Clare too. She is going with Uncle Teddy to California.

I want to tell you a little about the Goldstein family. Johnny and Jeremy are in a boys' camp in Pennsylvania with their father. Auntie Rosie, I think, is taking the train to Omaha Tuesday and Nason is with her. Alexander is in Council Camp and I will join him July 11, a week and two days from today.

I have been sick for a few days with an upper respiratory infection. The first two days of my sickness I was vomiting very much. The next two days I was getting better. The fifth and sixth days I was rarin to go and the seventh day I was my own self.

I was sick when Betsy saw Snow White so I will have to see it when it comes to the Uptown or the Granada. These are the nearest theatres to our house.

We have installed the fans in two places, one in the dining room on the buffet and the other on my dresser.

There are nine goldfish in the pool now because we originally had four and Miss Seidlitz and Miss De Smidt, Sammy's and Betsy's teachers, gave us the goldfish to keep for the summer. Miss De Smidt had two and Miss Seidlitz had three.

Uncle Teddy is very nice except for one blasted thing. He swears like the dickens. I acted as his mother by telling him that if he sweared any more I'd put him on my knee and give him a spanking.

It really is a shame that you cannot say much in your letters but then it is better for you not to say much than for our troops to be forced out of Cherbourg or for the rocket bombs to fall in the right place.

By the way, Ruth Amelia has ear trouble. Mom thought it was swollen glands that hurt her when she cried so much. Later she found out it was ear trouble. Yesterday poor little Ruth was crying her eyes out.

The letter you wrote June 19 to Betsy that you were sorry you could not write to Ruth Amelia because you did not know her very well is an easy problem. All you have to do is write letters to Ruth Amelia in baby talk. But maybe it is not so easy. I wonder if the censors would like it.

Love, David

⌐

July 3, 1944

Dearest Isabel,

Today Disney's "Dumbo" was shown at the camp. I thought it was a wonderful picture but I missed having David, and Betsy, and Sammy to watch goggle eyed beside me. It certainly is one of the best if not the best Disney production. The animals show such human traits still remaining animals. I thought the dance of the pink elephants was terrific. It may not have been strictly according to the text-books but it certainly caught the spirit of delirium tremens.

Tonight the Edelmans are coming to supper here. That is I think they are. This morning there was a loud noise from their neighborhood so I can't be sure. If they do come, I'll hear how close it was. I have a picture of them and me.

I called Abie on the phone this morning. He wants to come and visit me here but now it is impossible because of travel restrictions. We may be able to get together later in the summer. What I want to do is to take him up to Glasgow to meet the Naftalins. Abie has a good job in the hospital and no doubt is doing the very good job of which he is capable.

From Normandy come good news. From Italy, good news. And the same from Russia. Today we are on the threshold of Minsk. Do you remember a long time ago when I said that when Minsk or Pinsk or Omsk or Tomsk is in the news the war will be nearly over? Germany offers to quit the buzz bombing if we quit bombing Germany. What a laugh. We should stop our artillery and they'll stop firing pistols. But their offer has an encouraging overtone. The offer is definitely a peace feeler. And I don't think Germany would be feeling us out for terms unless they felt as close to the brink of disaster as we know they are.

Love, Reuben

⌒

July 9, 1944

Dear Poppy:

I went on a picnic and they had races. And in the races I got a prize. It was a gun. And at the end we all got prizes. And they were the same thing.

Love, Sammy

Dearest Reuben:

Sammy started the above some time ago but did not finish it. You can see that I did a pretty good job cleaning the typewriter keys. Insecticide did the trick. You can't buy kerosene without ration stamps.

I wonder if you have worried a little about David's note that Ruth Amelia has a running ear. I think it was July 2, that she had a fever of about 102 and a nose which had been running for about a week. That night she cried out in pain every few hours and by morning the fever was gone, the pain was gone, and the ear was running. I took her down to Dr. S. who observed an ear abscess and had me give her sulfa something and keep her in. She responded nicely to such treatment. The ear dried up in a few hours. July 8, I had her down for a check up. He said he could see landmarks in the ear and that she could go on a full diet and get up. Today, her nose is running again.

David had an upper respiratory infection beginning with a vomiting attack June 26. He had some fever and a running nose, but seemed well by June 30. July 4 he was rather quiet. July 5, he had a runny nose and a fever of about 101. I talked to Dr. S. on the phone and gave David aspirin. Oh yes, on July 1, he was down at Dr. S. office for a check up for Council Camp. He was just fine except for a sore throat and swollen gums. David has had a fever of 101 or 102 every day since July 5. Today Dr. S. ordered the same sulfa for him, six tablets in twenty-four hours. If David is not better by tomorrow Dr. S. is coming out. If he is better, I take him down. In any case, I doubt very much if David can go to camp on July 11. I hope I get our money back. I am inclined to substitute private lessons in Hebrew, once a week, for the present arrangement of five class lessons a week.

There seems to be a lot of summer flu in Minneapolis. I suppose this cold damp summer has something to do with it.

Last night I went for a walk with Dorothy Harris Israel and Jean Parsons; we were three wives with small children, with M.D. husbands now with the M.C. in England. Dorothy and I take it in our stride. But this poor little Jean Parsons is really getting gray hair over it all. She and her sister, with five children between them must find new housing by Sept. 1.

Love, Isabel

July 10, 1944

Dearest Isabel,

I know that you had a proper birthday celebration for Sammy. You must tell him to write me all about it. I was quite touched by your story of his treasuring my gift to him. The truth is that I don't even remember what I gave him. I don't like to give checks but there is so little here for children I hate to buy things.

This letter is sent in honor of our thirteenth wedding anniversary coming up in a few days. I hope it is the last we spend apart. My belief is that before the next one rolls around we shall be together again. Last year in the throes of homesickness shortly after landing here I wrote you about our twelfth. There isn't much I can add. Not having seen you or our family since then I can only repeat what I said then. We have had a very happy married life. I think we have solved the important secrets of how to be happy "though married." We have done very well with each other and with the business of producing and raising children. I think you have done very well to keep things going so nicely in my absence. I am needless to say proud of you.

If the children want a collie dog why not get them one? Get David to promise to bath it, Betsy to feed it, and Sammy and Ruthie to play with it. And Momma to clean up the mess in the house until it's broken. Perhaps you are right. A dog is a good thing for the neighbors to own.

Rafni has gradually become the hospital mascot. He [*should be she*] rarely comes home with me to sleep now. He prefers the mat on my office chair. So between him and me we occupy the office most of the 24 hours of the day. And he barks at any stranger coming in. A very good watchdog within limits. The limits are that all he does is bark and that for a few seconds only. Then he makes friends. He is a bit jealous of the hospital kitten acquired about three weeks ago. Kitten catches mice and has been promoted to Pfc. The little cat likes to play with Rafni but receives little encouragement from the pooch. Perhaps I can get a picture of both of them for the chollern.

Love, Reuben

July 11, 1944

Dear Papa,

I would like you to send us more British newspapers. They look a little bit like American newspapers except that we advertise more than they do.

I'm pretty sure I will be well tomorrow. But tomorrow's too late to go to Council Camp. I'll have to wait until next year.

Doctor Ershler's coming tonight. Mamma, Betsy, and Sammy are going to meet him at the airport.

I'm mad because all the captains got promoted twice while you were sent over-seas and you are still a Major but still they aren't getting fat.

Love, David

July 11, 1944

Dearest Reuben:

Today was the day David was supposed to go to camp. He is much better. His temperature was down to 98.6 this morning. This afternoon and this evening it was up close to 102. In between times it goes down, with aspirin. David looks much better than he did a few days ago. A slight peeling on his foot, which could be a mild case of athlete's foot has Mother convinced that David had a mild case of scarlet.

Tomorrow Peter's tonsils come out. I hope his appetite picks up. Peter talked to Joe on the phone. He said, "Dr. Garten, I'm glad to have my tonsils tooken out." He expects to eat more. We are going to have distinguished consultation at the tonsillectomy. Dr. Ershaler!

About five this evening I got a wire that Irving [Ershler] was coming in at NW [*Northwest*] airlines at 8:20. I dolled up Peter in his white suit and Betsy in her new blue silk and took them out there. It took about ten miles out of next week's driving. I had an extra six miles from this week's because I have stayed home so much with sick children.

Irving looked just grand, the same as ever. I think Betsy had forgotten him but Peter remembered him well. They pulled at his hands and climbed on his lap and bothered him for stories, candy and root beer. Irving tells me that your hopes for fall are based on rotation, not on peace. He even thinks he might get you a job with him in N.Y. or Atlantic City. Wouldn't it be wonderful? We wanted Irving to stay with us but he is staying at the Nicollet.

The other day I borrowed Peter's coin purse. He wanted to pay the tokens on the street car. For some reason, I think because the street car was going quite fast, I said no. He said, "Let me pay the token or I'll take back my purse."

I did read David most of your letter of July 5. David enjoyed the English paper very much. He likes to listen to the news and follow it on his map.

Love, Isabel

〜

July 12, 1944

Dear Papa:

I am having my tonsils tooken out today and I am in the hospital. Dr. Ershaler is going to come down & see me.

Yesterday I went to the airfield to meet Dr. Ershaler. I rode on a merry go round and I got some refreshments.

I'm in Abbott [Hospital].

There's such a thing as a rocket. A rocket is a great big bullet with a machine in it and if it hits you you'll die.

David is sick and Grace is home with the baby.

There is a baby in here with me. She is a year and a half. Her name is Doris.

Love, Sammy

July 12, 1944

Dearest Reuben:

I forgot to mention in my last letter that David's toes were peeling.

I haven't been home since 7:45 this morning. It's now 11:30. I gave David one sulfa & one aspirin at 6:30 AM. I called home at 10:30. David must have been feeling pretty well because he was playing dominoes with Grace.

Peter hasn't waked up from his operation. His tonsils, which you will see in a bottle, were large, deeply imbedded, & scarred.

Irving was at this hospital, Abbott, for a few minutes this morning. Then he went on to the General & maybe to 1127 Medical Arts Bldg.

Irving was in San Antonio twice on this tour he is making. He saw Ruth [Eldridge] both times. I suspect Ruth is holding up the deal now. Wouldn't it be wonderful if Irving married Ruth & they lived near us at Mitchell Field [in Milwaukee]?*

Love, Isabel

July 13, 1944

Dearest Reuben:

Last night Irving said to me, "Well, Ruth and I are going to be married in a couple of months." I said, "You have made Reuben and me very happy." I always thought they were made for each other but it took a long time for them to see it that way.

Last night I let Irving use the car to take Betty Hanson out to dinner. After dinner, Rachel Brin Helstein came over, then Irving and Betty. Edelmans were supposed to come but no nursemaid, so we

*The Ershlers settled after their marriage in Salt Lake City, Utah.

went there. Betty looks the same as ever. She sent regards to you. She and Gudrun, who teaches piano, and Claudia, the widow, now live out on 47th St. and 15th Avenue.

I asked Irving about the arrangements for psychologists in the proposed convalescent centers. He said there would be psychologists, and also that he could probably get me a job if you were stationed at one of the convalescent centers.

I stayed at the hospital with Peter till about two in the afternoon. It seems that 15 units of chloral hydrate are given routinely to all patients just after a tonsillectomy. But yesterday they were short handed for nurses so they gave the patients 25 units so they wouldn't bother the nurses. It worked too. Peter slept all day and all night. I took him home this morning and he slept most of the morning. He was very good in the hospital, didn't object when his skin was punctured for a blood test or when a thermometer was put up his behind, or when the anaesthetic was given him.

Today Peter was hungry all day. He had cantaloupe and apricots, canned mackerel, about four or five helpings of fried lake trout, buttered toast, buttered asparagus, custard, a piece of fudge, cookies and more of everything through the day. His temperature was 100 this afternoon.

David finally seems to be getting well. In the past few days his temperature has gone up to 103, then 102, then 101 and today to 100.4. Tonight it was normal long enough for him to take a tub bath, his first in about twenty days. He is still on sulfa, but if all goes well tomorrow I am to discontinue it at noon.

Love, Isabel

⤸

July 13, 1944

Dear David,

That was a very fine letter you sent July 2 when Teddy was there in Minneapolis. You always manage to include some information that I think is very important but Momma sometimes forgets to write me. Ruth Amelia's ear trouble for an instance. I hope sulphadiazine ends it and that she doesn't get mastoiditis. I don't suppose you remember your bout with that bad disease, but just put your finger behind your right ear and you'll see or rather feel what I mean.

That was a very nice report card Momma sent me from the Sunday School. David, I want to tell you that I'm very proud of you for doing so well. Maybe I shouldn't tell you that because you shouldn't get conceited. But then you aren't the type to get a swollen head over your own accomplishments.

Now I'm going to try a letter to Ruth Amelia.

Dear Ruth Amelia Berman:

A good baby eats and sleeps and laughs a lot. And you're a good baby.

Love, Poppa

⤶

July 13, 1944

Dear Betsy,

Letters cross the ocean each way so fast now that I can ask you a question and get the answer back in less than 3 weeks. This is the question: How many of your cousins can you mention by name and who are their mothers and fathers?

That was a wonderful report card Mommy sent me of your work in Sunday School. You know, Betsy, your school work comes naturally and logically to you. Both your momma and your poppa were pretty good in school.

The place where I go to dinner often on Fridays is called "Lindisfarne," the home of the Edelmans. Their daughters are 7 and 10. Natasha is 7, Sonya is 10. They have a dog named Terrier Terry. They have a great big lawn on which they play croquet with a wonderful

English set of mallets and balls. They have 20 chickens that lay 10 eggs a day. (Question: How many eggs per chicken?)

Love, Poppa

~

July 13, 1944

Dear Sammy,

I like to write to my children because I get such interesting answers. But it must be quite a task for Mommy to take all that dictation. You know that, don't you?

So you can swim now only you sink a little. When you get a little fatter you'll float better. I, for instance, float very well.

I'm glad you think you have a nice kind poppa. I try to be that way. I like to be happy, and it's a lot easier to be happy happy than to be happy mad.

I remember going through the Excelsior rolling tunnel and David couldn't walk in it and fell down and rolled around and around and I ran in to rescue him and I couldn't walk either, and I rolled around the barrel until we were both rescued by a guard. Boy, was that ever funny.

Now you are a very nice boy and I'm sure you try to be good.

Love, Poppa

~

July 15, 1944

Dearest Reuben:

I know you will be glad to hear that David seems to be over his sinus infection. He has had normal temperature for thirty-six hours. Today I took him to the lake for a while and he took a nap in the afternoon. He told Betsy he doesn't like her and hopes she dies soon and he told Peter that having his tonsils [out] didn't change him at all, he was as bad as ever. So you can see he is not sick any more.

Mother meant to help by staying with me. She did take the children out occasionally, sew for Betsy, cook, and do some dishes. But here are some of the things she said to me. "What is his temperature? If he gets to be a permanent invalid, it's on your head. Why don't you call another doctor? Rosie Schwartz says that Dr. Shapiro is a good doctor. Dr. Seham is too old. Why don't you have Dr. Garten come out? A Professor Swain from Stanford University told me that penicillin is released for the general public. Why not ask the doctor to use it for David? If you had given him a laxative the first day he threw up he wouldn't have been sick at all. What good is aspirin? I took it and it didn't do me a bit of good. That peeling on his feet must be scarlet fever. You mustn't give him any meat for some time now or he'll get a kidney infection.

The conversation with Dr. Seham was as follows.

G.: Doctor, do you object to a laxative?

Dr. S.: No, I don't object, if it's necessary.

IRB: He had a movement yesterday.

Dr. S.: He doesn't need a laxative, then.

G.: Do you take a throat culture?

Dr. S.: If it's indicated.

G.: Dr. Swain from Stanford told me about penicillin. Can you get it?

Dr. S.: It is useful for some things.

Well, it's all funny now as I write it down, but it wasn't so funny at the time. I hope you don't mind it. I have hesitated to tell you because a hostess should not bear tales about her guests and a family should preserve a united front. So please contribute this letter to the waste paper collection in England.

Love, Isabel

July 15, 1944

Dear Poppa:

I don't want you to practice in Sacramento.

Gramma Gertie is here.

Dr. Ershler came to town. He went away again too. He is going to marry Ruth Eldridge.

When the war is over, we are going to get a little house and a big garden and a cow and an apple tree out at the lake. We're going to have about five apple trees. We're going to have a man and a wife to work for us.

It is vacation now. I want you to operate on Rafni again so he will get baby puppies. Why does Rafni bark at civilians?

Momma has a beautiful picture of herself.

Do you think you will come back when the war is over or before the war is over? Well, if you do come back when the war is over or if you don't I hope you bring Rafni with you. Have you got a new medal now or a new ribbon?

We have a maid now. Her name is Grace. And she's a pretty one too. She has hair down to her shoulders and it's yellow and it's curly. She reads me stories.

I am taking swimming lessons now. I can go out to water up to my waistline and then sit down on the bottom. The water covers my head too. Also I can open my eyes under water. The first time I tried it, it wasn't so good. But the next time it was all right.

Love, Betsy

⤳

July 15, 1944

Dear Poppy:

I hope you can keep Rafni. Rafni is a very very cute little dog. I hope they'll let you bring him back. And I hope you come back very very very soon, before the invasion is over.

Now there is some flowers, some of those poison berries, up there on the buffet.

Betsy at about age six

Dr. Ershler came a few days ago, the day before I had my tonsils out. You might come back very very soon. You might come back in the fall, which is when school starts. In school I do lots of things. In school, one time I went to Calhoun Lake. I had lots of fun there. It was when Miss Seidlitz had Miss Hoyne's room. Miss Seidlitz is my teacher. When school starts I am going to be in Miss Affeton's room. Miss Seidlitz is my teacher now and Miss Affeton is going to be. Miss Affeton has her room in school right next to my room.

I had my tonsils tooken out. I was in the hospital and I was in bed. Dr. Ershaler came. Dr. Ershaler was in the hospital. He was down with Dr. Garten. I have my tonsils in a bottle. We are going to save them until you come back. And we are going to show them to you and you will say, "Those sure are bad tonsils. They should have been tooken out." When you will look at them you will see that they are real big and the looks of them doesn't look like marbles. But when you look at them, don't smell them. It's bad to smell it.

At Excelsior, that's the amusement park. There's a town called Excelsior, and the amusement park is in it. There is a house and it's called a fun house. And in the house there is lots of fun. And boy the way you get in! There is a pile of barrels and you go bum, bum, bum, bum. There's a record thing and it goes round and round, and that record thing I told you about that thing that looks just like a record, when it goes round and round, you slide off it. When you come back we might go to Excelsior and I'll show you where the fun house is. And at the fun house there is a great big huge monstrous barrel and you go through it and you go sideways and you go walking and walking but you never get to the top because it goes round. And if you walk straight you fall down and start rolling around and you can't get up. One time when Grace and I fell down in the barrel, and Grace took me there and the barrel tipped her over and she kept rolling and rolling around. And I couldn't get up till finally the barrel slowed up and I walked out of the barrel. Grace fell down in the barrel too and she kept rolling around and her purse opened up and the things started shaking and shaking and she was pulled out of the barrel.

Sammy

~

July 16, 1944

Dear Poppa:

I am completely well now. I have been sick for two weeks and six days and well for two days in between.

I think I might buy a camera today. My baby brownie one, you know, fell [*rest of the letter handwritten*] down from the mantelpiece.

Sammy is going to have a birthday party tomorrow. He's invited seventeen people. It will not last very long because Sammy just had his tonsils taken (tookin is the way he says it) out and he can't have too much excitement.

Old man Ershler arrived the day before yesterday and left yesterday night. He is going to marry Ruth Eldridge.

Now you look here if you dare go to Sacramento you can go by yourself because I'm not going to that horrible place with no lake. I'm going to Hudson Bay. Put that in your pipe and smoke it. I'm sorry.

Love, David

~

July 23, 1944

Dear Poppa:

Sometimes in the night the sky is a perfect blue. Then it's awfully pretty. When I say sometimes I mean that I didn't see it but I thought sometimes, but it's there.

I like to tell stories at night. I tell them to myself. Sometimes I tell a lot of stories. I tell one story and then make it run into another. Perhaps you do not get what I mean by that so I will tell you. Sometimes I tell the story of Gulliver's Travels but different. And then I tell another story about a little girl who was put in the same thing that Gulliver was. And then they meet. That is what I mean when I say that I add stories into one another.

I am now reading the book of Beautiful Joe. Or rather, I am through with it and reading it again. The first time I read it I started on Chapter V and went to the end.

Love, Betsy

⌐

July 23, 1944

Dear Poppa:

I hear you have ten pounds of fat under your skin. I haven't got so much. I only have a little bit. I hear you have a lot. Grace has seven pounds of fat. She is fifteen. And she's pretty too. I tell her she's very pretty. Grace is one of our best maids. She never did anything bad. She didn't do any damage. Doris, she was another one of our fifteen year old maids but she did one damage. She was carrying our phonograph upstairs and it broke and my mother had to take it down to Seyurs Roebuck and have it fixed.

Today I was swimming and often I would lie down, I would do what I told you I would do. I only got under water and I sink very very slowly, so slowly. Except in shallow water. I think it's lots of fun. Once I lay down on my back under water and opened my eyes and what should I see but some pretty army green and a circle going round and round real fast. I thought it was just a reflection of the clouds. I love to sink under water. And I love to blow bubbles. That is that you take a deep breath and put your face under the water. The water comes in through your mouth and out through your nose and you can see the bubbles.

I think it's fun to ride on the caterpillar. The caterpillar is quite old but I don't mind. I never did fall. Maybe it'll break. I think it's more fun when you go over the machines with the airplanes. Did you ride on the whip and go in that spooky place with the green eyes? I did, and I was scared too.

Do you really think you're going to come back in the fall? I would like you to answer this question. Why did the cow eat the light? Because the light was made out of grass and he wanted to eat the grass.

{ 159 }

It really wasn't grass but it looked like it. It was a cow pie. You know what that is. It is cow push. You have seen a cow pie in a pasture.

I ate some creamed chicken and I loved it very very much.

You float very well, I think. When you come back why don't we live at Grace's house in Deerwood? Deerwood is very far away from here. It's about a hundred and fifty miles away. I think it's a lot, don't you?

I didn't mind it when I had my tonsils tooken out but after I minded a lot. I threw up in the car and in the hospital. Dr. Garten looked at my throat. Six days ago he looked at my throat.

Love, Sammy

There is a ship and a Jap plane that the ship shot down. There is a submarine just coming out of [the] water. The ship shot down the plane and there is a picture of the pilot bailing out.

Sammy, July 23, 1944

July 23, 1944

Dearest Reuben:

David is not sick right now, but seems a little pale, listless, and quarrelsome. Last time I took him swimming, he said the skin just peeled off his foot. He also said that skin peeled off his hand a little. Yesterday I rode the big bicycle to Lake Street and he rode the little bicycle. He enjoyed that. Today mother took him along with her to the Grosby's. He could not resist the prospect of going fishing.

I resent your remark about girls being just other babies but boys being baby boys.* If I could choose the sex of just two babies, I would choose two girls. The way our social system is run, they might not amount to much when they grow up but they are easier to care for than little boys. Little girls do not drill holes through the wall paper, break clocks, start fires in waste baskets, break eggs on the basement steps or hide toothpaste in the ice box.

I see our anniversary is coming up in a few days. I have received some lovely letters from you. But the best present I could get would be your return.

Love, Isabel

July 24, 1944

Dear David,

I am glad to hear that you are interested in English newspapers. The last one I sent is historic. It contains the account of the Generals' revolt in Berlin. It failed in its prime purpose—to get Hitler—but it didn't really fail. Subsequent events show the effects of that revolution.

*On July 11, Reuben had written to her about their friends the Margets and their new baby, "Heard from Edith Marget. We have written of our new *baby,* neither of us naming the sex! I told her a boy is a son, and a girl is another baby."

I am quite friendly with a family named Edelman with two children, girls, one your age and one Betsy's age. You might care to write to

Miss Sonya Edelman
Lindisfarne
Chesham Bois
Bucks

Lindisfarne is the name of the house. All houses have names in England. It's a quaint and pretty custom. In Glasgow the house I visit is named Roslyn. Can you think of a good name for our house?

I hope you are well now. What did the doctors decide you had?

Love, Poppa

⌐

July 25, 1944

Dear Betsy,

Sometimes letters are as important for what they don't say as for what is actually written. For instance your letter of July 15 is the first one from home since July 11. The earlier letter tells about David being sick and Sammy being in the hospital. Since your letter doesn't mention this I know they are all right.

If you would like to write to a girl of your age here you might care to write to

Natasha Edelman
Lindisfarne
Chesham Bois
Bucks, Eng.

You will be interested to know that I am now wearing a very dressy battle jacket. It's cut like an army blouse only it has no skirts—it fits tight down the waist like a mess jacket. I'll send you a picture.

I'm very pleased about Dr. Ershler and Ruth. I shall write to both of them. When people get to be grown up they should get married. Single people aren't very happy very much.

Love, Poppa

July 25, 1944

Dear Sammy,

You must write and tell me all about your tonsillectomy. Also about your birthday. Did you have a party? I mean did you get over the operation in time. Momma would never pass up a party unless you were quite sick.

That was a very nice letter you wrote from the hospital. All about Dr. Ershler, and tonsils, and rockets.

I haven't seen any rockets. I haven't seen any buzz bombs. As Momma says, the odds are in my favor—about a million to one.

I think you are a very nice boy. Now that your tonsils are out perhaps you will get big and strong by eating everything your loving mommy sets before you. Mommy wrote how well you did eat when you woke up the next day.

How are you in the water? Do you swim like a fish or like a stone? Do you sleep well? What do you dream about?

Love, Poppa

July 25, 1944

Dearest Reuben:

Yesterday I received an air mail letter and a V mail letter from you both dated July 16. I went ahead with the red tape for your California license in a haphazard order. First I bought the one hundred dollar cashier's check. Then I called Dean Diehl's office about your certificate of schooling in medicine. They don't know anything about it, say they haven't seen it. And that could be. Overseas mail is often delayed. If it doesn't show soon, I suppose I can call the Minn. State Board in St. Paul or write to the national board for another copy. I can get a photostat of the diploma at Roger's with one day service. I was going to go downtown this afternoon and get two doctors to sign the paper and take care of the photostating but your momma is coming over to see the children before she goes to Duluth. I thought I had better be home for her visit.

The other day I was out in front of the house and Mr. Stafne asked me if I had a cold because my eyes were red. I finally told him I was upset about this California business. He told me, all in a nice Swedish accent, that Minnesota is the center of culture, that people here have a bright look, but just because it is the center of culture there is too much competition among professional men so that very few of them make a good living. But if they go elsewhere, their outstanding education and ability make them outstanding and they do very well. So after I had talked to him, I felt that I understood your point of view a little better.

Love, Isabel

July 26, 1944

Dear David,

Your ultimatum about living in Sacramento slew me. But as Wm. Jennings Bryan said when he was Secretary of State, "Between friends there is no last word." I don't say any more about Sacramento. All I will say is that I want to look into the matter.

Please spell it Reuben, not ue. In Hebrew it is ראובן meaning behold, a son. You should know what David means. It means beloved. Sammy means listen to the Lord (Shmu-el). Elizabeth means little Isabel. Ruth means compassion.

I must write to Ruth and Irving and congratulate them.

Thirteen years ago this afternoon your momma and poppa got married to each other. Both your grandfathers, whom you never saw, were there. Someday I must tell you about them. Good examples of grandpoppas are Uncle Dave and Uncle Ephraim.

Love, Poppa

August 1, 1944

Dear Children,

From a shortsighted standpoint, from the child's point of view, being an only child seems quite fascinating. All of the attention of Momma and Poppa is directed to one person only—the only child. But there are drawbacks. Everything the child does is altogether too highly spotlighted. He suffers from excess of attention. He can't develop his own personality. He tends to become an extension of his mother's and father's personality.

On the other hand when a child grows up sharing his parents with his brothers and sisters he leads a more normal life. He grows as all living things should grow as nature intended him, not necessarily as parents insist.

In your case I think there is enough love in Momma and Poppa to go around for all. We love you all. I am sure you know that. And I don't think it is a case of our dividing our love four ways. Each of you has it all.

I think you have all had and are having a happy childhood. Do you know what is one of [the] most important considerations for a happy childhood? It is happy parents. And we are happy because we have had such nice children.

I saw a picture in one of the newspapers of a child in France. I think I sent that paper home. It shows a little wan creature with legs wasted and belly swollen from starvation. That of course is an extreme example of an unhappy childhood. I remember when I was somewhere between the age of Betsy and David that my mother used to try to get me to eat saying that the poor starving Belgians would make a wonderful meal on just the scraps I left on my plate. I thought the argument was pretty punk at the time. Yet it is nothing more than an accident of geography that the struggles of the world have overflowed elsewhere and haven't engulfed our home.

Well, we aren't getting anywhere with this letter, it seems. You must forgive the old man for rambling on. Being away so long I fear you will forget me. There will be plenty of time to get reacquainted. We'll have a honeymoon when I get back. Fishing maybe. Yes fishing. I think that was a promise I made to David. I haven't caught a fish since those wonderful excursions to Passo Grillo. I like fish. And I like the way Momma cooks fishes. I wonder if you all realize that Momma ranks with the truly great cooks—the Rivkins, the Weinsteins, Charlie's, Harry's? I used to teach her how to behave in the kitchen. I mean what to do with food. What a laugh. The pupil was trying to teach the teacher.

Paul and David Edelman [*Maurice Edelman's nephews*] have a sister of three who doesn't talk yet. Or just doesn't talk. I told her parents perhaps it was because they dote on her so and indulge her every whim that she doesn't find the need for speech. It's good for a child to talk. Not too much though nor too often. I don't think any of you talk too much. I would give a lot to hear your unchanged voices. Another recording is in order. How about that?

Your dear loving, Poppa

August 1, 1944

Dearest Isabel,

If you repeat the word "Zoggle" over and over in a deep bass voice about two zoggles per second, you will have a pretty good imitation of the noise of a fly bomb. Or if you think of an old wash machine overloaded with clothes and the wringer going you'll have some idea.

Love, Reuben

August 2, 1944

Dearest Isabel,

The children's report cards came. It is very evident that the children like school and their teachers like them. I was impressed with

Katherine DeSchmidt's remark about Betsy's singing voice. I like the kindergarten (Blue) form of reporting better than the intermediate (white) report card. Miss Seidlitz refers to Sammy as Sammy. That, my wife, I take as a personal triumph of me and Sammy. How come he was absent 28 days?

It is not so easy to write a letter to the children telling them to love one another. As you once pointed out, you can't tell a person to love or appreciate another. They either do or they don't. Ingratitude is an overworked word. I think that the children like one another well enough.

How have you distributed the children in the house? David and Sammy in their room in twin beds? Where does the baby sleep and in what?

Love, Reuben

⌐

August 2, 1944

Dearest Isabel,

Forgot to mention in my airmail of this date that Ruth Amelia had a vaccination with a take in April of last year. She needs, unless you've already taken care of it, whooping cough vaccine, diphtheria toxoid.

Dear Ruth Amelia,

You are going to get stuck in the arms to keep you from getting sick. You aren't the youngest grandchild of Gramma Sarah anymore. Your cousin, Harry in Sacramento is now the youngest. How do I know his name is Harry? I don't.* I'm just predicting, that's all.

Love, Poppa

⌐

*It was Daniel.

{ 167 }

August 5, 1944

Dearest Reuben:

Last night David had a temperature of 100.6. Tonight it was 99.6. He has had some pain in the foot as well as the knee. Diane had the same syndrome last winter, including the slight fever and the pain in the knee and foot. David does seem to be getting better. He is very crabby. He leans his head out the window to tell the children to keep off the grass and to advise them not to play with his wagon. He complains that there are too many children around, that they come in the house without knocking, that Betsy feeds them peaches, that Betsy's singing annoys him, etc. I think Hebrew school and piano, perhaps Sunday school must be eliminated for some time.*

Love, IRB

⤶

August 7, 1944

Dearest Reuben:

Yesterday morning I met Nathan and two of his children at the main beach at Calhoun. Nathan took pictures of our children on the swings, on the sand and in the water. We also took pictures of his children, so the whole roll is finished and should be back in Minneapolis next week. Nathan will then splice this thirty feet onto the twenty feet he took some time ago and send you a whole roll. I haven't seen the first twenty feet he took but I talked to Charlotte Bearman who has seen them. She says they are just grand. Everyone who saw them remarks how much David looked like you. The picture shows him dealing cards and playing casino.

Yesterday afternoon we were all set to go to Bridgeman's for malted

---

*David continued to have recurrent attacks of fever and pain, and it was not until 1946 that he was diagnosed as having acute rheumatic fever. His earlier illness, in June and July, although diagnosed then as scarlet fever, may have been the onset of his rheumatic fever.

milks when the door bell rang. The Joe Gartens had come calling. Peter was delighted. He said, "Are you Dr. Garten who took out my tonsils?" The Gartens have a pretty little three year old. She got so interested playing for Betsy's dolls that she forgot to ask. When she finally did decide it was time to hurry down and ask momma she had waited too long—result—a wet trail down the stairs. I wiped it up quickly and assured Mrs. G. that in a house with children such things happened so often that we did not mind one bit. I read Joe your letter about the anaesthetic.

August 5, I took the children to see the Story of Dr. Wassell. Betsy wants to go again. You can be glad you are not in the Pacific theatre. I do hope the WD does not feel you are so valuable on combat zones that they will transfer you to the Pacific when you are no longer needed in the ETO [*European Theater of Operations*].

Love, Isabel

⌒

August 7, 1944

Dearest Reuben:

This morning I walked over to Sheffield's to order some flowers for Aunt Jean who is resting up at Edith's after a foot operation. I sent her eight beautiful gladiolas. Betsy took home one. The nine cost $1.50. David got a couple of small plants. Ruth Amelia loves flowers. She says "me" meaning smell. She knows she should smell and not touch.

Mother called up from the Hotel Del Otero. She wanted me to come out and bring some of the children. I took David, Betsy and Peter downtown on the bus and went over to the bus depot. My, what a crowd! Soldiers, sailors, women, children, old men. All tired, hot and dirty looking. I bought the tickets and then went back to the FF candy shop for candy and then to the kosher delicatessen for pumpernickel. David was rather bad tempered because he was afraid we would miss the bus. After waiting for about twenty minutes I asked the dispatcher who told me that the Mound bus was being loaded outside. I had to stand up till we reached Wayzata. I parked the children with various kind strangers, until there were more vacant seats.

Betsy and Peter embarrassed David. They stopped and talked to a lady who was working in her garden. They worked the lady for a few flowers. The lady mentioned some children who were real brats because they had held a parade right through her flower beds. Later David admonished Betsy and Peter by saying, "When that lady said brats, she meant you." David very much wanted to go fishing but was too polite to say so. He looked glum about swimming and about just rowing. But Ephraim realized the situation and said, "David, let's dig some worms and we can go fishing." My, how David brightened up. Florence loves it at the lake. She said that if she and Avner lived here, they would surely live at the lake all year round. David wanted to fish for quite a while. I had to get back because Mother was expecting us for supper. Eph. suggested I let David have supper with them. I agreed. But David was quite upset when he came up from fishing to find that he was expected to have supper there. He said, "no," and came on to the Del Otero cottage. David has no fever, but still is pale and still has a rather bad disposition. Sylvia said that he was not wearing his halo. Betsy stayed overnight with Gertie and Sylvia. I am to meet her at the bus depot tomorrow afternoon. I saw the Rubins from North Dak. Wigodsky is overseas now.

Love, Isabel

⌐

August 14, 1944 [*handwritten*]

Dear Papa,

I have a new job now. Every day except Saturday and Sunday I take a little wire haired fox terrier named Peachie around the block. That may sound easy but it isn't. He will not come with me until I carry him about half a block. The couple that own him both work and the dog is too well trained to go in the house. I get 75¢ a week.

I'm very sorry I got mad at you but Sacramento is strictly no good. If you really want to go some place let's go to Alaska and have some fun.

Your letter of August 1st says I might have forgotten you. I would never forget My Dear Loving Papa even if you were to stay away from home for 50 years. And when we go fishing let's catch 12 pd. Northern pikes and over.

Love, David

⌐

August 15, 1944

Dearest Reuben:

Peter is an uncompromising little soul. He saw David Gordon down on 36th and Holmes. David said, "Sammy, why don't you like me?" No answer. (I think it is because David G. and Jerry M. once locked Peter up in a garage.) David said, "This is a nice stick. Would you like it?" Peter said yes. David: "I'll give it to you if you'll like me." Peter: "I don't want the stick."

You know how Peter loves Sam Rush. They talk about such things as supplies to take on an ocean trip, about heaven, about the amusement park, etc. The four children and I were in the car. Peter in front was carrying on conversation with Sam. Anna asked Peter a question. No answer. Anna's feelings were hurt. When Peter left he said "Goodbye Sam." I told him to say goodbye Anna. He did, but she wouldn't answer.

Love, IRB

⌐

August 19, 1944

Dearest Reuben:

Peter was absent for twenty eight days because of influenza, car abscess twice, and German measles.

Ruth Amelia had whooping cough and diphtheria shots last fall. Is it time for the children to have repeat shots on anything? Did you vaccinate the older children before you left? Did you vaccinate me? Is it necessary?

Betsy sleeps alone in her room. David sleeps in his room. Part of the night, Peter sleeps alone in a twin bed in the boys' room, but he keeps coming back to our room. Ruth Amelia sleeps in a crib in my room. The maid sleeps in her room.

Love, Isabel

⌐⌐

August 19, 1944

Dear Poppa:

Betsy threw a party a couple nights ago and it was a great success. We put on a lot of different acts. First of all everybody danced to the Schottische. You should have seen it. Then the two greatest athletes of the century went to work, their names, Betsy and Sammy Berman, in a series of daring and wonderful stunts. Then for the closing act of the two, the great six foot jump reduced in size to one and a half feet. There Betsy goes. She's running up there. But she doesn't jump. What is the matter? David Berman, the greatest athlete in the world, comes up, makes a running leap and makes the six foot jump, and marches off proud. Next, the greatest play ever performed on stage, entitled Sir Richard and the Dragon. Here are the players: our two stars Sir Richard and the princess are Samuel Hirsch Peter Berman and Diane McFarlane. The housewife, Elizabeth Berman, and the terrible, most monstrous and ferocious dragon, David Berman. The play is opened as the housewife is sweeping. She is very mad at all the dust and spiders. In comes the princess weeping and saying that the dragon is going to eat her up. The scullery maid says she will go with the princess to the cave but when the dragon comes she must depart. The next scene is in the dragon's cave. The housewife is preparing to go. Then suddenly in rushes the dragon. At the same moment, from nowhere, in plunges Sir Richard the great and says, "I am invincible no one can stop me, dragons are as angle worms to my great strength." The dragon, seeing that a rescuer has come, lunges at him with three heads blazing fire. Sir Richard strikes out with his sword wounding the dragon very badly. Again he lunged out but this time to be killed by a stroke of the sword that cut off all three heads clear from the dragon's body. The next day the princess and Sir Richard are married and they live happily ever after. The curtain falls on the last act and everything else is drowned in the thunder of applause.

Yesterday, we went out to Lake Minnetonka to see Gramma Gertie and Auntie Sylvia. While we were there we went out fishing and on the way stopped to pick up Uncle Ephraim. We were drowsily lying there fishing without a bite when we decided to go home. Suddenly from Uncle Ephraim's pole is a terrific tug. And when he pulled it up we saw a fair size two pound northern pike. But as luck would have it, up it came to the side of the boat and down it went. An expert fisherman like Momma or me could easily have landed it. But Uncle Ephraim is not an expert at the sport and instead of swinging him into the boat he tried to pull him up the side of the boat.

Here are some of the books I have read in the last week or two: Exploring with Byrd, Pasteur, Gayneckis pigeons, Buffalo Bill, The Pony Express goes through, Florence Nightingale, Betsy Ross, Tactuk, an arctic boy, and many others.

Love, David

〜

August 21, 1944

Dearest Isabel,
    I left the 67th General* Saturday and stopped in at Bath on my return. There I met the Reuben Naftalins['] Dr. Robin Lynn. He

---

*He had been assigned to spend two weeks in Taunton at the 67th General Hospital to learn more about what, in deference to security restrictions, he called "a type of case for which I am not specially trained," meaning war injuries.

married Ruth Eban [*the sister of Israeli statesman Abba Eban*] and my mother attended their wedding in London ten years ago. I was entertained in the expansive Naftalin style. I took a tour of the city disguised as calling on patients. Bath is a wonderful old city of preRoman times. I didn't see much of the Roman influence because Robin's interested in the Georgian architecture and the city was largely rebuilt in Georgian times. He showed me several perfect specimens of Georgian houses. My reaction was very naive when I first gazed upon one of the great 18th century mansions: A good reproduction was my thought. I didn't quite realize that I was looking at the original.

I do hope the children are well. David's knee story sounded much like a complication of his non-scarlet fever.

I found several letters from you on my return. And Rosie sent pictures she took. When I first looked at the one of David putting a reed on his clarinet he looked so grown up that I scarcely recognized him. The picture of the family with Teddy as a standin for me was very good. Especially you and Betsy. I eagerly await the results of the movies Nathan took. I must get home soon. I am getting so out of touch with my beloved family.

Love, Reuben

⌐

August 24, 1944

Dear Poppa:

The day after tomorrow I am going to the State Fair again. I think it's lots of fun. Only this time I'm going to ride on more things. Mommy is going to see how much money it's going to cost. The State Fair is eight miles away from our house.

Betsy is out at Spring Park. She is to be here tomorrow.

Patty moved. A little girl named Patty moved. She lived across the street from me. A little girl named Marlys is out in the country. A little girl named Diane is out at the lake. I am going in first grade this

Uncle Teddy stood in for Poppa when the family
posed for this picture in August 1944.

time when I go to school. I am going to go in first grade in Miss
Affeton's room. Betsy is going to come back on a grayhound bus.

Well, and I went swimming today, today, today. And I went
swimming today.

We have a new cartoon. It's called Donald's Day Off. And Donald
gets the worst trouble. That time he ate a sandwich with a bee in it.
And he kept going baloom, baloomp, baloomp. And he got the worst
trouble, so much trouble, poor Donald. And the other time he drank
a drink and it had a bee in it and the bee got out on his nose, until
finally the bee, or the wasp went into his nest.

I go over to Rosalind Rush and I stay there and my mother and
David and Betsy are at home. There is two spooky trees there. One is

Sammy, August 24, 1944

called the old oak tree and the other is dead only it has a cigar hanging from it. If you had a ladder you could climb up and get the cigar. It might be some treasure there. Maybe it's even gold. Gold is worth a whole lot, almost five hundred dollars.

Sammy

⌐

August 25, 1944

Dear David,

I was worried about your illness all through July but you don't even mention that you are sick in your letter of August 14th so I know that now you are well. Because I can depend upon you to keep me informed about any changes in the health of my command.

That was a very nice letter you sent me about not forgetting me and about our fishing trip for Northern Pikeses. That will be about the first thing we do when I get back: we're fishing. I guess I didn't really believe that you would forget me any more than I will forget you. I got a picture of you in long pants taken by Auntie Rosie. You are standing with your clarinet outside fixing the reed. I had to look twice to be sure that big boy in the picture was my little boy David. Most people wouldn't know by looking at the picture what you were doing with the clarinet but we know.

Have you been following the news? The papers reported that Paris fell yesterday and then today we find them fighting again in Paris. Paris won't be liberated completely until our forces join with the Free French in the city. The news of Paris brings joy to the hearts of millions of people in Europe. It is a great symbol of the imminent victory and liberation of all Europe. You are living through days of great history, David. You should read the papers and Time and Life magazines.

I hope that you take good care of Peachie. She sounds like a good dog. My Rafni gave me a wonderful greeting when I returned from Taunton. Dogs know very well how to greet people. Rafni has been wearing a dog tag with my name and Isabel's on it. But she wore it out! The hole wore through from her shaking the tag.

Love, Reuben Berman

Dear Sammy,

Thanks for the letter all about the fun house at Excelsior. I think the fun house is fun too. But perhaps not as funny as it appears to you. Things have a habit of changing in value as one grows older. So what is very funny to you at six may appear quite sad later on. Things you want very much at six you may have little use for at eight.

I want to tell you what I did with my bike. It is getting dark early now and often I am out after dark so I need a light. I have rigged up a little generator that works off the back tire (tyre in England) and supplies enough juice to make a bright headlight and a dim tail light. I remember that Jack's bike had one on it but we didn't take good care of it and eventually that generator was junked. I am waiting for a good dark night to try out the light. There is a place in the headlight for a battery. On a very dark night you need that too because the generator doesn't work until you start up the bike and you are in the dark until you get moving.

I thought you looked very well in that picture of the family with Teddy. I thought it was a very good pose but of course I should have been standing where Teddy was. Soon I hope I shall be standing there. The war is moving so fast that Germany cannot hold up much longer. Then the Germans will whine for terms and soon I will get on a boat or on a plane and come home. I would like that.

Love, Poppa

⌇

August 27, 1944

Dearest Betsy:

Do you know what cow hide is? It is very tough leather that they take off cows and it serves many useful purposes. When I wrote to Momma that I had bought two new pairs of shoes I found myself with an old worn out pair that I thought was ready to throw away. But instead of that I decided to do some leather carving. So now I have a leather watch fob that I made myself. Do you know what is the most important use for cow hide? (This is no joke.) It's to hold the cow together.

I am going to ask you a lot of questions, and you can answer them in your next letter.

1. How much do you weigh?
2. When does school start?
3. What grade will you be in?
4. Who will your teacher be?
5. What do you want more than anything else in the world?
6. If you had wings like an angel and could fly anywhere, where would you go? Why?
7. Is Momma good to you? And are you good to Momma?
8. Do you get along with your siblings?
9. Who are your best friends?
10. What do you like to do best?

I think I shall answer some of those questions for myself.

1. 175 lbs. Over here they would say 12 stone 7.
4. A good physician has everyone for his teacher. He learns from experience.
5. This one is easy. I want a reunion with my family.

6. You can guess the answer to this one; it's too easy.

7. Momma is very good to me. She writes me often. She sends me packages. She does the family worrying over finances. She takes care of my children. She's good by day and she's good by night. I'm good to Momma too. I write every day almost and I send her money every month; sometimes more than I earn!

9. One never knows the answer to this question until he is in trouble. My brother Bill once served on a jury trying some "communists." It was a witch hunt and he refused to compromise justice by declaring obviously innocent men guilty. He lost some friends by doing this. But later on he realized that they weren't friends at all. A friend who won't stay with you in trouble is no friend at all. I suppose my best friend is Uncle Sam.

I wonder what happened to Lt. Jenkins from St Petersburg. I'll bet he is over here. I look at faces of officers on the street to see if any of them are Lt. Jenkins. One day he flew over to MacDill to see me. He came in a Thunderbolt and he dropped out [of] the sky like a god. One of the cherished moments of my life was when Momma and I were over to the Jenkins for dinner and Sammy came over by himself in the evening. When he saw his favorite people all together his face lit up with a tremenjous smile of perfect happiness.

Love, Poppa

⌐

August 28, 1944

Dear Poppa:

At the fair I rode on something. It was called the rocket. It went very very fast and it went slant. It went real fast and here's how it went, bum, bum, bum a lum bum, shoe shoe. David went on the giant ferris wheel and I went on the little one and I went in the fun house and I went on a little train. Betsy went on the things too.

Do you have a good time overseas and things? I hope you come back soon. Or else I'll go bym, bum. I'll be so mad.

And sometime I'll go to the state fair again. There was no fish in [the] pool but there was fish in the state fair. One fish was as big as Betsy. I'll bet you a hundred dollars you'll come back soon.

And I'm having a good time in Minneapolis. And you didn't know it but I went to the state fair today. And I saw the gardens that a man built and he died, but he left the gardens.

I think the rocket went a hundred miles an hour. It was going quite fast, it was going very fast. It doesn't make you dizzy either. It just makes you have to make push.

I think it would be more better for you to ride on a tricycle more than on a bicycle. It would be much better for you to ride on a house. But the best would be to ride on a desk, a desk is the best.

I got a long wiener at the fair. It was a hot dog. Hot dog! I had my picture tooken and while I was having my picture tooken I closed my eyes. And now I wish I'd stuck out my tongue. Look at the picture if you don't believe me. And I hope I stick out my tongue the next time. It would be more better for you to do it.

And on the rocket ride and on the ferris wheel it was fun.

Marlys is back.

I put what we rode on. Fun house, train, rocket, little ferris wheel, giant ferris wheel.

[Sammy]

⌐

August 28, 1944

Dear Poppy:

When we went to the state fair I got a pin. It was a little Russian pin. It had a card with it. It said, "I'm Tanya" and then some other words. There was also Gregor.

I listen to the radio program of Hop Harrigan once and I do it some more but I miss it most of the time. But Gregor was in it on one of his missions.

We saw some exhibits. I liked General Vitamin. There was a carrot with a face on it, and egg with a face on it, and apples and oranges and many other silly things like that. But General Vitamin was called General Vitamin because he had so many vitamins. He had some lettuce for his stomach and corn on the cob for his legs. I think his head was an apple but it might have been an orange. I forget which one it is. His arms were string beans. They had some little black stars for his eyes and nose and mouth.

Sammy and David and I went into a doll house. It was not really a doll house but [it] looked like one. It was a very pretty one. It had very very small candles which I saw. There's a little weensy book shelf. It was carved of magnificent material, very fine material. It had little books in it too. It had a little window at the top. When I told you about Snow White I only told you about the first and the end. I mean the show of Snow White. There is a window in it. And this window in this little weensy doll house looked something like that window. There is a little table set with glasses and things. In fact, when I remember it had two tables. There is a little tree outside of it and David said that it had jewels in it. It would not be so good if you imagined it but if you see it it is really beautiful.

There is a boy named Roger Tweed and he makes me lots of pretty things and I like it because he makes nice things in the sand box.

Love, Betsy

Betsy, August 28, 1944

August 28, 1944

Dear Poppa:

The descriptions of the state fair given to you by your two younger children only tell you about a few subjects. Now I am going to tell you the exact details from the time we left the house till the time we came back in the house.

We left at approximately 8:20 A.M. and reached the fair grounds at approximately ten minutes after nine. First of all we went to the conservation building. First we looked at all the different kinds of fish. There was a lake sturgeon that probably was as large as Betsy. They had some beautiful bass there. Next we went and saw a miniature iron ore mine, showing where they get the ore, where they bring it to the mine, the washers, and then the finished product. Next we saw a miniature dam showing how a lake is formed. Then we saw some concrete and tiles that had been affected by wood and good and bad concrete.

Next we went over to a desk and got a bunch of pamphlets. One of them was a poster showing Bambi and Thumper and Flower. And they are saying, "Please don't be careless, mister." Also there were samples of different kinds of wood.

Next we went to see some of the art exhibits. There were some by Fisasse. One of the prize winning pictures was made by a man that I met once. His name is Hac Le Seur [*Mac Le Sueur*]. His wife teaches art at the Walker art gallery and I took lessons there. One time she introduced me to her husband.

Next there were different booths representing the united nations. There was a Norwegian place, and a Chinese place, and a place for Palestine and Mexico and all the other countries. Betsy got a pin called Tanya for the Russian War relief. At Sweden they had a newspaper and I was going to get one but I couldn't read Swedish so I decided it wouldn't be any good to me.

Next we went to the amusement place where they had the ferris wheel, the merry-go-round and what have you. I learned that from the British. There was a fun house there and we went there but it wasn't as much fun as the fun house at Excelsior. First of all it was all dark and there were boards that went back and forth, and next you came to a tube and you slid down it.

Next, Sammy went for a ride on the rocket and I went on the ferris wheel. It was really fun. The ferris wheel must have been about a hundred feet high. It would go real fast till it got to the top and then the man would turn off all the power and let it drop. But it was really scary when it stopped when we were on the top and our seat began to rock. I am going to continue on another sheet.

Next we went to see a doll house. It was made by a retired movie actress named Colleen Moore, most of it with precious jewels. There was a little kitchen with tiny pots and pans. Then there was a dining room with a beautiful [table] and little dishes. There was a fireplace. Next came the living room. That was really beautiful. There were the book shelves that Betsy told you about. There was on a stand a tiny bible. There was on a table a tiny newspaper that you could read with difficulty and a little magnifying glass and a little letter opener. Then there was a tiny gun. The upstairs I didn't get a good look at but I saw there was beautiful bedrooms, tiny beds. Then out in the courtyard there was a beautiful little silver carriage and a tree made of pearls. Then there was another tree that was slowly rocking back and forth. Incidentally, the outside of the castle was all a beautiful deep blue. The room itself in which it was was dark, but the castle was lighted up so it would be more beautiful.*

Then we walked over to the Women's activity building, which also contains school exhibits. As we walked in there was a lady showing how to use a cookie press. Then there were beautiful quilts. And Dayton's and the big Minneapolis stores of Dayton's and Young and Quinlan's had exhibits of some of the things they have. Then there were exhibits of the schools of different counties showing the work the children did, mostly art.

Then we went into the 4H club building. That, I guess, was the most interesting of all. First there were some chairs and other furniture made by members of the 4H club made with boxes and barrels and other wood you may find lying around. One of the things was a regu-

---

*This fairy-tale doll-castle built by Colleen Moore became a permanent exhibit at the Chicago Museum of Science and Industry after its tour.

lar room made by all the 4H club. The bed was made by the boys and the sheets by girls. There was a chair and a dresser covered with cloth. There was a lamp that had been made from parts of an old lamp which had been thrown away but looked really like new. Then there was a mirror which they had decorated. Next there was the vegetable exhibit, with corn and other things raised by the members of the 4H club. Then there were miniature farms. One of them was made by Hymie. I know it was because I have one of them. Then there was a cute little army made up of fruits and vegetables. There was company A made up of most of the vegetables that have A in them and were standing on little pieces of paper that were shoes. And the same with B and C. General Vitamin Betsy has explained to you about.

It was getting late then but we decided we'd have a quick look at the dairy exhibits. It showed how butter was made and it showed the electric milkers. One whole table was filled with things about tuberculosis. There was a figure of a cow there and it seemed to be talking but probably it was a lady or a record a few feet away.

I forgot to say that we went to the poultry exhibits. There were a lot of ducks. And I looked at a duck and the duck looked at me and said "Quack." Then he turned to his neighbor and said "Quack, quack, quack." Then there was a rooster there that was crowing away like he was crazy. There was a goose and a gander there and were they ever proud. There were two turkeys there and they were strutting around like old maids.

Then we went to the street car but the streetcars all passed us up till we found out what was the matter. Then we took a streetcar downtown and transferred to the Oak and Harriet and arrived home at approximately 1:30 [5:30?] P.M.

There was [one] more thing I have to tell you. If you haven't sent our report cards yet, send them right away because it is very important that we get them. I would like to have you send them by air mail.

I am very happy to announce that this is the longest letter I have ever written in my life.

Love, David

P.S. [*handwritten*] You will soon receive a picture of us at the fair.

August 30, 1944

Dear David,

I enjoyed very much your letter describing the play that Betsy and Sammy and you put on. I would have loved to see you as the furious dragon and Betsy and Sammy in their parts. Where did you get the idea for such a play?

As I write this the hospital cat is sitting over the typewriter entranced by the moving keys. Every now and then she puts a curious paw across the paper trying to catch one of the flying keys. Have I written of the cat before? I think my letters have always been about the dog and never catty. Pussy arrived about two months ago a tiny kitten strayed from its mother. Now it's a great big black and white tabby who resembles our tom-cat from Cousson in everything but sex. And temperament. This cat is very loving to all people especially me and the cook. Oh oh! She just caught a key! Or the key caught her. I'm not sure which. At any rate she has four paws on the desk wrapped around with her tail and she doesn't seem to want to put a foot up again. She has taken to biting the space bar as an alternative. Cat is a good mouser and has cleaned out the kitchen cupboard of nocturnal intruders—four footed ones.

Did Momma tell you that Uncle Jack is thinking of getting married? He wants to marry a girl he met in Corsica.*

Here is a problem for you. A farmer has 100 acres of wheat. The summer drought destroys 25 acres and insect pests get away with 25 more. When he threshes the remainder inexperienced help lost him six bushels. He loads the rest on a truck to take to the miller. What I want you to tell me is what size shoes did the miller wear. This is a variation of the problem of the freight train with 100 cars. I think I shall have pussy sign this letter alongside of my scrawl.

Love, Poppa

*Jack Roston and Madeleine Porri were married September 14 in France.

The cat's paw print, August 30, 1944

August 30, 1944 [*handwritten*]

Dear Children,

On the bottom of this page are the footprints of Rafni. I made them by stamping with a stamp pad. Then I outlined them in ink. Poochie squealed when I pressed her feet so I couldn't get a good print.

Every day we make some new advances on all fronts against the Germans. Are you following the war on a map? Do you know where Romania is? The answer is beyond Poland?

Tomorrow the eagle screams. That is GI for payday. I send home money to Momma each payday. If you think it's any fun to be away from home you're wrong. Of course it isn't.

Love, Poppa

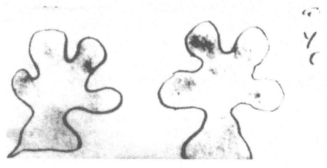

Rafni's paw prints, August 30, 1944

September 2, 1944

Dearest Reuben:

According to an article in Time, the rotation system works only to give furloughs and leaves, but not transfers to USA because positions here are already filled by limited service, overage, returned cripples, etc. So, I'll send you your rubber stamp and maybe I'll buy a fluorescent fixture for the dining room and one for David's bedroom. Maybe, I'll buy season tickets for the symphony. Maybe, in short, I'll admit I'm stuck here in this state of temporary widowhood, for the duration and six months thereafter.

I have not kept you as well informed about David's health as I should have. David had sinusitis, followed by tonsillitis. Part of the treatment for the latter was sulfadiazine. He reacted to the sulfadiazine by developing an anemia. With glucoferin and one month's time his blood count went up from 64 to 69. He still takes glucoferin. I kept him out of Hebrew school in August, but Dr. Seham says he can go now if he wants to.

Love, Isabel

September 3, 1944

Dear Sammy,
Here is the top gunner.
This is the tail turret.
This is a ball turret.
This is a [——] turret.

I tried to draw a fortress for you to show you some new things. You leave out some important parts in your drawings. For instance you should show the turrets. I'm afraid I'm not any better than you in drawing airplanes.

Can you recognize this tail? [B-24]
This airplane? [B-39]

English weather in September.
A German helmet.

Love, Poppa

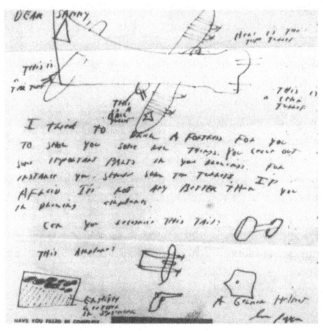

Reuben to Sammy, September 3, 1944

September 5, 1944

Dear David,

   I am going to tell you some stories about what I did when I was ten. Your age. First of all I want to tell you how it happened that I took up the clarinet. I was originally intended for the flute. Teddy, your Uncle Teddy, my brother was to have the clarinet. My father went downtown to Blakkestad's and ordered both instruments. He was a rich man in those days, my father was, and he loved to buy things for his children. Well, the flute, my flute came first. But Teddy was older than I so he pulled his rank on me and took it away from me. He got the flute. Next week the clarinet came and that was mine. We both took lessons in the Minneapolis School of Music on Eleventh and LaSalle. It really isn't a school at all but they call it that to make it sound more dignified. It's just an office building where music teachers teach.

Mr. Warmelin was my teacher. He was a great clarinetist in his time but he was thrown out of all the orchestras he played in because he got drunk. So he took to teaching. He was a wonderful teacher when he recognized talent and he developed some of the finest clarinet players of today. But the run of the mill pupil, the untalented clucks exasperated him. His only real effort he lavished on the chosen few. For the rest he got drunk and only just was able to sit through the fifteen minute lessons for $1.50. For me he got drunk too. Once he was too drunk to take me. His assistant Mr. Lowe gave me the next few lessons. One day Mr. Lowe called in Warmelin to listen to me play. "Listen to Reuben, Clarence," said Lowe. (Clarence is Clarence Warmelin.) "The boy has a good tone." Warmelin listened for a few minutes, heaved up a spirituous sigh and said, "I'm glad you called me, Lowe. Today it's a good tone, but tomorrow Reuben will be bleating like a sheep again with his clarinet."And he lurched out of his room and back to his bottle.

About that time I was having my teeth straightened by a dentist in the Physicians and Surgeons Building. It was all right for me to walk from my Music Lesson to the dentist but I wasn't allowed to go home by myself. My father insisted on coming to get me. One day I told the dentist I wasn't going to wait for Poppa because I knew the way home myself. But I reckoned without my father. He had warned the dentist and I wasn't allowed to go. The dentist threatened to tie me up in the chair when I insisted on going. I desisted. My two front teeth on top faced south and hid behind my lower teeth. That's why I had braces put on. It's no fun to wear braces. They hurt a little and they look so childish. Also, you can't play the clarinet well with braces.

Auntie Rosie played the piano, Uncle Bill the violin, and Teddy and I the woodwinds. We bought the orchestration of operatic overtures and we played them together providing our parents with ineffable joy and giving the neighbors an excuse to visit their relatives on the other side of town. Bill filled in for all the strings. Teddy played the flute and second violin parts. I played the clarinet and cornet parts. And Teddy and I both played the oboe parts and glared viciously at each other for taking the oboe cues. Then we would play louder and louder and more and more off key. I was all right as long as the music wasn't faster than four to the bar and played in the lower register. In the upper register I had a disconcerting tendency to squeak. Also I got flatter and flatter the higher I went so finally I would experiment with a note a half tone higher than what was written. Needless to say the result was anything but harmonious but our parents were an uncritical and ever enthusiastic audience so it didn't make much difference. The height of our family musical endeavours was reached when we played the overture to "William Tell." To be continued.

Love, Poppa

Dear David (Continued),

"William Tell" had everything. Resonant slow beauty, fast tricky brilliant passages, a storm where Rosie wiggled her left hand on the bass keys and Bill played fast runs on the G String. But best of all was the flute and oboe duet. Here Teddy didn't object very much to my taking the oboe cues—he couldn't play the two parts simultaneously. But when the flute part had a few bars rest he would join in with me for a few notes of the oboe part. I never edged over into his territory by playing the flute score because it was too hard for me. Teddy was much better on the flute than I was on my instrument. I think the duet represented the peace and quiet of the meadow after the storm. The storm was very stormy but our duets were never peaceful.

A great favorite of my father's was the overture to "The Poet and Peasant." Rosie got quite arty when she was fifteen or sixteen and started to play Chopin and Beethoven and such. "What would you like me to play?" she would ask. "Chopin? Bach?" "Play the Poet and

Peasant," Poppa would say and annoy Rosie no end. Music shmusik so long as the children played. His delight was visual not auditory.

We played those poor overtures to death. We played them on Friday nights and we played them on week nights. I took my clarinet part to Warmelin and he made me practice them. Every overture has a great big checkmark on the first page and a large scrawled "OUT" on the last. "OUT" meant I was through with that piece. It was a very descriptive word. Not "Satisfactory." Not "Mastered." Not even "Fair." Just "OUT." The manuscript took a terrible beating and finally fell apart.

I finally got so that I could play in passable tune and could execute some of the intricacies of sixteenth notes. I never had a good tone but that didn't bother me because I didn't know what a good clarinet tone was. At High School I played in both the Band and Orchestra. But I am getting ahead of myself. I'll tell you about that when you get to high school. How we played for operas and concerts and such.

David, my son, reaching across twenty-five years is quite a strain on anyone's memory. Many of the things I've written in this letter came back to me as I wrote. When I was around ten I remember asking for something that my parents denied me. I remember very clearly what I thought then: "When I'm grown up and have children of ten, I'll remember how a child of ten thinks and I'll be a better parent to them." I'm sorry to tell you David that I've forgotten most of the things I was supposed to remember.

This, David, is a very nostalgic letter. We, your father and his brothers and sister, had a beautiful childhood, a wonderful happy childhood; almost as nice as yours. I'm going to tell you more of our childhood in later letters because I like to tell these stories and I think you like to hear them. I think the best adults grow up from the best children. I think it is important for children to be happy, to grow up in a home of love and affection. I think the father of the house should stay home and not go off fighting wars and spending years in foreign countries. But I suppose that is important too right now or you children might never grow up at all.

Love, Poppa

September 6, 1944

Dearest Elizabeth,

Your mommy wrote and told me about your going to Minnetonka and coming back all by yourself. She said that you were gone for over a week. Now I want you to write and tell me all about it. I want to know what you did during the day. Did you go swimming and fishing? Did you go visiting? I know there are lots of friends and relatives who are spending the summer at the lake too. How did you get along with Auntie Sylvia and Gramma Gertie? Or have you already sent me all those facts? You know what Betsy? Once I thought you could go to Gramma Gertie to learn how to cook. But I know now that your own dear sweet loving mommy can show you that better than anyone I know. Oh, look what I did! I was going to call you Elizabeth all through this letter and then I forgot and said Betsy!

I'm very proud of you for being such an independent girl and going off visiting as you did and then coming home all by yourself. I think that children should do those things by themselves. Older and more experienced parents advise me that you don't need to push independent upon children. They learn to dispense with their parents soon enough without urging.*

I have some very simple ideas about bringing up children. I believe that you should have a lot of them so that you don't give too much attention on any one. I think raising children is something like raising flowers. You plant good seeds and then you let them grow. You give them light and water and food. You don't say to a rose: "Be a violet." And you don't say to a daisy: "Look, Daisele, why don't you grow big and beautiful like a sunflower!" Yes, our children, you especially, have been the flowers in our garden.

*He had been struck by the letter Isabel had forwarded to him August 22 in which Betsy had said that she would extend her visit to Grandmother Gertie and Aunt Sylvia if Isabel was not too lonesome for her. Betsy comments that the adults had misunderstood her; what she meant was that she was lonesome and wanted to go home but did not know how to say so.

All over England now the heather is in bloom. I am going to send you a bit of it to press in one of your books. You will see its beautiful color and perhaps catch a breath of the fragrance that makes the English people on foreign service homesick. The heather covers whole fields and hills. It changes the prevailing color of green to purple. I'll not forget England. I feel at home here. English people have told me, "Reuben, you could fit into English life very easily." It's because I value many of the qualities they prize: Tact, amiability, humor, sociability. This is a small country and there are many people so they must be able to get along well with one another. There are no wide open spaces. Everyone judges his surroundings by his personal experience. I've met nice people and have been well treated everywhere I've gone, in Ireland too, so I can't help liking the land. I hope you don't think that I've forgotten what is the best country in the world to live in—America. We're rich enough to afford a few words of praise to a poor country like England. It's in the same spirit that I get enthusiastic over other people's children.

But never a backward glance. My last letter to Mommy was perhaps a bit pessimistic from the irrepressibly optimistic poppy. I should be there for David's eleventh if not for your eighth. I have no plans for visiting the Golden Gate.

How are you coming on the piano? By the time this letter reaches you, you will be back in school. Also by that time we shall celebrate the end of the blackout announced over the wireless this morning for September 17.

Love, Poppa

~

September 7, 1944

Dearest Reuben:

I received two sets of pictures of you in the ETO. I gave your mother one set.

I talked Peter into making friends with Jerry Miller and David Gordon. I am not too happy I did it since those two are little wild

Indians and I would just as soon not have them around. But when Mrs. Miller told me how bad Jerry felt about it, I decided to remedy the situation. I told Peter he could have a half pound of FF candy if he would make friends. I also said he would not like it if he wanted to be friends with them and they wouldn't make friends with him. Betsy chipped in her little suitcase to the cause. Tomorrow night, I am showing movies to David G., Jerry M. and our children.

All three older children are in school all day. It's wonderful. Ruth Amelia cries when they go. Betsy took back the goldfish to Miss deSmidt and Miss Seidlitz today. I had a time catching five goldfish out of our pool. I used a large strainer.

Betsy is starting piano lessons Saturday. She took only a few lessons last year. Martha feels that Betsy should start now. David is not taking piano. Martha has felt all along that he was doing too much. I don't know whether his sickness this summer had anything to do with the clarinet, piano and Hebrew lessons last winter but it may have.

Saturday morning I am taking the children to Gene Garrett to have their pictures taken. The boys will wear white suits, Betsy a pink pinafore and Ruth a white pinafore. I was told to dress them in light clothes for a photograph.

Love, Isabel

↩

September 9, 1944

Dear Poppa:

We received your letter of August 30. Here is the answer to your problem. I don't know what size shoes the miller would wear and if you don't tell me I'll get mad.

When we were at Bridgeman's a couple days ago Ruth Amelia saw a little boy about a month older than she was and went over to make him nice, nice. And that bad little boy pushed Ruth Amelia over. Well, you might ask, why didn't Ruth Amelia fight back. The answer is that Ruth Amelia is probably much stronger than the boy but she doesn't know what it is to fight back. But that boy was very sorry that he ever laid a hand on Ruth Amelia because his mother was a witness and judged him guilty.

Last Sunday we went over to Hymie's for a picnic. Ruth Amelia wanted me to swing her on the swing but I didn't want to so to escape I climbed up a ladder. The ladder was just bars of wood, and it couldn't be moved around and it went straight up. When I looked around, Ruth Amelia was coming up the ladder. That started it. I went down to help her up and when we were leaving Ruth Amelia could climb up all by herself.

Sander was very jealous and said that his little brother could climb the other ladder. He said that that ladder was easy and he said it was hard, but it was easy. He was jealous, although I admire Sander for standing up for his little brother.

By the way, you might think that Ruth Amelia will not know you when you come home but you are very much mistaken. We were looking through some pictures and Ruth Amelia picked out a picture of you and said Poppa, then she picked out a picture of herself and said baby, and then she called other pictures other names.

Well, school started September 5 and I have not gotten my report card yet. My teacher is a very nice lady named Miss Cross.

Today we went to Gene Garrett and had our pictures taken. The report I have to give you is not satisfactory as you will see. We will start with Sammy. Sammy was sticking out his tongue but fortunately the man who took our pictures avoided the tongue sticking out. Just as we were about to leave and Mom was signing a check he started to run around as though it was a playground. Betsy was good while we were taking pictures but as we were about to leave, Betsy stood at a dressing room door and stared at a lady till the lady closed the door. Ruth Amelia didn't know any better so the report about her is OK. All she did is jump off the chair and we had to put her back on again. I must stop now because Sammy has taken off Mom's shoes and stockings and put them outdoors.

Love, David

In spite of the challenges the four children presented for the photographer, he captured them looking their best (September 1944).

September 11, 1944

Dearest Reuben:

It seems as if each day is a momentous day. Today the United States has entered Germany. I wonder if you will be released when Germany is defeated. Your contract is for the duration and six months thereafter. And I was looking forward to a trip to California at the expense of the government. Oh well, the trip will have to be at our expense.

I called Maurice and Marian [Goldberg] to make a date for a picnic. They did not want to come south and suggested I come north for a picnic at Maishie's. My gas tank was practically empty, but I agreed to come north. I took the bus to seventh street and walked up 7th street, trailing the four children, looking for a cab. Half the people on the street seemed to be looking for cabs, but one kind hearted driver turned away the man who hailed him first and took our party. We had a nice picnic, but, what do you suppose, no pictures!

When it came time to go home, Maishie drove us all the way. You would have enjoyed the conversation in the car. Sander: Think of a number, add ten, double it, add four, divide by two, subtract two, subtract the number and I'll tell you what you have left. David was mystified when Sander said ten, but quickly caught on after thinking it over. Then Sander said, "How much is 5Q and 5Q." To the answer 10Q he replied "You're welcome." Then Lael said, "How much is 1C and 1C?" She finally got Betsy to say 2C, but then Betsy didn't see anything funny about it. Then Betsy said, "Spell up backwards." And I think David asked Sander to spell Icup. When David is peeved at something I say he says with withering scorn, "Very funny, very funny." That is very rare, though. Generally he is very polite to me.

I think Betsy will make more progress with her piano lessons this year than she did last.

Love, Isabel

September 14, 1944

Dearest Reuben:

The pictures from Gene Garrett are lovely. The only trouble is that on no one picture do all four children look beautiful. But they do look alive and happy. In one picture, Peter is sticking out his tongue. I wish I could send you the proofs. The pictures are expensive. They will cost about five dollars apiece. I have nine proofs.

Love, Isabel

September 15, 1944

Dear David,

I have received many wonderful letters from you children in the last few days. Your longest letter was also the very best. I hope you liked my longest letter too. I became quite philosophical in it as I recall but I think you understand me all right. I called the Edelmans the other day to see if your letter to Sonia had arrived which it hadn't.

Do you know what is funny about the sentence in Betsy's letter: I will stay here a few more days if you aren't too lonesome for me? There is a rather subtle form of humor there, David. It is the humor of the unexpected. You expect a child away from her mother to miss her mother. This resolute specimen of beautiful girlhood puts it oppositely. And do you know something, David? I'm proud of that attitude. As a doctor I have seen too many people who have never learned to be self reliant. I think when a child shows that trait at seven we can be fairly sure that they will have it for life. You are quite self reliant too. I think you know that it is an unusual thing for children of six or seven to be allowed to go on buses or trains by themselves.

Sonia Edelman is having a birthday party tomorrow. I am invited and I will go if the press of military duties doesn't interfere. I hope you don't mind my reading your letter to Sonia. I haven't yet but I think she will show it to me. I am a particular friend to Sonia and she tells me all.

I haven't mentioned Rafni in my recent letters so I will bring you up to date. She is getting along very well. She has a companion now in another dog. A black creature belonging to one of the dentists.

I must go now. I'm off to a training film.

Love, Poppa

⌒

September 17, 1944

Dearest Isabel,

Even though I didn't go to Glasgow, all my plans for Rosh HaShonah didn't go awry. I was able to attend the birthday party for Sonia Edelman yesterday. 23 guests gathered around two tables. Rather foolishly Mrs. E. invited the children for 2:30. You can imagine how she felt around 7:00 when the children left. And then two adults including me stayed for dinner. Around 10:45 we left but by 9:30 Mrs. E. was making snippy remarks, something she never does! She must have been ready to drop.

But to return to the party. What went on before 4:30 I don't know because that is when I arrived. The children were gathered around two tables. The place of honor between Sonia and Natasha Edelman was reserved for me. I am the hero in uniform. To eat was the following simple fare: open sandwiches of lady finger size of egg salad, sardines, meat paste, and something else; tea for adults, lemonade (synthetic of course) for the children; about ten varieties of cookies (biscuits over here) all good; a trifle (raspberries, fresh peaches, and some other fruits in custard, very English and usually terrible but this one like everything Tilly Edelman puts her hand to in the kitchen was perfect and delicious); two kinds of pie, apple and cherry; and a peach flan. A flan is a fruit business on a crust. It is called a flan because the crust is usually like flannel. Then there were all kinds of sweets. You might think the above are sweets but they're not. Sweets are candy. I brought some of the FF. After everybody ate themselves more or less sick we went out in the garden where I told them a story—the Foxes with the Bushy tails. Then we played Charades (In England Charades is pronounced to rhyme with ye Gods). Then we played run-sheep-run which I taught them. All in all as you can guess it was a very successful party. But it wasn't managed as to games and food with the practiced care of a momma with four children whom I know in Minneapolis who takes care to have the children assemble *late* in the afternoon, who serves the children just a few very good things to eat, and manages games that blow off the children's steam without breaking up the furniture. There was a treasure hunt. Then everybody got a prize. David's letter hasn't come yet. It is going to be more difficult for me to visit the Edelmans in the future but I must return at least to read that letter.

By a very devious route I have contacted the Modern Music Library of England. The Modern Music Library turns out to be a trunk in a house in London. I made the mistake of calling personally when I was asked to communicate only by mail. Mrs. Library was not at home so I didn't even see what is in the trunk. Anyway I am getting the scores of two clarinet quintets by Joseph Holbrooke and some other music too. I've been on the trail of this music for three months ever since I heard Vivian Joseph's recording of excerpts from the quintets. From the Goehrs of Amersham, Walter Goehr is a famous conductor, I got the address of Holbrooke. I finally wrote to him and my letter was forwarded to the MML. I think I shall get Holbrooke to autograph the scores. These scores are in manuscript form and I suspect that some day they will be worth a great deal as collectors items. Holbrooke is one of the great contemporary composers interested in the clarinet. His son-in-law is Reginald Kell the clarinettist for the Liverpool Symphony Orchestra and the best in England.

Thank you for the three letters of Sept 7. I'll answer them specifically tomorrow.

Love, Reuben

∽

September 20, 1944 [handwritten]

Dear papa,

    I weigh fifty pounds.

    School starte sept 6th.

    If i had wings like a angel I would take some bombs and fli over to germany and japen and bom them. then you could come home sooner. I want you most if all.

    When sammy said that you were just like abraham lincoln he was right.

    Send us our Report Cards right away.

    Will you please send me a picture of natasha and sony.

Love, Betsy

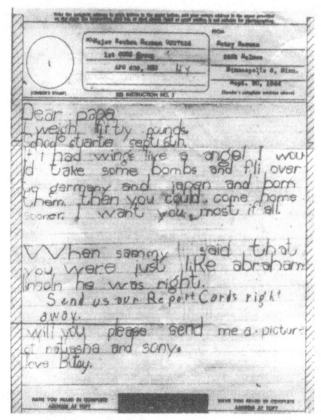

Betsy, September 20, 1944

~

September 21, 1944

Dearest Isabel,

David's letter came yesterday and until I write to him you might give him the answer to the problem I sent: miller's size of shoe problem. He wears size 9½ EE and the way I know is that he told me. There is no other way to find out. I'm afraid David will be mad at me for this.

At this late date in September it looks as though my prediction of the end of the month and the end of this part of the war is a bit early. Perhaps so. But I don't think I missed it by much, if I missed it at all. We move a country at a time. We have proved to the hilt that our command knows how to conduct war on a hemispheric or even a global scale. Every day brings reports of gains measured in tens of miles. And we are now only 300 miles from Berlin, within easy fighter range.

The buzz bombs continue to come over. I described the sound to you in a letter some days ago. Now I'll tell you how they look against the evening sky. We are warned of their approach by that characteristic throaty gurgle unlike any other thing that flies through the air. We rush out of our quarters and there in the sky is a bright yellow flaming thing hurtling through the sky. It flies so low we think it might hit any hill or high tree in the neighborhood but appearances are deceiving. Actually they clear the ground by perhaps a thousand feet. We watch the thing fade in the distance. Suddenly the light goes out! But the sound continues for seconds finally to end in a clap of distant explosive thunder. At night one doesn't see anything but the exhaust flame of course. It's a terrible and wonderful sight. The next day the BBC reports that "Flying bombs were launched against Southern England the London area again last night. Damage and casualties were caused." That tells us that these latest are launched from Heinkels flying perhaps over the North Sea.

There was a most interesting item in the paper recently about the treatment of a village that continued sniping after white flags were flown. This German town was simply razed to the ground. I don't think our armies will be too gentle in their treatment of German communities that leave booby traps around either. There is a very simple way to dispose of a house suspected of being booby-trapped.

Love, Reuben

〜

September 22, 1944

Dearest Reuben:

Tonight all four children and I had dinner with Toby Goldstein Silverman. Toby asked her children whom they would like to have for a dinner party and they said the Bermans. We had roast beef, apple juice cocktail, brown potatoes, sliced tomatoes, fruit jello, chocolate milk, ice cream and assorted candies. The children had a grand time and we went off with bobby pins and hershey bars and souvenirs.

Betsy has a new sweater, red wool, size 10, to go with her skirt of your scotch material. She doesn't really need a 10, but girls her age and up like the sloppy Joe style. David has some new all wool navy blue pants that he picked out of the Sears catalogue. They cost 5.35 and are really beautiful. It's hard to get all wool pants in David's size. With them he wore a dark blue sweater that my mother knitted for him and a white shirt and a dark blue tie. Peter wore his tan suit; Ruth Amelia a white dress and rose printed pinafore.

Toby, Mildred, Dorothy and I and I suppose many others have a strong feeling of "we army wives must stick together."

Love, Isabel

〜

September 22, 1944

1 CCRC Group APO NYC

Dearest Isabel,

David wrote about the trip to Garrets. Even an expert photographer would have difficulty in getting a family portrait of our active youngsters. I think individual pictures offer more chance of success. I have an idea about getting a good group picture that we may use when I get back: phenobarbital to calm down the children and benzedrine sulfate to pep up the parents administered one half hour before the lensatic ordeal.

Love, Reuben

⌐

September 26, 1944

Dearest Isabel,

The beautiful part of our marriage is our complete trust and understanding. I should say a beautiful part. I have never had the feeling that I couldn't do this or that because I was married. If I wanted to do anything badly enough, I did it and you agreed. But then I discovered that I didn't want to do it my way after all. I remember several times when we disagreed that we each took up the argument for the other's cause. Oh, I'm not kidding myself. I know you have given in to me more often than I have to you. But basically we both know that anything we want very very much we will have. And vice versa. These reflections follow your paragraph about Sacramento.

I love you very much and I miss you very much. I am annoyed that so many people don't realize that you have a big job on your hands taking care of four little ones and apparently do their damndest to upset you to the point where you can't be the proper momma you should. As the Sage next door says, they're taking advantage of my absence. To hell with them.

Love, Reuben

﹂

September 27, 1944

Dearest Reuben:

Sept. 24, Anna and Sam and Rosalind and children came over. Anna was simply impossible. Peter said to her in his sweetest way, "Anna Rush, if you let Sam Rush spend more time at our house, I'll love you just as much as I love Sam Rush." She answered, "Do you think I care whether you love me or not. You can't bribe me." She claimed that Peter was a bad boy because he called Don and Nancy toilets. She put on a lofty injured air when Peter tried to wedge in on a picture David was trying to take of her and Anna [*Rosalind?*]. She dragged Peter back across the street so he couldn't give Sam a second goodbye. I was furious.

Love, Isabel

﹂

October 2, 1944

1 CCRC Group APO 633 NYC

Dearest Isabel,

I came back to camp to find a beautiful haul of mail. Betsy's colored pictures are the very very best. I'm proud of her. The proof you sent is so wonderful that I can't see how you passed it up. David tried hard not to smile and screwed up his lips. The expressions on all their faces are so bright eyed and beautiful. Sammy's little tongue stuck out just adds to the gayety of the occasion. When you told me you were taking the children to Garretts, I thought it was kind of a silly thing to do but from this one rejected print I know better. I await impatiently the finished products. Please send small parcels such as pictures by air mail.

Love, Reuben

October 2, 1944

Dear Sammy,

Mommy wrote me about how she gave you a brown sweater and you didn't want to wear it. Do you know something Sammy? That is one of the things I remember what happened to me as a child that I promised myself to remember. My mother, your Gramma Sarah, bought a hat for me to wear. I think it was blue and made of straw. She thought it was lovely and wanted me to wear it. I thought it was terrible. It was a sissy sort of a hat and I wouldn't wear it. Gramma Sarah fought with me and insisted that I should wear it. "POPPY," she said. No that's wrong. "REUBEN, Mein Keend," that's what she said: "Reubkele, it's a beautiful hat and you look so cute in it." But I didn't wear it and I said to myself, "When I grow up and have chollern of my own, they can wear what they like." I'll bet if you ask Gramma Sarah about this she'll say I've got it all twisted. It wasn't a blue hat but a pink one. It was the blue one I insisted on wearing until it practically fell apart on my head. I think I was three then. Your mommy won't appreciate this story very much, but I'm so far away I can only be the loving father and not the stern parent.

I liked the picture proof Momma sent me very much. I liked even the sticking out tongue. Momma says she will get a picture made from a more dignified looking proof but I suspect I'm going to prefer this one where you all look like mischievous elves.

Momma also tells me that you like Sam Rush. Sam Rush is a beautiful man and a fine friend to have. There are lots of people that don't appreciate his fine qualities as you do. I'll bet he is proud to know that you like him so well.

Oh, Sammy, I forgot to tell about the moving pictures Momma sent me that I had shown to me at Eastman's in London Friday. It is a wonderful reel with all of you on swings and things and swimming at the beach. I'm not going to send it back just yet. I want to show it to my friends here, the Edelmans. They're not the same Edelman family that you know in Minneapolis. I have a set of pictures that I took around my last station. They came out very well. You'll see them soon.

I want you to write and tell me all about school. Did your teacher have David and Betsy too? Who is your teacher? Do you like school? Do you go all by yourself or do you walk with the other children?

Did you know that your Granduncle Jake died? I've known Jake ever since I can remember. He was a good man who thought only of the good of his family. He wasn't a very good pinochle player though as I recall. Do you know what Jake's five sons are going to do every morning and every evening for the next year? They are going to the Synagogue twice a day to say Kaddish for him. Yes, that is what Max, and Isadore, and Maurice, and Hymie, and Harold will do. And after that once a year on the anniversary of his death they will foregather in Shul [*Synagogue*] to say the prayer Yisgadal, Vyiskadash, shmeh rabboh* to commemorate their father. It is a beautiful custom.

Love, Poppa

‿

October 2, 1944

Dear David,

My thoughts reach out to the very distant past this afternoon as I sit here thinking about what to write to Etta Goldberg, Jake's widow. I think back to my childhood at 711 Elwood Avenue North. It was 1909 when we moved in there and I remember nothing about it because I was only one year old. But I remember very clearly when Jake and Etta moved in to 712 Elwood because I was all of five or six then. I even remember the house they lived in before at Sixth Avenue North and Fremont. So you see I've known Jake all of my life and about half of his. I can't say that we were ever very close to him or that I ever got to know him very well. He is a man deserving of considerable respect.

I wrote to Sammy about the Kaddish. I think I should tell you my

*These are the first words of the Kaddish, the prayer for the dead.

thoughts about this ancient Jewish custom of commemorating the dead. It is a very intimate sort of a prayer that is said only by children for their parents after they're dead. In the past people set great store by this Kaddish and you will read in Jewish tales of parents being congratulated on the birth of a son for he will say Kaddish for his parents. The custom was that only the sons say the Kaddish. I would like you and Sammy to follow in the footsteps of your father and your ancestors and say Kaddish for your parents when their time comes. I didn't mention Betsy and Ruth but they can do the same too.

Sometimes many months go by and I don't think of my father at all. But always on the fifteenth of November I remember and say those mysterious words that express so little and mean so much.

I felt a bit funny about aiding and abetting Sammy in his decision not to wear the brown sweater. From where I sit, it looks and sounds like a very silly thing to do! And it is silly: I'm following my judgment of the age of three and discounting the experience of the next thirty-three years. I would like to have your opinion on this. Also I would like to know what you have learned from your childhood that you might change when you have children of your own. Was there anything you wanted very much and couldn't have and that you think you will give to your children?

Your dear loving Poppa

⤳

October 5, 1944

Dear Betsy,

Your letter that just came was the very best yet. I am very proud of your letters and your drawings. They show that you have improved a great deal in your handwork the past few months. The picture of the house was very good.

I have sent your request for a picture of Sonia and Natasha on to the Edelmans. If they have one I think they will send it and if they haven't, perhaps they will have one taken.

Also your report card if it isn't there now will be home soon. I sent it some time ago.

If I had wings like an angel, I wouldn't fly over Germany and Japan. I'd fly over the ocean and circle for a landing at 3528 Holmes and gather all of you about me in the living room and tell you never never again will I leave you.

That is until you leave us. Children grow up and girls get husbands and go away to live with them. But fathers and mothers come often to see their grownup children, and the children come to see their parents so it isn't so bad. I have lots of things to remember about how to behave as a poppa ten years or so from now so that I can profit by the mistakes of your grandparents.

I am very glad that Momma took you all down for your pictures taken tooken. The one little glimpse I had of Garret's work makes me very impatient to see the rest.

Did I tell you that the moving pictures of you and the others came and I had it shown to me at Eastman's Kodak store in London. I was the whole audience and for one shilling they ran it through. One shilling is twenty cents.

I am buying a lot of clarinet music. I should say I have bought a lot because I am not buying much more here. I may get some more when I get to another country.

Natasha is just your age but she was brought up like an Englishman so she talks differently. When it's fall she says it's "Ohtum."

Love, Poppa

⌣

October 20, 1944

Dearest Reuben:

I can see that you need my influence. I notice you write to the children suggesting, or implying, that they say Kaddish after you are dead. What difference can it make to you? You won't know. I told

David that I didn't care. I also told him my story of the girl in my Latin class. She heard with great interest the story of how the Romans believed that dead people went to the river Styx, there to be met by Charon the boatman, and ferried across to Hades. "My," she said, "they must have been surprised when they died." I am also surprised at you for going to services. Your patients come to you whether you join the Shul or not. David is quite devout now but I expect he will change. Betsy and Peter also believe in God. Betsy was invited to two birthday parties this afternoon. She went to Rosalie's because R. invited her first and because she was the same religion. I told Betsy, that she had to go to the one who invited her first in any case. I hope you and Abie had a nice holiday in Scotland.

Love, Isabel

⤙

October 21, 1944 [*handwritten*]

Dear Papa
    How are you? How is Rafni?
    Do you ever go fishing?
    I am in the back seat in music.
    Our morning book at school is we grow up. Our afternoon book is it happened one day.
    You are a vary handsome man.

Love, Betsy

⤙

October 27, 1944

Dearest Isabel,
    To start with first things first. I am somewhat concerned over the report's of David's continued anemia. I do want a sedimentation rate

done on him. I don't think Seham will be offended if you take him down to Monica Storsh and have her do the test there. All I want is to have the test done and the findings sent to me. Also she should check his blood counts and HGB.

We had a lecture on continental affairs recently by a prof of History. He was quite a dope. He suggested that a certain European tribe is going to throw in our faces our treatment of the Indians. He elaborated a long spiel to show that we really have treated the Indians nicely, paid him for his lands, etc. etc. Some Indians in the audience burned up. I certainly don't intend to let a man who lives in a house piled high with dreck abuse me because of dust on the bookcases.

The main trouble with the "A" Clarinet is that it is out of tune due to the improper barrel I have on it. When you send it the Conn people, tell them to send it as soon as possible. I shall notify them independently of any change in address though none is contemplated for several months.

Love, Reuben

October 30, 1944

Dearest Reuben:
Sunday afternoon I took the children and your momma to Glenwood park for a picnic. Ruth Amelia is talking fluently. She said, "I want gwangwan" meaning your mother. Your mother loves the children but she is always a little sad to be called grandma, even when it's gwangwan. We stopped in at Uncle Dave's where the children collected their customary quarters. They love to go there because they like Dave and Etta, the cookies and the quarters. They looked at the picture of the Bermans about twenty-five years ago. Betsy looked at your momma in the picture and then said, "She isn't so ugly now."

At Hymie's they have a vertical ladder, then a horizontal platform, then a slide. Ruth Amelia climbs to the top of the vertical l., drops down to the horizontal platform and rushes over to the slide and slides down either on her tummy or her bottom. As you can imagine, your momma was appalled at the sight. Hymie just wanted to know which side was the monkey heredity.

Love, Isabel

⤳

October 30, 1944

Dearest Isabel,

The picture is simply beautiful. Along with yours it graces my bureau in my room. It was quite a photographer's feat to get all four looking so nice a the same moment. David looks very big brotherish standing up behind the three. Sammy and Ruth seem to be loving siblings with the boy's hand on the girl's knee! And Betsy has a lovely smile looking her best as she always does for pictures.

I visited the Edelmen a few days ago. They showed me the letters that David and Betsy had sent and one of the answers. The other had been already mailed. David's letter shows his grown up attitude and his remarks about the bombs and the blitz really amazed the Edelmans. They wanted to know where he had found out about all those things. I off handedly remarked that he reads the newspapers. They thought his handwriting was better than mine but still not good enough for a ten year old.

Betsy's letter was a scream. She really is going to train her pets. What was bothering her little mind about "Texas and Florida are cut out by the circle in the United States" we'll never know.

Love, Reuben

⤳

October 31, 1944

Dear David,

What grade are you in school? Mrs. Edelman showed me your letter to Sonia and it said that you are in the sixth grade. I thought that was too high for a boy of ten going on eleven. Incidentally that was a very good letter and the Edelmans were quite surprised to see that you know quite a bit about what is going on in the war, especially in England. I told them that you kept informed by reading the newspapers. They sniffed a bit at your handwriting but who am I to complain?

Momma may have told you that I have been buying a lot of clarinet music. Most of it is quite advanced and rather difficult but some of it you will be able to play easily. This music is extremely valuable and almost impossible to get. They don't publish much clarinet music first because there isn't much written and second they couldn't sell many copies when they do publish. But I am meeting the people who have collections of unpublished clarinet music and I am having some things hand copied for me. It is rather expensive to be sure, but I will be the only one in the US to have certain numbers for our instrument. So you can see what I mean when I say the music is valuable. I am going to take the A Clarinet. It has to be sent to the Conn Factory for tuning and repairs and then to me. You will need the A when you get to high school and you start playing in the orchestra. Can you tell me why there is both an A and a B flat clarinet?

Love, Poppa

Dear Betsy,

That was such a nice long letter that you wrote to Natasha Edelman. I was over there and they let me read it. Also I saw Natasha's answer to you but I won't tell you what's in that. I am fine. Rafni is fine. I never go fishing first because I am rather too busy and second because I haven't any fishing equipment. I am glad that somebody thinks that I am a handsome man. I think that you are a good

{ 213 }

looking girl. Your picture proves that. It was a very nice group picture that Momma sent me of you and the other three. What I did well I did it like this: I set up your picture and Mommy's up on a table and I sat down beside it and made like I was musing about my family and then I set the delayed action shutter and took me a picture of me and my family.

Love, Poppa

⌣

October 31, 1944

Dear Sammy,

What should come from you Sammy yesterday but three V Mail letters. That is a very lot of mail and all the boys here were envious of me when they saw the great stack I carried away from the mail room. I like your pictures you draw for me and I'm proud of them and I show them to other officers as well. I hope you don't mind. I hope that you will continue to write often to your dear loving poppa.

Dear Sammy, I didn't intend to end my letter so fast but I got started with an ending and I had to finish. If you learn to play the violin you will have a good basis to learn all the string instruments. I want you to be able to play in a string quartet. I want you to start on the violin and then when your fingers are bigger and your arms are longer to switch to viola or cello. You could play a little violin now. If you want to. But if you get one you must practice every day because there is no other way to learn. You must have a good sense of pitch to play the violin. Ask Momma to test your voice for pitch. She plays a note on the piano and then you sing just that note, and some day you will play duets with your dear loving poppa.

Dear Sammy, I seem to run into endings all the time. Write often to your dear loving poppa.

Dearest Isabel,

The children's letters and yours of October 20th and the account for Sept have arrove. Sammy has the damndest habit of mirror writing, writing backwards, upside down, all different ways. Did you notice he spelled witch "mitch." The J. K. and R. in "jackolantern" were turned around. The G in ghost was upsidedown. I wish we could look inside his head and see where he short circuits! These letters must be put in a scrapbook. We should have a book for each child.

Love, Reuben

Sammy, October 20, 1944

November 2, 1944

Dearest Reuben:

Peter came home with a thin little stray white kitty. So we have a cat. I feed the kitty my own patented cat food. I buy a pound and a half of inexpensive fish like smelts or herring. I cook it about an hour or more in water with salt, onion and celery added. Then I add bread crumbs and an egg and stir vigorously. I put it in the ice box and feed a little at a time. The cat thinks it is the best food in the world.

Today the cat was lost. David Gordon told Peter that a bad boy had put the cat under a barrel. I asked D. G. what the bad boy's name was. He said his first name was David and he didn't know his last name. It looks suspicious for D. G.

October 31 I had a Halloween party for the children in the neighborhood. It's the first party I ever ran with no other grownups present. It went pretty well. Betsy invited Fisher, the policeman, and her teacher but neither of them came. Betsy and Diane were witches and Peter was a ghost. David skipped Hebrew school to be at the party. I served hamburgers, carrotsticks, some celery and lettuce, root beer, squares of Egequist chocolate cake with orange sprills on them and Bridgeman's icecream roll, chocolate icecream on the outside and orange ice inside.

Love, Isabel

November 15 [3], 1944

Dear Ruth,

Today is your second birthday anniversary and the second one that I'm not home to give you two kisses for it. I hope you have a nice birthday. You're still a baby and Richard Hughes argues [in *A High Wind in Jamaica*] that babies are animals and they don't become human until they're children. But don't worry. Poppa and Momma and your brothers and sister all think you are quite human. And when you get to be three you will have a birthday that you will always remember. You don't need to pay too much attention to this second one because you will forget it.

This letter is really being written November 3rd but I dated it the fifteenth to fool Momma.

Be a good girl and many happy returns of the day. With love from

Poppa

↬

November 5, 1944 [*handwritten*]

Dear Papa,

We have a kintten. Her name is tiny. Tiny is a white kintten.
She is a cute kintten.
We all love her.
We almost love her as much as we love you.
I can read very good is [*in?*] school.
I hope you can bring Rafni home. But tiny would fight with him and that would not be so good.
Everything is happening hear.

Love, Betsy

↬

November 6, 1944

Dear David,

Would you criticize the English way of spelling criticise?
If a monkey is hanging to the side of a ship with his feet one foot above the water and the tide rises one foot, will he get his feet wet?
A farmer has 100 feet of fence wire and he wants to fence in as

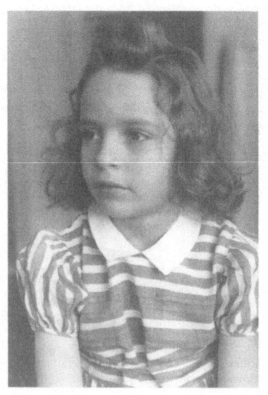

Betsy at about age seven

much ground as possible. What shape field does he enclose with his 100 feet of wire to include the most ground? He could build a field 45' long and 5 feet wide or one 40 feet long and ten feet wide but notice the difference in area of the two! Neither of my suggestions would be considered a good answer. I want you to figure out the good answer and then Momma will tell you the best answer. I'm a mean father for giving you problems like this.

Dear Betsy,

When I was over at the Edelmans last week, Natasha, that's the little girl who is just as old as you, was sick. She had a fever of 102 and was dizzy. They didn't call a doctor because I was there. I'll have to call back now to find out how she is. She had the flu. Did I ever tell you that the English children wear school uniforms? All the children who go to the same school wear the same clothes. The school uniform for boys is a tiny cap like a jockey cap, a blazer which is a striped coat, and a special tie. Girls wear a uniform hat and dress. Some schools have ridiculous uniforms like Eton where the boys wear cut-away coats and plug hats. Parents worry about all the clothing coupons they must spend to keep the children in school uniforms.

Dear Sammy,

I think you must be a very busy boy to turn out so much art work. Your pasted work that Mommy sent me was very good. Sometimes I pass around the pictures of airplanes you send me and all the pilots here think that you draw a Flying Fortress very well for a six year old boy.

Dear Ruth,

Did you have a nice birthday party?

Your loving Poppa

ᔐ

November 11, 1944

Our cat was stuck up in a tree for four hours. Peter is sending you three pictures showing the cat up in the tree [*watched by Isabel, Sammy, and Ruth*], climbing down, and on the ground.

We have received seven letters from you in the past few days. Will write more tomorrow.

Love, Isabel

ᔐ

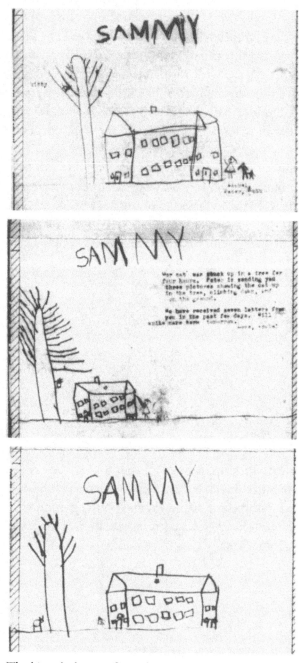

The kitten's descent from the tree, November 11, 1944

Dearest Reuben:

Well, today was Ruth Amelia's birthday. I did not have a party for her. But the first thing in the morning, David, Betsy and Peter sang Happy Birthday to you and she got that pleased, embarrassed expression. She learned the song too. It sounds something like hoppa boppa a boo.

Ruth Amelia was quite impressed when the kitty was marooned in the tree. She says, "Kitty in tree."

The other day I took all four children to Dr. Seham's office for Schick tests. There have been a few hundred cases of diphtheria here this fall. The test is recommended. The children were very good. Not even an ouch when they were stuck with the needle. Dr. Seham was very busy running from one little room to another. Ruth Amelia thought he was playing a game. She said, "Docka hide."

Love, Isabel

⌐

November 15, 1944

Dearest Reuben:

I haven't written you about my latest adventure with the turkeys. One day last summer, Peter, Diane and some other children not belonging to me were playing in the back yard. Mrs. turkey had been shouting at the children in a mean voice. They threw wet blobs of sand at the turkey house. I stopped them but there were a lot of sand blobs on the wall. I thought rain would come and wash it off. It didn't rain for a long time and when it did the sand stayed on the wall. On October 28, I went to a ritzy tea. While I was gone, Peter and Diane threw small stones at the turkey wall and toward the basement storm windows. Denise stopped them and lectured them. Mr. turkey came out and said, "Why can't she keep those damned brats at home. Always running around and letting the brats run wild." He thought

Diane was one of my children. Denise said, "If you weren't so damn mean to them they wouldn't do such things to you." A couple days later I got a nasty letter from Mr. Turkey—his name is really Evans but we call them the turkeys because of Mrs. T.'s funny walk. He said I had been warned repeatedly to keep my children off his premises. And that I should repair a broken storm window and clean up the wall as early as possible. I looked and sure enough a couple panes on a tiny storm window were broken, but I have a definite impression that they were broken some time ago. I got the repair price from Warner Hdw. Then I got the ladder, a pail with soilax solution and a brush. I scrubbed the sand off the wall. Then I wrote a note on the bottom of Mr. turkey's letter. I enclosed a check for $1.25 for repairing the window and explained that I had cleaned the wall. I have heard no more from them. When you come back, you and David must play the Marche Slav on two clarinets at 8:30 Sunday morning.

Love, IRB

↬

November 16, 1944

Dearest Reuben:

Yesterday I received a very nice letter from Tilly Edelman. Betsy got one from Natasha. Natasha has better handwriting than you or I have.

Today was a busy day, the paper sale, the [Minneapolis Symphony] children's concert, and the Temple Sunday school committee in the evening. Even Peter works on the paper sale. The wagon has a loose wheel but Peter managed to use it to get a load of paper from Mrs. Grove. He also got two sacks of waste paper from Sam Rush. At 8:30 AM I took children and paper to school. During the morning I sorted and wrapped and tied paper that David and Peter had not finished. We had a quick lunch of weiners and chocolate custard. Then Mrs. Wyman took care of Ruth while the rest of us went to the concert. In my group were David, Betsy, Peter, also Stephen Diamond,

Stanley Shapiro and a little girl. Judy Gordon, Osher Altrowitz, and Phyllis Igo were among those you know who went to the concert.

Miss Probst reminded the children that if anyone had to be spoken to twice by one of the mothers, his season ticket to the concert would be sold to someone on the waiting list. The children did behave pretty well. We all, about five mothers and thirty children, waited on the corner of 31st and Hennepin for a chartered car marked "Calhoun, Jefferson, Douglas." The street car went all the way to the University.

Can you imagine 5000 children pouring into the auditorium? Carle Fischer is a very fine program noter for the children. He starts by saying "Good afternoon" and a few thousand children answer "good afternoon."

You would notice many changes in the orchestra. There is a girl harpist. Nicolai Graudan has been replaced by Ives Chardon. Mrs. Chardon also plays the cello in the symphony. Jenny Cullen, now white haired and old, is back. There is a lady flutist. The personnel of the orchestra looks old—Nacherly as L'il Abner would say.

The first number was the overture to the Barber of Seville. The second was a theme and variations by Mozart for oboe, clarinet, bassoon and French horn. David enjoyed that very much. Then came a selection from Hayden's Symphony with the kettle drum roll. Most of the children were a little bored with the first somber slow part but they perked up when the music did. The last selection was a group from Bizet's L'arlesienne Suite including Prelude, Minuet, Adagio and dance form.

I know all this from notes I took at the time, special for you.

Peter was quite bored. He drew pictures which I shall send you.

Love, Isabel

⌐

November 6/18, 1944

Dearest Isabel,

You haven't mentioned taking any movies of the children for a long time. I wonder if you can arrange with the long suffering Nathan to take a reel of snow pictures if there is any snow. What I want is close ups of the children playing. Those are the best shots. And I want them to be my children. Also I want you to get into the movies. I want to see what my family looks like. I'm away so long I'm beginning to forget.

Love, Reuben

↩

November 18, 1944

Dear Betsy,

Momma told me all about how you invited Fisher, the policeman, and your teacher to the Halloween party but they couldn't be there. I haven't had any of your art work for quite some time now. I like to get examples of your work. Also ask Momma to line out a V Mail blank and sit down and write me a letter. I think you are a very nice girl and will grow up to lead a happy life. When I get home I'll tell you all about life and how to live it.

Love, Reuben

↩

Dear David,

A set of two books are sitting on a shelf. Each book is two inches thick plus bindings ¼ inch thick. A book worm eats his way from page 1 of volume 1 to page 500 (the last page) of volume 2. How much of a distance does he cover?

Love, Reuben

Dear Sammy,

I think your drawing of the house not burning that you sent me is the best thing you have ever done. I hope you learnt what I was trying to teach you about perspective. I think a good idea would be for you to sit down and draw for me a fast train of modern design going from Minneapolis to Chicago.

Love, Poppa

Sammy, house with three sides, October 30, 1944

November 21, 1944

Dear Betsy,

That was a very nice letter you wrote about the kitten. Aside from the fact that cats fight with dogs, I couldn't bring Rafni home because of governmental restrictions on importations of small animal pets.

Love, Poppa

November 23, 1944

Dearest Reuben:

Today was Thanksgiving. I caught the dickens from Betsy and Peter because I did not have a turkey. Peter said, "Momma, the capon is very delicious but I want you to get a turkey. Can't we go to someone's house where they have a turkey?" Betsy said how unhappy she was because of no turkey.

In some parts of the country there was a turkey shortage. I read in the paper that the turkeys were available in NYC only on the black market at seventy-five cents a pound. Here there were plenty at ceiling fifty-one cents. Davis's charged fifty-four cents a pound. I did not get one because the smallest weighed twelve pounds and I did not feel like having company.

The capon weighed a little over six pounds. It has a lot of meat. And what a delicious flavor. I roasted it yesterday and we started it last night.

We had our dinner at noon. Sylvia was here. Your momma had a previous engagement at Grossmans'. I had capon, baked potatoes, baked squash, cabbage and spanish onion salad, tea and the orange and raisin cake I once wrote you about.

Sylvia was invited to Rosalind's for Thanksgiving supper. I was supposed to take her just to the street car but she missed the Oak and

Harriet car and after twenty-five minutes another one hadn't come so I took her. Peter got an unexpected chance to see Sam Rush. He does not talk about Sam so much anymore. I do my best to keep away from there and it works pretty well.

Love, Isabel

⌣

November 24, 1944

Dear David,

I visited some friends of the JNaftalins in London and I found a boy of thirteen doing some arithmetic problems. I don't think he could do them as well as you. He was working with circles though and they're hard. I had to answer the silliest questions for him such as "How can I find the diameter? It only gives the radius!" The boy's father was helping him. Says the father, not a graduate of the eighth grade: "Dummkopf! It says here you mullipy w wiv da diamter aber gott vaist vos iss w." David, how much is a half of a third of a fourth of a fifth.

Love, Reuben

Dear Betsy and Sammy and Ruth,

Tell your dear loving Momma that now is the time to get some more movies made. You must be growing and changing rapidly now in the manner and habit of small children and I want our pictorial record of you to be complete. Also you might use your influence with the mater to get me some more 620 film. I know that I have just received three rolls but unfortunately two of those rolls went to repay my debt on borrowed film. I borrowed three and paid back two.

Love, Reuben

November 26, 1944

Dearest Reuben:

Yesterday I took the three older children to lunch at the Rainbow. At the cashier's desk, Peter noticed cigars. He had me buy two for Poppa. They will go in with the package of rayon—not nylon—hose, peanuts etc. that I shall send in a week.

After lunch I took the children to Dayton's. We walked through Toyland. But I firmly said no to rides on the toy train. Our destination was the book department on the fourth floor reached by escalator. I bought them the Walt Disney Surprise package—a large volume of lovely stories some new and some old illustrated by the Disney staff. Betsy got a Raggedy Ann book. Peter got Wanda Gag's Nothing At All. We had that book before but it has become lost. David got Robinson Crusoe. David also wanted a book called Caddy Woodlawn but I promised it to him for later. I also got three fifty cent single stories from the Jungle Book with illustrations by Rojankovsky, to put away for presents.

I picked up your clarinet at Bakkestad's. It has a new mouthpiece, barrel repaired, new reeds, entire instrument gone over and packed for overseas shipment. I stopped on Lake Street to mail it and was unpleasantly reminded that The Lake Street Post office is closed Saturday afternoon.

Diane got paddled for something that was most likely Peter's fault. It was the absence of forty ripe olives intended for a Stafne party. If I served a meal of shrimp cocktail, blinces, water, ripe olives, pumpkin pie, apple sauce and chocolate ice cream, Peter would enjoy every bit of it.

Did I tell you that Peter goes to [Temple Israel] Sunday school now and likes it? His teacher is Ethel Brooks Brody.

Love, Isabel

November 26, 1944 [handwritten]

Dear Papa:

I am sorry I have not written to you but I am so busy with Hebrew School, clarinet lessons, and such so I have not had much time.

We have a new kitten her name is Tiny. She is pure white. Momma is going to have her operated on so that she will not have babies.

You have been gone to long, 18 months, without one single leave home. If something doesn't happen pretty soon I'm going to write to General Isenhower. I went to the Symphonic Concert. Among the things they played were the Overture to The Barber of Seville and a quartet by Motzart for Clarinet, Oboe, French horn, and Bassoon.

Your loving son, David

⌐

November 26, 1944

Dearest Isabel:

Last night was my big date with Josef Holbrooke. The Authors' club has 1500 members. They have a wing of the second floor of a five story building in Whitehall place right in amongst the government buildings of the district. This building houses nothing but clubs. There is a concession to wartime in a common bar on the ground floor. I arrived about 5.15 and found a little old man with a waggling goatee playing billiards. I recognize a faint resemblance to his photograph and he recognizes my obvious accoutrement so we get over the difficulties of introduction easily. "Come in Major Buhmen, I've ordered tea for you." We drink tea. We play billiards. We talk music. Our conversation is mostly he talks and I listen. "I always write with some musician in mind. Now this Kell fellow. Wonderful clarinettist. He married my daughter but that's beside the point. I wrote my second clarinet quintet for him. Very difficult to play too. I write a good deal for the saxophone. Wrote something for the London Philharmonic and I wrote parts for five saxophones! Including a double B

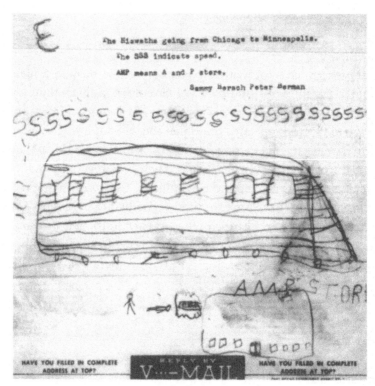

Sammy's drawing of the Hiawatha train, November 26, 1944,
requested by Reuben, November 18, 1944

flat bass. They wanted to dub in the parts for the clarinets and bassoons. We had a devil of a row. We couldn't get the saxophones. They were all built for band work which is high pitch (Circa 1920). Had a set of five saxophones in low pitch built specially for me. There were only two such sets in England at the time. Mine and Sir Henry Wood's. Saxophone puts a lot of color into the woodwind section, don't you think? Major Buhman, I'm writing a concerto for four woodwinds: clarinet, flute, bassoon, and cor Anglaise. Wonderful combination don't you think? I prefer the English horn to the oboe. I suppose this will be my valedictory work. Wonderful idea—concerto for four woodwinds.

"I talked to Kell about you. He doubted the ability of an amateur to play my compositions. Have you seen Spohr's clarinet concertos?

He wrote four and they're all out of print right now. He must have had a superb instrumentalist in mind when he wrote those most difficult and well nigh impossible passages."

I told him we had played Brahms' quintet.

"If you are willing to tackle the Brahms," he gurgles in his throaty voice and waggles his small white goatee in my ear, "you'll tackle anything!" The necessity for my speaking directly into his "good" (Comparatively!) left ear inevitably leads to his intimately whispering into my right ear. "Very difficult for a composer to be deaf. I've got a Sonotone, you know, American instrument, the best; and it's very good for conversation. I hear better in noisy places, strangely enough." My comment that an electric ear-phone is very useful especially to shut off when the conversation turns dull is lost somewhere between the battery and the receiver. My questions sometimes got strange answers. When I asked him what he thought of my sending some of his numbers to Dmitri Mitropoulos, I was told that unfortunately not all of his works are published.* Then he wanted to know if Mitropoulos had a lot of musicians in his band.

"Joseph is a very clever cellist. He shouldn't have gone off to the war and got shot up. That's not the sort of work for artists."

Love, Reuben

⌐

November 27, 1944

To continue the story of my visit to Holbrooke.

You can see that I had a most interesting and stimulating visit with the old goatee. I came expecting to have dinner with him. But shortly after seven he excuses himself to catch a train and that is the end of our party. I didn't come empty handed. My shack-bag was filled with his scores all of which he autographed. And knowing the similarity of tastes of old English composers I brought a gift for him, ½ a precious pound of Fanny Farmer chocolates.

*Mitropoulos was the conductor of the Minneapolis Symphony Orchestra.

Holbrooke lost his hearing through what he calls catarrhal deafness twenty years ago and his story sounds plausible. He blew his nose very hard and felt that he blew some nasal secretion into the ear through the Eustachian tube and started an infection in the middle ear. It is difficult to distinguish the totally deaf from the very hard of hearing. A quick intelligence in a deaf person can gather so much from gestures and attitudes that one thinks he hears a few words. I think the old man is stone deaf.

Altogether a most interesting, stimulating, and exciting evening.

Love, Reuben

⤶

December 3, 1944

Dearest Reuben:

I am going to copy out the report cards because they must be returned immediately. David did not get one just now.

Sammy Berman, Grade 1, Dec. 1, 1944

Sammy is experiencing no real difficulty in first grade. His reading is very satisfactory. He needs help with printing and music. His contributions to our discussions are very worthwhile. Sammy's one trouble is completing his work. He has no regard for time and consequently we must supervise his work constantly. When he learns to work independently and faster he will be a better member of our group.

Days present 48½, days absent 5½, School-Calhoun, Teacher Marion Atherton, Principal E. M. Probst

Betsy Berman, Grade 2, Nov. 1944

Betsy is friendly, alert and cooperative. She shows much interest and enthusiasm in our activities and makes some fine contributions in social studies and elementary science. Betsy has a fund of general information and expresses herself well orally and in writing. Her papers are neatly and carefully written. She reads well and with understanding and enjoys reading. She is making good progress in spelling. Betsy has a sweet singing voice and is a help in our music work.

Sammy by the living-room fireplace, 1944

Days present 51½, days absent 2½, tardy 2, Teacher Janet Gittens etc.
I think Peter's small failings are somewhat common in first grade. I think he dawdles and day dreams because his thoughts are more interesting than his school work. He can sing nicely when he pays attention to the music. Betsy, I think, should be skipped, but far be it from me to say so. David is no longer in the primary grades. That is why his report comes later and in more standardized form.

Ethel Brooks Brody taught the first and second grade Sunday

School children a song. Betsy had every note perfect after one hearing. She tried to teach Peter and David to learn it too. Betsy gets exasperated at the failure of David and Peter to sing perfectly. David sings and says, "How was that?" "Four notes wrong," says Betsy. The first lines go "Candles in your lights I see, friendly pictures beaconing me." David and Betsy both picked it out on the piano as being in the key of G, but Betsy insisted that the ning in beaconing is F#. David thinks it is natural. F# is a hard note to hit exactly and David misses it two times out of three.

Love, Isabel

⌒

December 7, 1944

Dearest Reuben:

Tuesday, Dec. 4, I went to see Janie. I went to the Lyndale by myself. Right in front of me was Dr. Lefkovitz. He really has nobody close to him here, but he has his work and is attached to the city. He asked me if I had my car. I said, yes, but I didn't have it. That was a trick I learned from you.

Janie was very entertaining but it had a lot of flaws. The seven year old was like no seven year old I have ever known. Janie was like the relatively small proportion of popular, pretty, giddy young females. Most girls have no such plethora of dates.

Dec. 5 was the paper sale. As usual I had to stack and tie paper that the children collected but did not have time to tie up. Dec. 6 was the presentation of the Babes in Toyland at the University. Mrs. Wyman took care of the baby. This time there were six chaperones and seventy-two children. The street car went right to the University. As you will see by the review, the performance was very good. They sang Toyland, toyland, little girl and boy land, Don't cry Bo-peep, Put down six and carry four. They also played the famous March of the toys. The children were especially tickled at the remark that the hero would have to go where the angel food cakes come from.

Today I went to the A and P store, the dime store and Egequvist's. At noon, Peter came home and decided he would have to give Jerry Miller a doughnut. I called up Mrs. M. to see if Peter should call for J. Then I gave Peter three doughnuts in a bag. I told him that if David Gordon went along he should give him one doughnut, otherwise he and J. M. could each have one and a half. When Peter came home, I asked him what he had done. He smiled sweetly and said, "Mrs. Miller said I shouldn't give J. any doughnuts, but he wanted one so I gave him a half. I ate the rest and gave the empty bag to David Gordon. He opened it up and found no doughnuts."

I think David is a dream boy for the little girls but they mean nothing to him. I know Lynn Green, Manny Green and Marlen (Dizzy) Ophen's little girl, said, "Hello, David," all sweetness and David said, "Huh, Lynn" in an unenthusiastic tone. The little girls in David's room are very polite to me.

Love, Isabel

⌇

December 10, 1944

Dearest Reuben:

Yesterday noon I took all four children to lunch at the Rainbow. The last time I took Ruth Amelia to the Rainbow for a meal, I had to send her out to the car with David. This time she was pretty good. It was noon, this time, and the service was faster. For .45 they serve a plate of turkey croquettes or chicken wing and giblets, mashed potatoes, green peas, crusty rolls, butter, milk or coffee. I got two Masetto cigars which I shall enclose in my next package to you.

David took some of the money he has earned and went shopping in the dime store. He bought Peter a plastic bugle, Betsy—I forget. Then Betsy had to go shopping. She bought Peter a box of colored toothpicks, David a cardboard Santa Claus box with candy kisses, and Ruth Amelia two hair ribbons. Then Peter went shopping. He bought himself a set of toy airplanes. He didn't have enough money to buy presents for the others. Betsy got herself a tiny doll that looked like a dancer. David is going to get me some flowers.

Love, IRB

᠆

December 14, 1944

Dearest Reuben:

I have been having trouble with the stoker. The coal cokes up. The trouble may be in the coal. Anyhow, yesterday a tub full of live coals stood in the basement. Peter looked worried. "The house may burn down. I am getting the kitty and I am getting dressed and getting out of here." He put on his overshoes and with a worried look hunted to [out?] his jacket, his hat and the kitty. To persuade him to stay I had to pour cold water on the live coals, which process raised a terrific smoke and stink. Tonight the furnace is full of coke again. I am going to let it get cold in the furnace this time.

Love, Isabel

᠆

December 15, 1944

2nd Air Disarmament Wing (Prov)
APO 639 NYC

Dear David,

Your wonderful package I found waiting for me when I got back to the base from Ireland yesterday. I want to thank you very much for buying the things for me. The candy we eat up right away and there is none left for anybody. The fruitcake we will use part of here and the rest we shall take to the Edelmans. I found a lot of mail waiting for me when I got here including two letters from you. But one after

I opened it, I found was for Sonia. It so happens that I am going to see Sonia and her family tomorrow, so I shall take your letter there to them then. That's how Betsy used to like to say it.

As I mentioned I have just come back from Ireland. We went up at the beginning of the week intending to stay overnight. We ran out of engine trouble yesterday and had to come back. Ireland is a wonderful place to visit and I liked it well enough as a place to live. This time I looked up my old friends, the Hurwitz's of 9 Old Cavehill Road, Belfast. I discovered that Lewis Hurwitz, the youngest and just entering medical school at Queen's, is a chess player. I admitted that I knew the moves so we played: two games at his house; four games in my hotel in downtown Belfast the next morning; two games the next night at his house, etc. I think he is a good player even though I beat him most of the games. He is a medical student just beginning his freshman year. I asked him some questions about physiology and he snapped out the answers so well that I know he is the brilliant student type. I have invited him to come to America for an interneship with the idea that we might be able to arrange an exchange with perhaps the Royal Victoria Hospital here. If you happen to study medicine, that exchange might operate in your favor. But an American student would do better to interne in his own country and come here as a postgraduate. And then of course the place to go is London.

Yes, you are entirely right when you say that I have been away from home too long. It is now nineteen months almost since that fateful day when Momma put you all in the car with Teddy and drove down to MacDill to say goodby to Poppa. No, it is closer to twenty months. But there is nothing we can do about it. We have to stay here until the war is done and that, my son, is that. But when the war is over I shall put on a terrific campaign to rejoin my family. It makes it a lot easier to stand this separation to know that all of you at home remember me. When I wrote that the younger children had forgotten me, I was really quite unhappy about it but your letters convinced me that as far down as Sammy I am still a real poppa. As for Ruth, I'll need some sort of an introduction. And packages mean a lot too not nearly as much because of what's in them but who sent 'em. So a package from you boughten out of your own money will be treasured long after the last crumb of fruit cake has been gobbled up and the last piece of FF candy rolled under an appreciative palate. David, my lovely son, I must repeat to you the words of my mother and father: I hope you get as much happiness from your children as Isabel and I have had from ours.

Your loving father, Reuben

↬

December 23, 1944

Dearest Isabel,

Poochie got herself a bath today. The Edelmans think she is a nice dog so they will visit her too and she has to look her best. She is very big about the middle and I'm afraid she is that way though I refuse to admit the possibility.

Love, Reuben

↬

December 24, 1944

Dearest Reuben:

Last Sunday, Dec. 17, I went with Sylvia to the Elaine Keaton–Douglas Sweet wedding. It reminded me of our wedding. Hans Brecher[*] was there. He told me [he] had such nice calendars this year that he was going to send one to the children.

A couple of days later a large envelope addressed to "Master Berman, Junior" arrived. It was a calendar with a beautiful picture of a police dog on the cover. Each month had a different dog. I hung it in David's room. Peter raised a fuss, he wanted the calendar. I suggested they toss a coin. David said, no, they would guess a number

---

[*]Hans Brecher was the husband of Isabel's cousin Rhodessa Rosenstein Brecher.

between one and ten and the one who came closest to the number Momma was thinking of would get the calendar. Never tell David, but I contrived to have Peter win. But still, David takes the calendar into his room and as soon as Peter sees it is missing, he takes it back. I am hoping Bill's calendar will show up soon.

Love, Isabel

December 29, 1944

Dearest Reuben:

Last Friday, David was the star at the services put on by the Adath Jeshuran branch of the Talmud Torah at the Adath. David looked very beautiful in medium blue knicker suit, white shirt and blue striped tie and blue and white yamelke. For the first few minutes, Rosalind Fryer (Irene Sussman's little girl) sang with him. But for about fifteen minutes he sang alone.

I took Betsy and Peter with me. But they got so tired and crabby that I wished I had left them home. Peter pulled my hand so hard that I lost my balance and nearly fell down the stairs. I gave him and Betsy each a cup of tea. Peter spilled his tea.

Mr. Kahz worked very hard with David. One night Mr. K. came here, about six times David went there, and the night before the services David sang his part on the phone. He had to hang up to let the Stafnes use the phone, since they are our party line.

Your momma was thrilled. She wept when David sang. I told David afterwards, "I don't see why Gramma Sarah wept. I didn't weep and I have to do the work."

I want to make a record of David's singing to send to you, or at least to save for you. Nathan is so busy with his own affairs, that I don't dare ask him to make a record. The Beck studios charge 2.50 for a ten inch record, or seven minutes of playing. Uncut, David's part runs for fourteen minutes. Your momma could not bear to think of a part to cut out. I imagine Mr. K. would feel the same way. Yet I don't feel like spending five dollars just on David's voice. Your momma said that when David grew up the record would inspire him to send his children to Hebrew school. I want to include some of David's clarinet playing, Betsy's piano playing and singing, Peter's singing and stories and perhaps even Ruth Amelia's reading. So I don't know what to do. Sylvia wants me to make a record of David reading the story of the Tar Baby because David has such a good southern accent.

Love, Isabel

The Slow Return: 1945

January 2, 1945

Dear Children,

Yesterday morning when I got up I couldn't get Rafni to follow me out of the room. "Oh, oh," I said, "This is the day." I got back to my room at 11.30 in the morning and Rafni was still sitting in her chair and I couldn't get her to move. At 12.30 when I got back she had, I swear, a big smile on her face, and a little black puppy sucking at one of her nipples! I had to leave right away so I didn't know about the other two puppies coming until later that day. So Rafni has three little puppies, one dog, and two bitches. They're tiny and shiny black and their eyes are closed and they squeak like little mice. They aren't much bigger than mice either. And Rafni is absolutely a changed person. I mean dog. She won't leave my room. She spends all of her time cuddling up her pups and lying on the blanket beside them. She'll hop out of the box I got for her just long enough to lap up a few laps of milk then back into the box again. She makes mistakes on the floor only they aren't mistakes. She just won't take the time to go out on the grass. When I take her outside she turns around and sits by the door waiting to get back to her little animals.

The poppa dog is a little black squirt, a Schiperke dog. He paced up and down the corridors when Rafni was delivering just like any anxious husband. When we took him in to see his children, Rafni let out the loudest yelp I've heard from her and wouldn't let him near the puppies! Skipperkee tucked his tail between his legs and beat it.

The whole medical detachment is taking a keen interest. My room has never been so well heated and policed. About ten boys want one of the pups. I shall give them away but one of the requirements of the prospective owners is that they live at least a mile away from the sick quarters! I don't want a menagerie here and I almost have that already.

I want you all to write to me as often as you can spare the time. Your letters and pictures and everything you send me is very much appreciated.

A lot of people think that it is a hard job to bring up four children for a mother all by herself with no maid to help her and no husband to comfort her. I would like to suggest to all of you, especially David, Betsy, and Sammy, that you try to help Mommy as much as possible and most important of all, help by not doing things that make extra work.

Yesterday I flew around in a little cub and had a very good time in the air. Today if all goes well, we're going to fly to a nearby field to pick up some safety equipment for a demonstration I'm cooking up.

Love, Poppa

David—I practice the clarinet every day now.

⤺

January 3, 1945

Dearest Reuben:

I can't remember whether I wrote you about Martha's recital or not.

Only David and Betsy were invited to the recital. Mrs. Wyman stayed with Peter and Ruth. I drove Betsy and David to Baker's house which is on East Lake Harriet Boulevard. The brother who was in the south Pacific with Don MacKinnon and Mr. Zenne, is now back. Remember I sent you the picture of the enormous shell? One room has such souvenirs as belts of shells, a Japanese gas mask, a Japanese sword. The other brother, who was injured in a crash off of Miami and hospitalized for nine months, is expected here shortly.

Betsy played three pieces including the Jolly Fisherman, the March of the Wee Folk, and one other. David played, on his clarinet, Silver Threads among the Gold, accompanied by me. I already wrote that one key of the clarinet stuck. We figured out later that it was probably because of moisture condensing on the clarinet in the warm room after we had come in from zero outside.

Love, Isabel

⌐

January 4, 1945

Dear David,

We didn't think when we left in 1943 that we would be writing to you in 1945. But that is what has happened and we have to make the best of it.

I have your letter describing your Chanukah gifts. Gramma Sarah wrote how pleased she was at your performance at the Friday services. She says you remind her of me. I don't see where that is any recommendation but she seems to think it is.

I am very glad that Momma sent me the clarinet I am practicing every day now. It didn't take me long to recover a decent tone and now I am working on technique. It is important to move your fingers in unison. Try to play G sharp then D in the upper register. Can you do it smoothly so it comes out Da da and not Da t'da? Can you play a chromatic scale so that all the notes are equal in loudness and similar in tone? Or are some notes loud and others soft and some clear and some fuzzy? The clarinet tone is a pure and sweetly mellow note. It shouldn't sound fuzzy like a throat full of mucus. Try tiny changes of the setting of the reed and see exactly where the best sound is produced. Sometimes it is with the top of the reed flush with the mouthpiece and sometimes with the top of the reed just a fraction below the top of the mouthpiece. The reed must always be exactly centered. See if you can tighten the corners of your mouth without tightening the middle of your lips. That helps in producing a nice tone in the higher notes. Tone is everything.

Some day perhaps you will play some of the lovely music I have bought. I'm looking forward to the day when you and I can sit down to play a clarinet duet. There are lots of nice ones and I have a few of them.

I am your loving father, Reuben Berman

‿

January 6[?], 1945 [handwritten]

Dear Poppa:

I am writing this letter to you from school. I have just finished alphabetizing my spelling lesson. I got 3 words wrong today but it was only because I incerted a letter after I was through writing the word.

Ruth Amelia is a nice baby but she likes to be the boss of the house. For instance, I had hung up my wraps and Betsy's too because she could not reach the hook when up comes Ruthie and makes me (no one else will do) hang up her wraps too.

Love, David

‿

January 6, 1945

Dear Poppa:

It is winter now. I have fun going tobogganing and sliding. Wednesday I had supper at my friend's house. I had bacon and some scrambled eggs.

Betsy and David call the kitty Tiny but I call her Snowball. The kitty goes to the toilet in the basement. But every time she tries to do it I grab a hold of her and put her outside. She does not like it outside. It is cold.

The little girl next door froze her cheeks because she was outside and she was coming home from school I think. Her father came home from Italy.

The baby drinks out of a tiny glass.

I went to hear David sing at the Adath Jeshurun. But I did not like it. I wanted to be at the Temple Israel.

Sammy

Dearest Reuben:

As you see by the above, Peter was not especially inspired in his letter writing today. He had lunch at the Rainbow today. Peter looked very thoughtful and said, "My, how I wish Poppa would come back. It makes me very sad."

David said to me the other day, "Momma, bitch is not a bad word. All it means is a little dog." Don't ask where he hears swear words. It is from me. I don't smoke or chew, but I do swear once in a while. Not often, I hope.

Today, David was invited to lunch and a show with Albert Kapstrom. The show was 30 seconds over Tokio. Mr. Weinberg was willing to change David's lesson to the morning. With some small misgivings I sent Betsy alone on the bus to her lesson this afternoon. I put a dime in her mitten and $1.35 in her purse. $1.25 was to pay Martha for music. Betsy just returned in her usual high spirits when she does something by herself.

Love, Isabel

January 9, 1945

Dearest Reuben:

We have had below zero weather almost steadily now for three weeks. Last summer I had the bin filled to the ceiling with coal. I felt like the miller's daughter in Rumpelstiltskin when she looked at the room full of flax to spin into gold. Only no Rumpelstiltskin came to shovel that roomful of coal into the furnace.

I think I'd have enough coal to last two weeks. I'd better have because NW Hanna, who have absorbed Campbell coal, are two weeks behind on deliveries. Furthermore they deliver only one ton of coal. For a few days, some soldiers from Ft. Snelling were helping to run the idle coal trucks. But, according to the Star Journal, the Union objected so the soldiers were withdrawn.

Saturday, Jan. 6, I had an appointment to make records. I picked up Mr. Kahz and with all four children we drove to 2025 S. 6th St. There a very nice Armenian by the name of Thomassin makes records. I had two ten inch records made of David's singing.

Peter was supposed to tell a story on the record but he wouldn't tell me ahead of time what the story was. With the record going he started in with the obvious purpose to fill up as much of a record as David had. Very slowly he told a long and pointless story about how the lion met a bear and said to the bear what is your name and the bear said my name is lion de lion, then likewise for other animals. When I stopped him he lay on the floor and cried. Betsy played the piano very nicely and Betsy and David sang. Ruth Amelia contributed a scream when she was removed from the piano. Mrs. Thomassin and I contributed some unnecessary conversation in the background of the Hash kee ve nu.[*] Next Sunday, Mr. T. is bringing a portable recorder here to make a clarinet record.

Love, Isabel

⌒

January 10[?], 1945 [handwritten]

Dear Papa:

I have a new complaint to make to General Of The Army Isenhower. You've been a Major for 3½ years. It's about time you get to be promoted to a Lieutenant Colnel and a week after that Colnel.

We are studying the British Empire in school and so I took some

---

[*]"Hashkivenu Elecho" (Restore us unto thee) is a prayer in the Sabbath liturgy.

pictures and photographs of England that you have sent home to school to show to the children. Please send me more things about England.

How is Rafni and her puppies? Shame on you. I thought you were the great Dr. Reuben Berman M.D. You operate on Rafni so she won't have puppies and she does. But if you want to get rid of them send one home and give the rest away to other people.

Your loving son, David

⌐

January 12, 1945

Dearest Reuben:

I notice your address has been changed again. You have gone from a wing to a group. Does that mean you stay a major for a while longer?

Have you ever thought about applying for the command school at Ft. L [*Leavenworth*]? It would bring you back to this country at least.

Tonight Betsy high pressured me into serving a Sabbath dinner. Do not tell Rosie about this. She would gloat. David blessed the candles, then he blessed the root beer served in his kiddush cup, then he blessed the cholla.* We had tongue, lettuce, and tomato salad, bread and butter, milk and raspberries and cream for supper. Betsy got dressed up in her wine color velveteen dress and Peter wore his sailor suit.

Tonight I took David to Jefferson J. High to hear a pop concert given by the glee club and orchestra. Anita Tweed sold me the tickets. She is a new member of the glee club and did not appear in the concert. Jean Jackson plays the cello in the Calhoun orchestra. She is a tall, rather hefty, very pretty girl. Mrs. Jackson feels rather bad because Bobby, her eighteen year old, was drafted, given three months training in the infantry and is due to be transferred elsewhere. She said that Bobby liked to play with Gerald and David,

*Challah is fine white bread, often baked in an ornamental braid, for the Sabbath.

that he never had a gun in his hand, and that he seemed too young for all this.

Mr. Weinberg tells me that David is doing very well. I hope you will be able to hear the record we are going to make in a couple of days. Mr. W. says that David has a good tone and nearly perfect timing. David is now in the glee club at school. They told him there that he had good timing and could read music very well but that he occasionally went off pitch. At the end of one piece tonight, David said to me, "Was that C?" I didn't know.

Do you still think you might buy a French clarinet? Mr. W. would like a Buffet, or is it Busset [*Buffet is correct*], for himself.

I hope my remarks about coal did not worry you. I talked to Mr. Derby today and am to get a load, not a ton, of coal in a day or so.

Ruth Amelia did not fall asleep till 10:40 tonight. She went to the toilet, drank water, listened to stories, jumped out of bed, cried, got spanked and finally fell asleep.

Love, Isabel

~

January 18, 1945

Dearest Reuben:

Last Saturday night Mr. Thomassin brought a portable recorder over here and we finished up the records. He did not charge for the record where Peter told about how a bear saw a lion and he said what is your name and the lion said my name is bear de bear. That record had surface noises. But the record is included in the collection and you may get to hear it. I had two records made for your momma. They are copies of David's sabbath singing. Your momma wanted to reimburse me for them. David said, "Oh, no, I wouldn't take a thing from you for these records but a kiss—but without lipstick." Peter read the story of the three billy goats gruff for the record. I nearly wore him out and myself too coaching him to read fast enough so the story would go on one record. If you listen carefully you can hear me prompting him, also Ruth Amelia saying trip, trap, trip trap and wah, wah. The wah stands for walk. She wanted to walk on the piano bench. I spent 13.50 on records. Five unbreakable ten inch records at two dollars apiece and two breakable records for your momma at 1.75 apiece.

Sunday I wore myself out again by an overdose of hospitality. I took David, Osher, Albert, Judy Segal, Betsy and Peter to the rose gardens for tobogganing. We had one toboggan and two sleds with us but no one wanted to use the sleds, everyone wanted to use the t., the big boys wanted to go down alone, the little children did not like to take turns, etc. Your momma and Sylvia stayed with the baby.

Your momma finished a beautiful afghan for me. It is made of strips in different shades of rose. There is room for two people to take a nap under it.

Love, Isabel

January 23[?], 1945

Dear Poppy Poppa:

Momma has made me a jumping bean. She made it by taking a capsule and putting a little bean in it. When you drop it, it bounces; it makes a little noise too. Like this.

Movements of a jumping bean as drawn by Sammy

Today is the paper sale. Sam sent me a big heavy heavy sack of paper, and Momma can hardly lift it. But I think you can lift it better than Momma can.

Momma had the car all fulled with paper for the paper sale, but she had a flat tire. The spare tire didn't have much air in it. We went to a garage, the closest one. The air pump in front of the garage was broken. So Momma drove the car into the garage and they put more air in the tire.

My girl friend is in my room in school. And her name is Judy (Segal).

Momma sends the papers that are 100 but almost every one of my papers is 100.

We are going to make a challa cover in Sunday School. The challa cover is for the bread on Sabbath. Sabbath is on Friday night. If you were here, you would say the blessing but you are not here so David says the blessing.

Sammy

↬

January 23, 1945

Dear Poppa:

Mommy got Sammy some new pills. Now in the United States at school they happen to have something called jumping beans. These little beans are just capsules with little beans inside of them. The object is to shake it up and down and to rattle it. These capsules of the pills Mommy got Sammy happen to look just like the capsules of the jumping bean. So we ate the medicine and Mommy put a bean in the capsule. The medicine tasted very bad.
(The medicine was calcium glucenate and viosterol, on special sale at Sears Roebuck. I figured it wouldn't harm them and might do some good.)
The first time Mommy put in the bean, the bean was too big. But then after I told her, Mommy put in a smaller bean so now I have a smaller bean; that is, a bean that wiggles.

I might get a couple of cards for them at school. We trade cards and pretty cards for pretty cards and all the while you get pretty cards, and ugly cards for ugly cards for ugly cards. The reason we don't trade our ugly cards is because nobody wants to trade them. I am trying to get all the cards I can and I hope you will send me some; be sure they are all different kinds. I like horses and dogs the best but I'm saving Mexican cards.

Today we had a paper sale. We all had a whole lot to bring. David, because he collected a whole lot; Sammy, because Sam Rush gave him a bagful; and I, because Barney gave me some and Mommy gave me hers. We tied with another second grade and so we both got second prize for the paper sale.

I hope you will come back soon because I love you.

Could you send me some pictures of Rafni's puppies to take to school? I can just imagine them.

David and I were both on the honor roll in Sunday school. I came first so I must have been the best child. I think it was alphabetical, I guess, though. Sammy would have been on the honor roll but his room didn't have any honor roll. A little girl named Genevieve Berkwitz gave me a beautiful party dress. It had a very long tie in the front but I liked that. It had little pink ribbons and flowers. She also gave me a silk yellow blouse and a white linen petticoat. The blouse was too big and I wanted it big too but Mommy insisted it shortened. Mommy got me a gardenia for my hair. It was white and synthetic. It's for Sabbath.

Love, Betsy

⌐

January 27, 1945

Dearest Reuben:

Your bad handwriting is coming home to roost. David has written you a very interesting letter about a sleigh ride, but you may have trouble reading it.

Today I overheard Peter saying, "Last night my brother went to a sleigh ride. My sister went out for dinner with my mother. I had to stay home. I was very sad."

David and I were invited to the Maurice G.'s for dinner, but David's class was having a sleigh ride. I asked Maurice if it made much difference which child I brought. Of [course] he had to say no. Betsy wore the beautiful print silk dress that Josephine Berkwitz had sent over to her. She had a gardenia in her hair. She wore a John Frederick's hat. I bought it for $2.50 at Dayton's, on sale. It is a wine color beret with the hours in blue embroidery thread and the hands in felt.

Love, Isabel

⇜

January 27, 1945 [handwritten]

Dear Papa,

I went sleigh riding with my class at school last night. It was sponsored by a boy in our room's father and mother and cost us 50¢ a person or two nickels and two tokens. We met at the corner at Lake and Hennepin and caught the St. Louis Park bus then got rid of one token. We rode from there to the city limits and caught another bus which took care of one nickel. We got off at the stables and we looked around the place. That smell. (*It stunk*).

We had to take on sleigh wheels because the man said there wasn't enough snow. We stopped at a gas station to refill the horse's [——] but we decided the tires needed the air hose.

By the way the horses names were Joe and Choklate Chip. While the tires were getting air we saw some children (29 children in all) taking a sleigh ride in the back of a truck. Well we finally got started the first part was uneventful except that a Huge girl poked at a little boy and sent him back mad as a hornet we all had to chase after him and bring him back. Later we all started jumping on and off heaving snow at the children left on it. I was wondering how to get off because there was a boy beneath heaving up snow finally I solved the problem by jumping on top of him. This kept up all the rest of the way. On the way home we stopped off at the Wiggins house and had hot cocoa and took some doughnuts.

Love, David

January 27, 1945

Dear David,

I've been meaning to tell you about why the clarinet key stuck for a long time but I always forget when I am writing home. I think you brought the instrument out of the cold and started to play immediately. The cold metal made the oil around the springs in the keys sluggish and stiff. You must always thoroughly warm up the clarinet before you play in public. Five minutes of playing generally does it. A cold instrument will be out of tune too. I would suggest that you pay a visit to Bob Clarke at Blakkestad's and have him show you about the springs in a clarinet. You will be fascinated to see the beautiful engineering in the articulation of the keys.

I hope you like the Haggadah* that I am sending you for [*from*] the Edelmans. I know it isn't necessary for me to tell you that you must write to Sonia and Natasha to thank them for it.

Dear Betsy,

I would certainly like to hear you play the piano and sing now. I've been away so long that it isn't fair at all. They should let me go home. I remember you as you were in the beautiful spring of 1943. Now I suppose you've grown so you're as big now as David was then. I think if I try to place each child the size of the next one up, I'll have it straight in my mind. But that doesn't tell me how big David is. I'll just have to remember how I was 26 years ago and that's David.

When you visit England when you are grown up, I will tell you just where to go and what to do and you will probably be a sensation. I'll explain that later.

Did I ever tell you that all the little girls wear uniforms to school? They're generally little blue dresses with round hats and some sort of crest on the hats indicating what school they attend.

---

*The Haggadah is a book containing the liturgy for the Passover Seder.

Dear Sammy Hirsch Peter,

Your pictures are very nice and I want you to know that I like them very much. I often show them to other officers because I am proud of your work. I like the way you sign your name writing right to left or left to right or upside down or whatever way your fancy pleases. You are a very good boy and I want to tell you that your dear loving poppa is going to hurry back to you just as soon as his Uncle Sam lets him.

Dear Ruth Amelia,

You are better off at home.

My puppies are now big enough to growl in falsetto, bite each others' ears, play nicely together and in general provide some amusement to their master, me. I have a picture of them that I will send if it comes out.

I also took a snow picture, rather rare in England. The trees are loaded with frost.

Dear all four children:

Mail has been very scarce lately and I always assume it is due to the service and not to the failure of my correspondence. I think you should all write often to me and David and Betsy should be able to complete the address and return address too.

Love, Reuben

⌐

February 3, 1945

Dearest Reuben:

Tonight David made supper for the children. He opened up a can of vegetable soup, put it in a pan, added a can of water and heated it to boiling. He made a salad of lettuce and tomato and French dressing, sliced bread, poured milk, made a butterscotch custard from Ann Page butterscotch mix. Then he said to the other children, "Now, I'm not straining this soup. You take it as it is." But Betsy put up a good argument about eating the salad. She finally did eat it though. Peter refused to touch the milk. David said, "Such spoiled children. My children won't be like that." I asked David if he wasn't going to eat. He said, "Oh, yes, I'll eat when the children are through." Peter was very angry because he had not made the butterscotch pudding himself.

David did this for two cub scout tests. One is to prepare and eat a meal with at least two hot dishes and a green vegetable; the other is to have some duties at home. Every Saturday night hereafter, David is to make supper.

Morris and Edith had a feeding problem in Nancy Beth, until Morris took time off from work to try a cure which Dr. Seham said is exactly what [——] would have done. For three days in a row, he stuffed three good meals, unemotionally but firmly, down Nancy Beth. At the end of that time she ate. That was at Xmas time. Since then she has gained two and a half pounds. It is possible that some such cure, administered by you or your momma might work on Peter. I think his melting brown eyes would get you, and his inexorable logic would get your momma so the cure would not be complete. He looks well even though he eats little.

Love, Isabel

⤺

February 19, 1945

Dearest Isabel,

Today I played the records. I can't tell you how much I appreciated them. David's Hebrew singing was astonishing to me. When I left he didn't know more than a dozen words of the language. And he has made wonderful strides on the clarinet. I was amazed at Betsy's sure touch at the piano. I couldn't be sure all the time who was playing the piano. You played some, I think, and did David too? Sammy was very cute in his story of the three Billy Goats gruff read with such expression. And I liked the background noises that Ruthie made to let me know she was there too. What a day you must have had! David makes a fine MC. I want to tell you that I think those five records are a wonderful success. I am sending them home very soon because firstly I am lightening my baggage and secondly I know Sarah wants to show them off in Omaha and California when she goes. Now the next thing I want is another movie of you and the children. I must admit that there were many sounds on those records that went straight to my heart—including your sweet, reasonable, lovely, and loving voice.

I am sending home all the negatives I've collected in my 20 months here. There are two sets that haven't been printed. One is marked for printing. The other will require special treatment because they are underexposed. The main group of negatives has all been printed. Put them all aside for me.

The sleigh rides that you described—the one you went on—sounds like it was more fun than the one that David went on without you. Yes I should have been along and I assure you that I would have had I been home. I may be an old goat of 37 but I am still young enough for sleigh rides. I remember that we used to ride to the Talmud Torah on the ice sleighs as they swung down 8th Avenue from Kegans lake. If we were lucky we could ride them full down and later empty back.

I hope that the war is over soon. I am going to put on my own peace offensive but not until VE. The Germans have had enough, I'm sure, but it is difficult to make peace under the present circumstances. Peace will have to be made for them. My estimation of their position is that it is hopeless. It is interesting to conjecture what will happen to the pockets of resistance remaining behind the allied lines—Dunkirk, the Bay of Biscay, Koenigsberg. I think they'll stew until VE.

I would like to get Thomas Mann's "Joseph the Provider." I ordered it months ago from Powers but they never sent it. See what you can do.

Love, Reuben

⌒

February 20, 1945

Dearest Isabel,

My first view of France was obscured by low lying clouds. We broke through the overcast slightly east of Paris into country that differs greatly from anything I've seen in England. The farm houses here are clustered into little villages. A group of farm buildings enclose an inner court where sheep, cattle, and chickens are corralled. From our low level most of the roofs appeared to be thatched. In a group of six Frenchmen whom I met first I found none who could speak English but one spoke German and I found my first use for my Deutsch. Those six helped me unload an airplane. We paid them in cigarettes and to the interpreter we gave some shoe dubbin to waterproof his shoes. "Dieser Schuben kann ich nicht wasserfrei machen," he answered me sorrowfully and showed his shoes with the sides gaping wide from the uppers! Don't jump the gun. I am still tethered by a thread to my station in England.

Tonite I sleep in a French girls' school but there is not a skirt visible among my male Paris friends.

Love, Reuben

Friday March 2, 1945 [*handwritten*]

Dear Papa:

I went to see the play Huckleberry Finn yesterday. The actors were very good even with their southern accents. I saw it at the Music Hall in the U. of M. The actors were students. Thursday March 8th I'm going to the Northrop Auditorium to hear the Symphony concert.

Did you enjoy the records? Since I made them we have learned to write Hebrew. I have also improved on the squeak stick.

Mr. Weinberg says that I'm good in time and tone but not so good in tonguing.

I am ready for a $4.00 Klosé clarinet book. Do you have it and where?

In school we have learned the addition and subtraction of decimals. Please DO NOT send me any more of those doggone algebra problems. I'm not that good.

Would you please send me some English money because we are studying England. In fact send me anything.

Lovingly, David

⌐

March 5, 1945

Dearest Reuben:

Yesterday was my birthday. I got perfume from Jack, the promise of a slip from Sylvia, six bars of blue florama carnation soap from David, silk underpants size forty from Peter, and white candlesticks with rose decal transfers from Betsy. Betsy also bought the happy birthday decorations for the cake. Betsy used her own money which she earned by drying dishes for me. David used his money for taking care of the dog. Peter's money was partly his own and partly earned. He also dried dishes.

If you had not told me you bought a new pen, I would not know it. David's writing has improved tremendously since the introduction of a new handwriting system in the public schools. His teacher tells me that it seems to do wonders for the left handed children. David says that the handwriting chart for their room goes from 30 to 90. In September, he had 30, and now it is 85.

Love, Isabel

⌐

March 7, 1945

Dearest Reuben:

Peter said tonight, "There are three reasons why I am so popular in school. One is that you are so nice. One is that I play with all the children and they play with me. One is that I do such good work in school. Only Michael Goldman doesn't like me. It's just like Alice (Stafne) said, the boys are supposed to go after the girls, not the girls after the boys." My visit to school with cupcakes, fancy paper napkins, and movies made quite a hit with the second grade.

Ruth Amelia says to me, "Finga polish." This she proceeds to apply liberally to fingers, toes, hands and face. When David came home and saw it he said, "How many times have I told you not to have any of that red paint around?"

Did I tell you that we bought a dozen dinner plates for $23.50 in Syracuse Romance pattern to match our dessert set? David did not approve. "Now, Momma, we didn't really need these plates. You know, you are supposed to wear it out or make it do." Actually, what is left of our Fiesta is relegated to the kitchen, and the Romance pattern is second to our practically unusable Lenox.

Love, Isabel

↩

March 10, 1945

Dearest Isabel,

The children will want to know about Rafni. I have her with me now.* She came on the convoy and I picked her up on this side. She gets lost an average of twice a day but so far she always comes back. I think she feels at home here now which is more than I can say for her master. She is the belle of the town being so far as I can see the only bitch among a hundred dogs.

Love, Reuben

*On March 6, Reuben was sent to France and was stationed there, following the advances of the American army.

March 10, 1945

Dear David,

Here it is the tenth of March and your birthday is just a month
away. You will be eleven years old and from what I hear you're a fine
big boy for an eleven year old. Congratulations on your birthday. I
think I can safely promise you that it is the last one you will spend
without your poppa. We have crossed the Rhine; the Russians are
over the Oder. The most formidable barriers to Germany are crossed
and now the allies are in good tank country all the way. It will take
us about two weeks to get sizable forces across the Rhine but after
that the campaign will be a fast moving affair. The Germans were
smart enough to blow every bridge but one across the Rhine from
Coblentz to Cologne. That one is doing us great service now. But of
course you can't send an army across one bridge. We'll have to build
many others. But I never thought we would get across without a
gigantic combined operation with paratroops and all. Incidentally
the general who was responsible for the demolition of the bridge at
Remagen, the bridge that didn't blow up, he's going to catch hell
from the Nazis. He'll probably be executed if he doesn't commit suicide first. Do you remember how terribly upset we were in America
when we learned in 1940 that General Corap of the 7th French Army
had failed to blow up the bridge over the Meuse? We thought then
that defeat or victory was a matter of a bridge being down or up. It
wasn't so then any more than the presence or absence of that one
bridge on the Rhine can make any important difference to the campaign. The bridge simply means an accelerated campaign with fewer
American lives lost.

Reuben Berman

I have got some postcards but unfortunately only two. When I get
four, I'll send them home. I think you will like the French postcards.

I hope that soon I shall reestablish contact with my family in

Minneapolis. As I wrote to your mommy, my Isabel, I can't expect
mail until the APO finds out where I am now.

Love, Reuben

⤶

March 11, 1945

Dear Betsy,

It has been some time since I have written a letter just to you
alone. I want to tell you how pleased I was to read your fine letter
about why I must stay in Europe taking care of the sick and
wounded. I don't want to disillusion you but the fact is that most
of my work is administrative and has little to do with ministering to
the sick.

I think you are growing up to be a fine girl, the sort of a girl a
father is proud to claim as his daughter. Since I have never been a little girl, I find some difficulty in talking to you of your present activities. But I am pleased to know that you are doing so well with your
piano playing. Do you dance too? I've forgotten whether you learned
to swim or not. If not, you must be sure to learn this summer at
Calhoun. I remember you were very pretty in your yellow bathing
suit at the beach. Please write often to

Your dear loving Poppa

⤶

March 20, 1945

Dearest Reuben:

Today Betsy and Peter brought home their report cards.

March 13, 1945

Betsy has a fine attitude of friendly helpfulness. She is very interested in all of our activities and makes some very worthwhile contri-

butions in civic league and social studies. She is doing very good work in reading and spelling. Betsy expresses herself well. Her papers are always neatly and carefully written. She is a teacher in music. She has good self control. Her stories are original in ideas and interesting. She is thoughtful of others.

Present 50, Absent 2, Calhoun School, Jane Gittens, teacher.

March 15, 1945

Sammy's reading ability is remarkable for a first grade child. His keen enjoyment and understanding of reading are marked. He is improving in ability to work independently and faster, which makes him a better member of our group.

Marion Atherton-Teacher

Our children are all joys to their teachers. Peter's report card shows quite an improvement. I think the school work is more interesting to him now. At first, he found his own thoughts more entertaining than school work.

Love, Isabel

᷎

March 21, 1945

Dearest Isabel,

How would you like to take a bath in a helmet? It really isn't as difficult as it sounds. You need a helmet full of water a wash cloth and some soap and some sunlight. Otherwise it is very cold. Anyway it is very cold. You use the cloth with the soap first and you must be careful to wring out the rag well before rinsing it in the helmet. The water in the helmet becomes rather unpotable. I have rigged up a hot water heater out of the alcohol burner that comes with something. I set the burner in the bottom of a C rations can, punch holes in the sides for ventilation, and set a cup of water on top. It works fine for shaving.

I suppose the reason my information of affairs at home is fragmentary is that I move around so much my mail is delayed and sometimes lost. You never can depend that any single communication will arrive.

I don't need a thing really. I'm getting along fine. The nights here are invariably quiet which is quite a relief from England where the frequent alerts for buzz bombs would keep us up often.

Love, Reuben

⤿

March 21, 1945

2 Air DSR WNG-PRV, APO 149 NY

Dear David,

I was very pleased to receive your nice letter of March 2. Any mail received the same month it is sent is considered to be delivered in good time. I was afraid that this recent move of mine would separate me from my mail for a long time. You will notice that I am using a different unit address also. It means that I am on loan from a provisional organization to a provisional parent organization The word provisional means lot of things but the most important thing that it means is no promotions.

I am glad to hear that you are doing well on the squeak stick. Now wherever did you get such a name for the clarinet? Go ahead and buy the Klosé exercise book for $4.00. Study especially the duets in there. I am looking forward very much to playing them with you. Is it easy for you to get reeds? It was next to impossible to find any in England. Those that I did get were worthless. Now that I am in France, I should be able to get them easily. Reeds come from French Africa, you know. Or did you know?

Sorry I have so little to send you. This is a very poor country right now. I don't think you can imagine how poor. In France too they give a lot of consideration to the ladies and their perquisites. Thus if I wanted to send you some perfume, it would be simple. Their picture post cards have a lot of loving on them too as you'll notice. But if a man wants to send his son a simple present like a knife, he can't find it. And if a person has four children and wants to send something for each the matter becomes almost impossible. I have some English money and it goes home in the next package of letters. One of the coins will be very familiar. To convert to American money values remember that there are 12 English pennies to a shilling; 20 shillings to a pound, and a pound now is worth about $4.00.

Love, Poppa

⌐

March 25, 1945

My dear sweet Betsy,

I want to tell you how much I enjoy your letters to me. It is perfectly all right to write a second letter before the first one is answered. I often do that especially to my family at home. It takes three weeks for a letter to cross the ocean so if I wrote and then didn't write again until I got a reply I would wait six weeks between letters. Then I would catch it from your momma who wants me to write more often than that. I think. Then again I am the kind of a person who likes to get mail from home and I have discovered that the surest way to get mail is to write letters.

What I like about your letter is how well you spell and how nicely you print with faces in the Os. I like your stationery too. But most of all what I like is the way you take a complicated idea and reduce it to a logical paragraph. I am referring to a previous letter of yours where you correctly deduced that we must stay in Europe for a while.

I am sorry I can't oblige you with a picture of Rafni or her pups. The difficulty is no film. This is a request for a package of what I want.

Speaking of Rafni I flew her from L to V and then forgot her at the airport here. I waited in town an hour expecting that she would find her way in. Then I climbed onto my bicycle and went back to the airfield. I found poochie about two miles from the field heading the wrong way! She isn't as smart as I thought. This was my first cub flight in France. I will tell you about it. We took off from an airstrip in Eastern France. We flew over the beautiful Vosges country with its many hills, valleys and rivers. We flew over the Moselle, one of the prettiest rivers I've ever seen. At this upstream point the water flows in rapids. It is pretty pretty from the air. Landing on an airstrip with the wind 90 degrees off turned out to be a difficult affair. I'm used to coming in into the wind. I made a very bouncing landing but I set it down all right.

Rafni's pups are scattered now over a good corner of France. One pup she sees fairly regularly. This one is the male that I gave to the 9th Group dentist. He is called Dinky and is black and fuzzy. I mean the dog.

When I was up at the town where the group is, I saw a little boy of nine hopping about on one leg. The other was machine gunned off by a German who was having some fun with French civilians coming out of a church one Sunday morning. I am telling you that because I saw the boy myself. I want you to know what is going on over here. Also I think that it is a very good idea that you should know how the war is going day by day. Today for instance we are across the Rhine in force in many places. There is now no good natural defense line separating the American and British forces in the West from the Russians in the east. That means the war in Europe is nearly over.

Love, Poppa

⌒

March 26, 1945

Dear Sammy,

I am sending you an Air Force shoulder patch. I am sending enough patches so you and Ruth and David and Betsy can each have one. Some of the patches say 8 and some 9 for whichever Air Force it belongs to. We wear the patches on the sleeve below the left shoulder. I would suggest that you don't wear it—carry it to school to show the other children.

For Momma in the package is a knife she may find useful in the kitchen.

Rafni may not be a bird dog but she flies with ease and aplomb. In the Cub she sits on the ledge behind me with her forefoot on my shoulders. She rides like the lady she is and never gets sick.

Sammy, my dear son, the war news is so good that maybe it will be over here soon and then sometime we can go home. I do appreciate and enjoy your letters, pictures, and work. So continue to write to your dear loving

Poppa

⌒

April 1, 1945

Dear Sammy,

Do you know what HP stands for? It stands for hot pilot: a pilot who flies fast and does a lot of stunts and dies young.

Soon you will be having another birthday. How old will you be on your next birthday? Maybe I can come to the party. I'll ask the Colonel. Germany is getting a good whipping. Soon this war will be ☺ver. I made a smiling over because that will be a happy day I think. [Can you figure] this out? I think I'm being very [*duncecap*]. (Silly I mean. My puzzles are pretty punk.

Love, Poppa

Reuben to Sammy, April 1, 1945

⌐

April 8, 1945

Dearest Reuben:

Today was David's birthday party. I let him do his own inviting. He invited Albert Kapstrom, Osher Altrowitz, Sanford Raihill, Mendel Abrams, Sander Berman, Julian Berman, and Gerald Jackson. He did all his inviting last night or this morning. Julian could not come because he had the flu. Gerald said he could not come because he was having company.

In regard to this last, note the following conversation.

Albert K.: So Jackson ain't coming because he is having company. I saw him riding a bicycle with Nancy Sclamberg. That flirt. She is almost a disgrace to our religion.

Osher: Is she Jewish?

Albert K.: Oh, no—just goes to our synagogue and spouts a little Hebrew now and then.

David got a dollar bill from Mendel and four quarter defense stamps from Sander. Maishe also gave Peter a quarter and Betsy a fifty cent piece. Otherwise David was told, "I'm sorry, Berman, I didn't bring a present because you didn't give me enough notice." Anna Rush gave David two decks of cards with his initials on them. I had to brush up on Casino in the rule book so I could explain it to Betsy and David.

I took some of the children and Maishie and Hilda took the rest to the main picnic ground at Lake Harriet. It was about 67 degrees but very windy. I asked M. if he wanted to stay and he said Frankly he didn't like it. But he did stay long enough to get the fire going. I had Anita to help me. Sylvia came along too. Just as we were ready to leave, Rosalind Simon and Anna Rush and Sally drove up. They took home a few of the children.

The food was hamburgers, fried potatoes, Egequist buns, mustard, sliced raw carrots and celery. After we got home we served milk sherbet and cake—Bridgeman's don't sell ice cream right now. Then I showed movies. David announced proudly that the movie of MacArthur captures Manilla and the Landings on Iwo Jima was a gift from his father.

The boys played baseball and then investigated the bird sanctuary. Peter and Betsy went along with the boys. Betsy was having a wonderful time, dressed in slacks and sweater and trailing along with five or six boys.

Rosalind had a bad trip up from El Paso but looks just fine now. She had to petition, with tears, the ration board in Lincoln, Nebraska, for a new tire to replace a redcapped one that went bad on the way. She was late for the picnic today because of a flat tire.

Love, Isabel

April 13, 1945

Dearest Isabel,

News of President Roosevelt's death came to us this morning over the radio. We have lost a great friend. We needed him very badly for the first year of peace. Both the republican and the democratic parties have lost their greatest leaders in the space of twelve months.*

Love, Reuben

⌣

April 14, 1945

Dearest Reuben:

Have I told you this story about Peter? We were having lunch at the Rainbow. His lunch was a ham sandwich and a malted milk. The rest of us had turkey croquettes. Betsy wanted some of his malted. When he was looking the other way I gave it to her. When he realized that he was missing some of his malted milk and a straw as well, he was very upset. "Why didn't you ask me," he said again and again. "I would have said no."

Love, Isabel

⌣

April 14, 1945 [*handwritten*]

Dear Papa:

We received the Natzi pin a little while ago. I am going to show it to the children in my class at school.

Arnold is talking about building a cabin along Lake Placid for $2,000.00. He says that he would sell the rest of his property there

---

*Wendell L. Willkie, Republican presidential nominee in 1940, died October 8, 1944.

except for the part which the cabin will be built on. You, him, a carpenter, and myself would build it.

On the Klosé book I am doing pretty well. We will have much fun playing the duets when you come back. I did not know that reeds were made in North Africa.

How do you like France? Have you met any nice French people there? Have you been to Paris? If so, how is Paris?

I got an answer from Dr. O'Brien today. When I read it at school I think that this anti-vivisection thing will stop in our room.[*]

How did you feel about the President's death? I felt horrible.

Love, David A. Berman

April 20, 1945

Dearest Reuben:

Today I received your letter to dear folks, with a note enclosed for me. The date of your letter was April 9. If I receive many more letters to dear folks I'll begin to think I'm just one of the folks, not your wife who should get a special letter of her own. Not that I don't appreciate your letters for posterity. They are very good. But they should supplement, not displace the letters you send to me.

Tuesday, all four children and I went to Nathan's and Teresa's for dinner. I brought along some 35 ml. color film. Nathan took some pictures which, I hope, will turn out very well. In one picture Peter kissed Ruthie. This morning he was angry at her for something. I said to him, "You like Ruthie, don't you? Then why did you kiss her when Nathan was taking the picture?" He said, "I don't like her but I want Poppa to think I do." He really does like her.

Love, Isabel

*David had written to Dr. William O'Brien at the University of Minnesota Medical School to ask for information on why vivisection, experimenting on live animals, was considered important in science.

April 21, 1945 [*handwritten*]

Dear Poppa:

I have been wanting to tell you about my birthday but I keep forgetting to write. I only had 6 children but we had a lot of fun. It was a picnic. Before we ate we plade baseball then after we had eaten we went to the bird refuge. We had hamburgers, carrots, fried potatoes, and milk. After the picnic we went home and showed movies. One of them was the battle which Momma bought for me with the money you sent me.

I showed the Nazi pin and band of cloth to the children in my room. Thank you very much for them.

Momma showed movies at school yesterday. The children liked them very much. Momma is getting very good at showing movies.

Please send me some more German stamps and other souvenirs.

Momma got some beautiful Mexican glasses from Gramma Gertie the other day.

We expect Uncle Jack home any day now because he is sending his things here.

Please don't go where there's any fighting.

Au Revoir and Love, David

May 2, 1945 [*handwritten*]

Dear Poppa:

How is Germany? How do the German civilians feel about the war? How do the German prisoners act?

I am going to plant a Victory Garden in the vacant lot. It will have beets, carrots, cucumbers, lettuce and radishes.

Tomorrow we are going to the play Mary Poppins at the University of M.

It may be that when this letter reaches you the war in Europe will be over. 7 yrs ago Nazi troops marched into Poland. At last they are about to be defeated.

Thank you very much for the patches, fishing knife and coins. Please send us many more souvenirs from Germany. But beware of booby traps.

David A. Berman

↜

May 5, 1945

Dearest Reuben:

It finally turned almost warm enough for me to let the fire go out. It is still chilly in the morning and evening but I am almost out of coal and do not want to buy more. For one thing, any purchases now apply on next year's supply which is rationed to eighty per cent of normal. We have burnt here from ten tons of coal, in pre stoker days, to thirteen tons. Mr. Derby told me I could ask for eighty per cent of thirteen tons. Besides, I still cherish hopes of being elsewhere next winter and would just as soon not buy coal to sell to the next occupant of the house.

Last Sunday I took the children to the wild flower garden at Glenwood Park [*the Eloise Butler Wildflower Garden in Wirth Park*]. The flowers were very pretty, but rather few in number and the day was cold and windy. We saw cowbells, may flowers, dutchmen's britches, blood root, hepatica, wild ginger and marsh marigold. Betsy said that if she couldn't pick the flowers she didn't want to see them but when the rest of us came back she decided she wanted to go. David took her through on a quick trip. I listened to the remarks on the opening of the San Francisco conference. The radio reporter for this occasion was Professor Quigly from whom I took a course in world politics in 1927.

Thursday, Mrs. Wyman came to take care of Ruthie and the other children and I had lunch at the Rainbow and then went, in the

Calhoun school group, to see the play, Mary Poppins at the University. Sylvia gave the children the book of Mary Poppins. Both the book and play are enchanting. If books go duty free, I should send it to Natasha and Sonia, though Sonia may think she is a little grown up for it.

Last night Dave Goldstein came in town with his four boys. He parked two with Belle and himself and the other two with Toby. Today, they took David along to Alan Goldstein's Bar Mitzvah. I conveyed my thanks to Belle and will forward a gift sometime next week. Hymie Lurie brought David home. Mollie Mersky's mother fell down and broke her hip so Mollie will stay in town about a week but Hymie will leave tomorrow.

David was bored with the Bar Mitzvah. I suspect that the religious phase in David is on the wane. We now eat Friday night suppers in the kitchen again.

Ruth Amelia surely pushes the other children around. Last night David was sitting in a chair listening to the downstairs radio. She pushed him out of the chair and turned off the radio. I lay down to take a rest. "Gup oo mornin, Momma," she said so I got up. Today I found that Peter had got off the toilet and on to the potty so Ruthie could have the toilet. The general rule is second come gets the potty. Ruthie insists on dividing up candy giving the most to herself, the next most to Peter and equal but smaller amounts to the rest of the family.

Love, Isabel

⌐

May 6, 1945 [*handwritten*]

Dear Papa:

At long last we have had victory over the would be destroyers of mankind. For 6 years the Nazis oppressed humanity in ways which have never been exceeded in the history of the earth. But now I want to get to the point. I believe that now that we have won victory over the Nazis, you and other men should be allowed to come back home again. I think that there are many people who would agree with me on that.

I am glad you are sending Betsy a flute because I think that will suit her very nicely. But what will we do with the violin from the Goldsteins?

Have you seen any of the prison camps? Please for God's sake Don't.

Love, David

↩

May 7, 1945

Dearest Reuben:

This morning I was listening to John Raleigh who gives the news over WCCO at 8:30 AM. He told of the German surrender report that had come in earlier in the morning, of Admiral Doenitz' calling the U boats in from the sea, and finally of the imminence of the VE announcement. Then came the commercial telling us to use blue white which blues while you wash. Right in the middle of the commercial, another voice broke in announcing the surrender. It came only on the associated press ticker. By afternoon the radio people were sure that the news was authentic but not official. Tomorrow it will be official.

I predict no big celebration here. The false announcements of surrender, the war in the Pacific, the knowledge of the price of victory, and uncertainty of the future conspire to make one thoughtful rather than gay.

Does VE day make any difference in your plans? I heard over the radio that those overseas since 1943 had a good chance of getting home. Does that mean you? Or are majors with four children exempt? It looks as though you have a better chance to transfer to the US than to get leave here. Lots of officers, overseas two years or less, have been transferred here, to the USA. I don't know how it's done but there must be a way.

Love, Isabel

This is, of course, a tremendous victory and I am very proud of the part you had in it.

~

May 9, 1945

Dearest Reuben:

I have just been listening to Henry Kaiser's plans for the post war home. It will cost, including the lot, from 4000 to 5000 dollars and will include air conditioning, garbage disposal, sink, stove, laundry, also two bedrooms. We would have to buy two of them. Putting out homes like that would surely puncture the inflation in real estate. The Lou Winers are moving to Cal. and want $15,000 for their house at 3900 Beard. An outlandish price!

Love, Isabel

~

May 9, 1945

Dearest Isabel,

You bawled me out a small bit in a recent letter for not writing individually to you. I suppose I had it coming all right but I've been so damn busy the past month that I can truthfully say that I have done nothing else but eat sleep and work. And my work has been so absorbing and interesting that when I write about it as you say, it is for posterity. Today is VE day commencing at 00013 this morning. The troops in this area celebrated by shooting off assorted captured German ammunition and pyrotechnics throughout most of the night, scaring the town, Rafni, and me. Me, I went to bed. The second Air Disarmament Wing has only just begun to fight. The atmosphere here reminds me of Kelly Field about December 8, 1941.

I want to tell you that I love you and I appreciate you and I think you are just the person I want for a wife. I appreciate your criticisms of what I do as much as I do the packages and the other ways you take care of me. You're a very smart person and in spite of what Dr. Irving Ershler thinks, I do appreciate you.

As the children would say, now that the loving is over, let's get down to business. Yesterday we all got together in formation and the head adjutant read us a letter from Eisenhower telling us that the war was over. As soon as the flag was taken down, we strung up a German soldier of the luftwaffe on the pole and there he hangs still. He is well stuffed with straw but up there forty feet in the air he looks startlingly real. Today some German women came back into our area to look over their homes and see about reoccupation of their property. The idea in back of their Teutonic heads is now that the game is finished we should clear out and let them prepare for the next season. Some of these dopes are in for a rude shock when they discover that we don't mean to take the attitude of a winning football team

A German mobile low pressure chamber has two trailers and weighs thirty tons on the road. It is like taking a railroad train down a road. It would be a good souvenir to bring home to you. We could have a mountain climate right in our own backyard.

David wrote about his birthday and Betsy about everything. I also have a letter from Sylvia about how she took care of the children.

It shouldn't be too long now, I hope. You gather that the organization is in for a good deal of work but I hope that the men and officers who have been over here a long time will be relieved by officers and others of less total and foreign service to do the job. I've given up any idea of staying here and of bringing you. Europe won't be a pleasant place for years and with all the displaced persons roaming around spreading disease it may be considered a dangerous place to live. Our Grand Tour will have to wait. But I will be a good guide for England and Germany and a fair one for France. With our trilingual abilities we'll get along fine.

Love, Reuben

May 12, 1945

Dearest Isabel,

Today came the package with the cake mix. As you warned me, the flour was suspiciously salty. It will work out all right though: I am going to dilute the mixture with flour and I think it will work out all right. And you mustn't scold Sammy any more because of this misdeed, but it was a naughty thing to do.* Food is very scarce these days. I never waste any if I can help it. When I am out on trips and we open a can that is too much for us, we generally find a DP (displaced person) on the road to give the rest of it to. Not every soldier is as careful as that.

Love, Reuben

May 13, 1945

Dearest Reuben:

Today was mothers' day and, as you will see by Betsy's air mail letter, I got lots of presents and cards. David took his bicycle to the Fanny Farmer shop yesterday afternoon and had to wait fifteen minutes to get candy. Betsy stopped at the dime store on the way home and bought a candy jar full of jelly beans, a glass serving dish, a plaster tiny shoe with tiny flowers, and a pretty handkerchief. She stopped at Sheffield's to get some pink ribbon and fixed the hanky

---

*Several attempts had been made to send him the fixings for a fresh-baked dessert, usually for an American apple pie. British apple pies, he felt, were too low on apple and too thick on crust and served with the point out instead of in. Sometimes the package had gone astray, and sometimes travel restrictions kept him from visiting his civilian friends. This time, the dessert was defeated by the mischievous admixture of salt in the flour. Sometime during that summer, he finally received an apple pie package in apple pie order when he could visit the Edelmans. When he set about making the pie, however, Tilly Edelman, fearful that he might spoil the precious ingredients, supervised. The result, although served with the point in, was a British pie.

up in a handmade green paper envelope. Peter kept his present hidden till this morning. I heard him talking about it the first thing when he woke up. It was a set of six coasters made by coloring and shellaking circles of cardboard. There was also a pretty card. I'll send the cards on to you.

Today was the last day of Sunday school. Betsy got a large certificate for being on the honor roll. There is some question whether David is on the honor roll or not because he may not have attended Saturday AM services often enough. David says that if the services were good the children would go anyhow and would not have to be bribed by the threat of losing their Sunday school promotion or honors.

May 10 was the spring concert of the University band. Mrs. Fryer (Irene Sussman) called to see if I would take Rosalind along. Rosalind is just David's age. When I picked up Rosalind David insisted that she sit in front and he in back. Then I picked up Mildred Pass and Teddy and I had all three children sit in back. Teddy was simply enthralled at the conversation. At the concert David didn't want to sit next to Rosalind but had to for a little while because two available seats with clear vision to the stage were adjoining. On the way home Rosalind said to David, "I won't tell anyone I went with you if you don't." He agreed but he did tell Albert Kapstrom. Albert felt bad because he had not gone too.

You should really be on your way home soon.

Love, Isabel

༆

May 15, 1945

Dearest Reuben:

Today Betsy went to Louise Altrowitz's birthday party. Peter was not invited but he wangled an invitation this way. Peter, Ruthie and I were sitting in the car waiting for David and Betsy, near school. Mrs. A. came along. Peter said something about the party. She said,

"You can come if you like but there will be just girls." "Oh, that's all right," he answered, "I like girls." He brought along fifty cents and a card, presents he selected himself. I buy a number of birthday cards at once and keep them. This one had a fuzzy bunny and a rhyme, "All the joy that life can hold to a darling one year old." Peter especially wanted to go to the party so he could give this card and have some fun. Louise is nine. Betsy gave a very pretty Raggedy Ann book and managed to read it first.

David wants to do good when he grows up. I mentioned that having a movie is a good way to make money. David couldn't see that it did people any good. He wants to be a doctor. Peter wants to make money. His latest ambition is to make cars and sell them.

Last night Ruthie picked up your army flashlight and conked Peter on the head with it. When he cried, she was quite upset and sat down to make nice Peter. I cautioned him not to hit her back because she didn't mean it and went to get ice for his head. Of course he hit her, but not as hard as she hit him, and pulled her hair. Then she cried.

David wanted a victory garden. He finally asked Mrs. Bland, who lived at 3516, if he could use the vacant lot at 3520 and she let him use it. He got gardening books from the library, is enrolled in a junior gardeners organizations, and works hard at it. Tonight before he went to bed he had to go out to get a look at his garden. So far he has tomato plants and carrot seeds set out.

Love, Isabel

⥲

May 18, 1945

Dearest Isabel,

I'm looking forward to the possibility of coming home. On the point system I have 105: 45 months service plus 24 months overseas service plus 36 children. I mean 3 children at twelve points apiece. That is a lot of points. I don't know whether I get credit for battle stars or not.

I'll write as often as I can. Please don't let up on your writing because my letters have become less frequent.

Love, Reuben

~

May 20, 1945 [*handwritten*]

Dear Papa:

I have a skin disease. It is called contact dermatitis. I got it from a weed in my garden that I am planting in the lot next to Stafnes'. It seems as if there are touches of poison ivy too. I have a bottle of white medicine that stops it from itching but it's always wearing off.

As I mentioned before I am having a garden. It has weeds, bugs, radishes (red and white), lettuce, beets, carrots, and tomatoes. There is also a package of mixed flowers each.

How is Germany? Do you like your work? I don't. It's high time you came home.

Have you seen any German youth? If so what is their attitude to you? What is the attitude of all the German people?

Love, David

~

May 23, 1945

Dearest Isabel,

A Lithuanian Jewish physician was in yesterday. He is taking care of 400 Jewish patients in various stages of malnutrition and disease after four years in concentration camps. He wanted vitamins mainly but there was little I could do to help him. The released prisoners are dying at the rate of many a day from malnutrition and several other diseases. He told about two Jews that died the day of liberation. An American captain from St. Louis whose first name is Otto and who must be of immediate German descent forced ten German officers to act as pallbearers. He turned out the entire German garrison and spoke to them in German for forty-five minutes. He told them they were not burying just two Jews. They were burying the German nation, he told them.

I remember how some of our friends used to say what they would do if they only could lay their hands on some Germans. Well, I have my hands on fifty. They are little Germans. They are not Nazis. They didn't want war. They want to go home. They're thoroly disgusting. But I will say this for them: they work like hell. They act as though they love to work.

Leaves to England started today. I don't think I shall have any leave in the early future, but I can fly up there as a crew member. When I looked at England with the eyes of an American fresh from the states, it seemed to be a poor country. Now when I consider England in comparison with France or Germany, I think of it as a pretty nice place. This change in opinion is universal among Americans who served in the three countries.

I think I am entitled to three battle stars: Air offensive, Rhineland battle, and whatever this deal will be called. If that is so, I have 121 points which is considerable. The point system entitles us to three children only but I can't pick out the extra one so we'll have to keep all four.

I hope my packages are coming home.

Love, Reuben

⌐

May 27, 1945

Dearest Reuben:

Yesterday I took the children on a picnic at 46th and Lake Harriet. Anna and Sam Rush and Rosalind and her two children and Clare and Harriet were also there. I fried hamburgers. They were the first hamburgers we had had in a few weeks. Meat is quite scarce

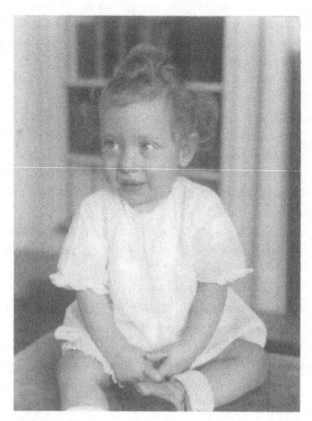

Ruth Amelia, about 1944

here. We are grateful for whatever the butcher has. I no longer say, "I want some round steak." I say, "What do you have?" It is lucky I take from the Jewish butcher. They have a better supply of chickens and, at least once a week, meat.

Ruth Amelia had a wonderful time at the picnic. She said to me, "Lovey dovey go on picnic." She learned how to go down the slide by herself. She wouldn't let Sally take her turn away. She said, "My turn." After about thirty slides, Ruthie was quite tired. When she started landing on her seat and flopping flat on her back, I decided it was time to go home. As usual after a picnic, I was all tired out but the children were as full of pep as ever.

Today I took the children to a show. I wanted to take them to see

Thunderhead, son of Flicka. It was showing on Lake and Nicollet. We were told there would be a fifteen minute wait. The wait was a half an hour and still no seats. The war bond rally was over and Thunderhead had started. What had happened was that the show was full of youngsters intent on seeing the show twice. So I got my money back and took the children across the street to see Thirty Seconds over Tokio. All except Ruthie had seen it at least once before. There was a fine picture story of the carrier Franklin. Hell sure broke loose when the Jap suicide plane crashed through to the explosive laden carrier. David was very upset at the delays and wasted time. I told him that Poppa made it a rule never to wait for a movie and hereafter we would stick to that rule.

Here it is almost June and still cold. I let the fire go out but must start it again.

Love, Isabel

⤶

May 28, 1945

Dearest Isabel,

I've been travelling continuously the past 4 days doing my work. Yesterday I spent all day at Dachau Concentration Camp. I will describe it in detail in an epistle to posterity. I don't need any hearsay or cinema evidence of German atrocities. Isabel, I've seen for myself. I've never had such an interesting and important assignment. I'm on the go 16 to 18 hours a day. I love it, but I hope it's over soon and I can go home. Forget the film requests. We've "captured" enough to snap pictures of everything and everybody in Germany. Thanks for being such a good wife always. I love you.

Love, Reuben

⤶

May 30, 1945

Dearest Reuben:

Well, here it is the third decoration day that we have been apart. Do you remember the lovely time we had when you and Ershler and Miriam Friedell and I went up to see Friedell? Do you also remember the time Ruby and Leon and Myron and Stepha came to visit us and how Stepha and Ruby were pursued by mosquitoes?

Today, Mr. Kapstrom took David and Albert to Excelsior on the bus. David visited the fun house, rode on the scooter, went through the hall of mirrors and had his picture taken. He will send you the picture. Peter, Betsy, Roger Tweed, Ruthie and I went to the Granada to see the Three Caballeros. I had not intended to go but when Ruthie said she wanted to see [a] movie I decided to give it a try. After a while Ruthie got restless and I took her home. The other children sat through the whole show twice. I got worried and went back for them. On the screen they were singing and dancing the title song. The children were simply entranced. All reviewers agree that the mixture of Donald Duck with gorgeous live females is bad taste and poor entertainment. Otherwise, the picture was wonderful.

A couple nights ago I heard on the radio that the eighth air force of which, I presume, you are a part, is being transferred to Japan. The information appeared as a short news item in the Star Journal. The New York Times elaborated so that I know that part of the eighth air force under Gen. Doolittle is being transferred to the Pacific and part is still in the ETO. With all this shake up, I hope you can manage to shake yourself clear.

Love, Isabel

⌣

June 6, 1945

Dear Poppa:

I went to the Como park. And I didn't get to ride on anything. But I saw the animals in the zoo. I saw a lion and I saw some baboons. There was one baby baboon. He would always follow his mother. The biggest baboon was hungry and everytime he wouldn't get food for a long time he would scream like a lady being killed. Every time he screamed the children who looked at him would laugh. I saw some swans. One swan went into the water. And he would put his head down and he would put his head up like he was saying hello. I saw some monkeys. They were cute. And they were very funny. And I saw a polar bear. He was not in the building. He was outside. He was not in a cage. And where he was there was a hole where he could go in when he wanted to. In the building I saw an anteater. He had a long nose. He was tan and black. And he had a bushy tail. And he was very very funny. But he did not do funny tricks. He just walked around.

The reason why I didn't get to go on the water bicycle was because there was a long long line and it took a long long time for them to come in, because the water bicycles went so slow. And I waited in line for a half an hour. If I did ride on it I would have to wait in line for an hour. And the train and the horses were too far away.

I went into the tropical gardens. And I saw palm trees, and I saw banana leaves. But I didn't see any bananas on the banana leaves.

I climbed up in the archway while we were waiting for the street-car. And I had a lot of fun doing that. Osher, that was a boy that was with us, he would push me a ways up and then I'd climb up the rest of the way. It was hard climbing up but when I got to the top it wasn't hard to stay up. And then when I wanted to get down I would slide down. So Momma owes me thirty-six cents. Now I'm through with about when I went to Como park.

Two weeks ago I went on a picnic at Lake Harriet. I went with Momma and Sally was there and Stevie was there and Clare was there and Harriet was there. Sam Rush and Anna Rush were there too. And Rosalind was there.

Yesterday I was let out of school at 2:30 instead of 3 o'clock because we brought so much paper for the paper sale.

My birthday isn't far away. In six weeks it will be my birthday. And if it's warm I will have a swimming party at Calhoun Lake. I am going to invite Judy Segal. She is a girl in my room in school. And Jerry Miller. He is a boy in my room in school.

Love, Sammy

ᔐ

June 12, 1945

Dearest Isabel,

No word from Rafni. I guess I won't see my poor little poochie again. She was nice company for the year and a half that I had her. She saved me from boredom many times. Isabel, I warn you, I'm going to have me a dog when I get home and no objections on your part will carry any weight. David, Sammy, Betsy, and I suppose Ruth Amelia too, will join me in the chorus shouting down your objections, if any. Poochie wouldn't have been a good dog to take home anyway (sour grapes). She was so used to adults in uniform that she barked at civilians and women and growled at children. She didn't understand them. She was entirely a one man dog. She tolerated GIs and accepted other officers on an equal basis. She never fraternized. That is what makes it so difficult now. She is lost in a German prison camp.

Love, Reuben

ᔐ

June 17, 1945

Dear Ruth Amelia,

I promised you that the next letter would be for you specially and now you see that I am keeping my promise. I know that to you I am just a picture on the wall but I promise you that I'll do my best to come home before your next birthday and you and I can get acquainted. It is very wrong for papas and their daughters to be separated so long. And sons. And mommas. I will never leave you again like this.

Ruth, my friend, I am going to go to England for a week starting the 19th of June. I expect to stay with the Naftalins and the Edelmans in and around London. I don't think on this trip that I will get to Scotland.

And now I am going to let you in on a piece of news. I think I can almost promise that I will be home in time to celebrate your birthday. I think I stand pretty high on rotation plan or whatever they call the present system of getting home.

Once upon a time a major of the medical corps was riding through a town in Germany when he was stopped by a guard. The guard saluted but poppa I mean the major didn't salute because his driver was pinning his arm to the seat by holding a driver's trip ticket across the major's chest. After a moment or two the guard said, "Aren't you going to salute me, Major?" I snarled at him and drove on. As we drove away I began to mull over the situation in my mind. In Germany we never salute Germans who salute us. The guard was rather dark skinned and was probably an Indian. I could almost reconstruct his thoughts as I drove away: "That goddam major treats me like a nigger or a German!" The next day I came back through the same town. The Indian was not on guard but I saw him lolling in the grass behind the guard house. I called him over and I saw his face fall when he came up expecting to get his backside chewed again. I said to him: "The reason your salute wasn't answered yesterday was that my arm was pinned to the seat by my driver handing you his trip ticket. I think you didn't notice that." "Yessir," he said, "Thank you sir" and a smile covered his face from ear to ear. There is no great point to this story except to enhance the Abraham Lincoln tradition.

So you won't get the wrong idea of your poppa I'll tell you another story: When I was investigating houses in this town, I knocked on the door of a house. In about 5 seconds the curtain on the door raised a bit and an eye peeped out for a moment. I waited about 2 minutes then I figured they were playing not at home. So I started to kick at the door and Ruthie, I was kicking to kick it down. Immediately a woman appeared with a key and opened the door explaining that she knew I was there but had trouble finding the key. I'll never know whether her story is true or not. But for a few minutes I was behaving in a manner completely approved by the Nazis, the SS and all the other things we think we are fighting against.

I look forward to seeing you again soon.

Love, Reuben

⤷

June 18, 1945

Dearest Reuben:

Yesterday I took the children to the cub scout picnic at Glenwood. It was cloudy and rained enough so that the picnic was scheduled for the Adath Jeshuran. Then it cleared up and the picnic proceeded according to plan at Glenwood. I had Mrs. Cantor Winter and son David, aged nine, in the car with us. Betsy looked at David Winter and beamed. Like Peter, she appreciates good looks.

The picnic was a wonderful success. First the food. There were weiners, buns, pop, chocolate milk, cheerios, bags of marshmallows, boxes of cracker jacks and lollipops. Every one of those items is hard to get. But Norman Stillman is in a good position to get out certain things for the cubs.

David won a baseball bat as a prize but traded it in for a compass. All the children got felt hats studded with airplane pins for favors. These hats were supposed to be obtained from your grocer for ten cents and three package tops from Kellogg's Pep. David, Betsy and Peter each got a billfold contributed by Mr. Kapstrom of Alexander's.

Yascha Goldberg, the accountant, evidently belongs to the Adath and the Temple. His wife is on the Temple Sunday School committee and he is on the Adath Cub scout committee. Mr. G. told me that both you and Teddy were once in an orchestra that he directed at the Beth El. He wants to have a cub scout orchestra and has already bought the music. The music has a simple melodic part for each player.

Dutchy Strauss took the children off on a nature hike through the wild flower garden. Peter got so tired that David carried him, horsy back style, part of the way. The three-legged race and the hobble races and all those things that recreation leaders know how to run off, were progressing in fine style when it started to rain again.

Love, Isabel

⌐

June 20, 1945

Dearest Reuben:

Your letters to the children were very nice. Peter was so thrilled that he said, "I could go to Sears Roebuck and buy a present for David, but I won't." Peter has just recently had a hankering for money. He gets a fifty cent weekly allowance. Bus fares are supposed to come out of that. Besides he sometimes gets extra money for refraining from saying push and pee. At the picnic he received a bill-fold. So all in all he was extremely happy to get two dollar bills for the billfold.

David answered your letter and mailed it today. David is really a good boy. He mows the lawn and insists he wants no money for doing it. He is very nice looking. Betsy sometimes says to him, "My David, you are handsome. If only you were as good on the inside as you are on the outside." Then David says, "But my ears are so big." I assure him that Clark Gable and Bing Crosby also have big ears.

Love, Isabel

⌐

June 23, 1945

Dearest Reuben:

Last Sunday, June 17, after the cub scout picnic I noticed that Ruth Amelia had a lot of mosquito bites. The next day, when the bites failed to go away I got a little suspicious, and when more appeared on Tuesday I called Dr. Seham to ask if Ruthie had hives or chicken pox. He said it sounded more like chicken pox but if they did not disappear by Wednesday I should bring her down. The reason I was doubtful was that there was no fever. Wednesday I took Ruthie down to Dr. S.'s office. I first explained the situation to a nurse who assigned me an end room. Then I rushed Ruthie in, giving a short snobby greeting to Hortense Deinard. After the diagnosis, which was chicken pox, I took Ruthie out by the side door. Since our three older children and Diane and Marlys have all had chicken pox I have kept Ruthie confined to the house, the yard the sidewalk for about a half a block up and down, across the street and the car. She has continued feeling fine. The pox have not "gratched" after the first couple days.

Love, Isabel

⤶

June 24, 1945 [handwritten]

Dear Papa,

My garden is coming along. Everything I told you about has come up. The weeds are under control. I cleared away some more space and planted four rows of beans. My radishes are almost ready to eat.

In my Klosé book I have just finished the first 12 weeks. I have a duet that myself and someone else might play for you over the record.

Betsy has started lessons on the flute from Mister Weinberg.

We are missing one of the boxes which you sent us for blocks.

I have decided on a plan for all my letter writing. Every Sunday will be my letter writing day. If you think this is not often enough, tell me and I will increase my letter writing to twice a week.

We have gone swimming 4 days in a row. I got a bad red sunburn which, however, turned into a beautiful tan except for my shoulders.

Do you think you will be home before November? I certainly hope so.

Your loving son, David A. Berman

↩

June 25, 1945

Since the above was written we have talked to you on the phone. What excitement! At eight the overseas operator called to ask me if I would accept a collect call from Major Berman at 12 PM eastern time. Of course I said I would. When I told David that poppa was going to call up, he cried. I said, "David, why are you crying?" "Because I am so happy," was the answer. I put the children to bed and assured them I would wake them up when the call came. First we drilled Ruthie on saying "Hello Poppa," "Goodbye Poppa." At eleven, our time, the operator called to say the call would be delayed. At 12:15 I was resting upstairs when the call came. I woke up David and rushed downstairs to answer the phone. Then I went back for Ruthie and Peter while Betsy and David talked to you. Ruthie was too sleepy to say anything. After you hung up, the operator called to tell me that the call took five minutes and would cost twenty dollars plus tax. But it was twenty dollars well spent. David tells me I told you to call again. I mean from New York, though, not from London. This morning each child took turns calling up favorite friends and relatives to tell them the news about the phone call.

Love, Isabel

↩

June 29, 1945

Dearest Reuben:

Our little white cat that we had last winter disappeared. We now have another cat. Every day for a week Betsy had gone across the street to 3517 Holmes and admired some baby kittens. Finally the lady gave her one. It is a little Tom cat. Betsy wanted to call it shining star and David wanted to call it Geronimo and Peter wanted to call it Star Journal, so they have compromised on plain Star.

Love, Isabel

◡

July 1, 1945 [*handwritten*]

Dear Reuben

I am terribly sorry I have not written to you about the phone call but you called right after I had written a letter to you and I had no more news. It was the best phone call I had ever received in my life. But please try to phone us very quickly again and make it be from N.Y.C. and another one from the Minneapolis train station. It was $20.00 for 5 mins. and very much worth it. By now practically everybody in town knows about it.

I have an idea. There is an art exhibit at the Walker Art Gallery drawn by Russian children. Many of the children that drew them are as old as I am. With Sonia, Aunt Madeleine's brother in Italy and a Russian boy I can have a writing club. I'm going to get more members from countries.

David

◡

July 4, 1945

Dearest Isabel,

Waw! Waw! I'm crying to go home. I got the pictures of David and Betsy from a birthday party in our house and the children have grown so nicely and they are so beautiful. I searched them again to see if I could find a trace of Sammy Hirsch Peter or Ruth Amelia but they weren't there. Such a wave of nostalgia hit me when I looked on the shining faces of David and Betsy—when I saw the background of the familiar corner of the dining room with the oak sideboard and cupboard—the curve of our beautiful table around which we used to have such wonderful family meals. I say a birthday party because I can't be sure which one it is. I count 9 candles on the cake. As I study the cake more carefully I see one candle is out and one is leaning over so it should be David's. But even more microscopic study shows "Betsy" on the cake so it's Betsy's happy birthday. The pictures bear the stamp of Morris Goldberg's artistry. Right?

I'm very restless. The period now is the most trying of all. We think our job is all but done and we want to go home.

It is easy to read in your letters how restless you are too. And how you miss your man. Well, let us hope that soon he will be home to provide and be provided with the necessary spiritual and physical relations conducive to a happy married life. I love you very much and the knowledge that you are home waiting for me has meant a lot in keeping up my spirits, yes I can say my courage, to face what little troubles we have had to endure.

Photography has become a great hobby with me here. I sent you two rather poorly posed shots of me. But note the wonderful clarity of the pictures. You can tell the time of day on my wrist watch in one. I'll have many more pictures to send you shortly.

Love again, Reuben

⌐

July 5, 1945

Dear Betsy,

Mommy sent me a picture of your birthday party and I liked it very much. In fact it was four pictures, two of you and two of David. But let's talk about the pictures of you. One showed you with your hand raised up like at school and the other showed you getting ready, I think to blow out the candles. The pictures were taken in our dining room and you and the room and the look of home about it make me quite homesick.

I want to tell you how much I liked your letter telling about how you teach Ruthie the ABCs. You know what letter I mean. The one that ends with "an alphabet of love for poppa." You write very good letters. I like to get your letters and the samples of your work that Momma sends every now and then.

Love, Poppa

Dear Sammy,

You must tell your momma that I was disappointed not to find you in the pictures that she sent me. I looked and looked for you. I searched the corners of the four pictures and looked for you in the reflection of the mirror. But no. No Sammy. & No Ruthie. I want to see both of you in the next set of pictures that comes.

Your letters in your own handwriting are what I like. I am glad that you are able to write so well. If I could write as well I wouldn't have to use pictures to [show] what I mean. [Sticks out like a sore thumb] my [hand]writing is so bad. Soon [I] hope to climb aboard an [airplane] or maybe a [boat] and I'm even ready to go home like this: [walking]. I want to go [home].

The [sun] is shining now. I'm going outside and take some pictures to send home.

Love, Poppa

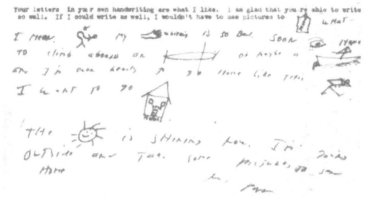

Reuben to Sammy, July 5, 1943

July 10, 1945

Dear Poppa:

I am taking flute lessons from your flute. I am taking flute lessons from Mr. Weinberg. Tomorrow will be my third lesson. Mr. Weinberg showed me how to clean the flute. Mr. Weinberg is the same Mr. Weinberg that teaches David. We both have our lessons at the same day and Mr. Weinberg gives us each fifteen minutes, then a rest and fifteen minutes more.

I can ride a bicycle, but I cannot ride boys' bicycles; I can only ride a girl's bicycle. The bicycle is colored blue. One time when I went out I got a flat tire. It took a long time for the gasoline man to fix it on account of every time they fixed it it got flat again but they got it. Another time when I went out the pedal got broken and it still is. But we can ride it.

Ruthie can say about a million words now. Sometimes she says to one of my dollies, "Go to sleep, stinky brat, dolly." But she says tinky instead of stinky and bwat instead of brat.

When Ruthie goes to the grocery store with Mommy they call her "Curly head." When Marlys and I (Marlys is one of my new friends that came here while you were away) play ball, Ruthie always wants the ball. When I take my piano lessons I ride down on the bus alone.

Miss Baker teaches me. I started last fall. I finished a lot of books since last fall.

A piano full of love, [Betsy]

Dearest Reuben:

Betsy has filled up a V mail and an eighth. She sometimes reads three books in a day. You can see her reading reflected in her style which is occasionally literary and involved.

I read the Watch birds to Peter. Do you remember the Foodfusser? It goes "This is a foodfusser who is much too old to be still sitting in a baby chair but it fussed about what it should eat so much that it doesn't eat anything new and it is so thin that it isn't strong enough to get up." Peter thought about that for a while and then said, "I'm not a food fusser. I can get up." David says Peter is just as funny as Jimmy Durante but he doesn't know it.

Peter said to me the other day, "When Poppa comes back, will we have another baby?" I said, "Would you like another baby?" "Oh yes," he answered, "I would like a pretty little girl." The other day we were at Maishie's, and I heard Lael say to Hilda, "Sammy is a jerk. He kissed Happy and me."

At Maishie's, Ruthie saw Boopsie sitting on the stairs. Boopsie was wearing a shirt and sucking on a thumb and blanket combination. Ruthie looked at Boopsie, beamed and said, "Can I kiss him?" I said, "Yes," and she kissed him. Boopsie does not mind having Ruthie kiss him when Hilda is not around but when Hilda is there he yips and runs to her for protection.

David is taking the summer reading course and has already passed the finish line. He reads only non-fiction, preferably biography. He did not particularly enjoy the Life of Emerson.

Love, Isabel

July 11, 1945 [*handwritten*]

Dear Papa:

Grandma Sarah is coming to Minneapolis tomorrow. We think she will stay at our house.

Sonia Edelman says she thinks she will come to the U.S. to visit her cousins. She might come to Minneapolis.

Ruthy is so funny. It used to be that she would love baby boys, but once one of them pushed her. Now she beats up the baby boys. Once I got a bobber. Ruthy took it away and said that's mine. Once I had a magazine and I let Ruthy carry it. But then she wouldn't bring it into the house. So I took it away from her. She came into the house and said, quote "Momma, David taked away mine magazine." end quote.

I had my picture taken at Powers [*Department Store*]. There are 12 proofs of them. Everybody likes number 6. In it I am smiling.

Your loving son, David A. Berman

↜

July 12, 1945

Dearest Reuben:

Here is a poem that David wrote:

My family
My family is fairly large, 6 to be exact
I love every one of them and that is a fact.
First there is my father, big, strong, and bold
He's an officer in the army, that can proudly be told
Then there's my mother, beautiful and sweet
She always keeps our house looking prim and neat.
Then there's my sister Betsy, reading books all day
But when she sees handsome boys she gets into a fray.
Next comes brother Sammy very thin and frail
But when someone gets him mad he lets out with a wail.

Last is baby sister Ruthy, she is very dear
She's the best baby of them all. Do you hear?

David Berman

The last two lines were originally written to read
    Last is baby sister Ruthy, she is only two
    But when she goes to the bathroom, O.P.U.

Love, Isabel

⌐

July 18, 1945

Dearest Reuben:

Today I received your air mail letter of July 6 with the bilingual menu enclosed. If I were you I'd go easy on the kartoffel and brat.

I did not give David your message about not wishing to be called Reuben. If he wants to call you Reuben you should be flattered. Your momma's contemporaries might have been shocked to hear you call her Sarah but our contemporaries will not be shocked to hear David call you Reuben.

Yesterday was Peter's birthday party. I had planned a picnic but the weather was too uncertain for an outdoor party. The guests and presents were as follows: Sam and Anna Rush, one dollar; Sally Simon, one dollar; Betty Tweed, twenty-five cents; Marlys Miller, fifty cents; Jerry Miller, twenty-five cents and some games; Uncle Dave Berman, one dollar and twenty-five cents; Isabel Berman, two dollars; Diane McFarlane, one dollar; Stevie Goldberg, suspenders; Buddy Silverman, polo shirt and stockings; Teddy Pass, Parchesi; Judy Erickson, a beautiful book on bird migrations with pictures by Weber; Auntie Sylvia, a nice book; David, a book about the bunny with the magic nose with pictures you can feel; Betsy, a book about a kitten; Happy Berman, a game; Lael Berman, ten dime war stamps. I'm not sure whether Sam and Anna gave Peter a separate present or whether Sally's present included theirs. Anyhow, what with some

saved up allowance and the $1.25 from Dave and Rosie, Peter had
$10.75. He had me take away all his one dollar bills and give him a
ten dollar bill. David and Betsy were consumed with envy. David
said, "Peter, can I see the ten dollar bill." Peter was all set to buy a
bowling set for $6.50 but I told him that maybe after the war he
could get a rubber boat with the money so he is saving it for a while.

The games were spin the bottle, drop the clothespin in the bottle,
and going to Jerusalem. Betsy played the piano for going to
Jerusalem. She played Climbing, Gavotte, and some etudes with
great fluency and grace but she threw the game off when she tried to
play a new piece she didn't know very well. Every time she stopped
to figure out a note the children started to sit down. The refreshments included weiners, buns, carrot sticks, milk, hamantaschen
(that by special request), and birthday cake. The cake was from
Egequist. I had made one which was as bad as one I made for you in
Cussen some years ago.

Anna Rush is going to write you this but Peter's birthday wish was
for the war to be over and Poppa to come home.

Love, Isabel

⤸

July 20, 1945 [handwritten]

Dear Papa:

Rosalind Rush [Simon] took Betsy, Sammy, and me to see the
Aquatenniel parade [in Minneapolis]. All of the floats were very
beautiful. There were also men of the Minnesota State Guard and
many different bands.

Here is a bit of advice: Next time you visit the coast see if you can
get a ride home or better yet go to an airfield and get a plane ride
home.

We are sending you a picture of Ruthy. And I think you could get
her the title of pinup girl of your outfit if you'd try. I wish you would.

Lincoln has been promoted to a Lieutenant Colonel. Why in the

world is it that in the army the men that work the hardest get promoted the least and get sent home the last?

Your loving son, David A. Berman

↬

July 28, 1945

Dear David,

Mommy sent me your poem about the family. I think it is a very
beautiful poem and I intend to save it. Me, my rhymes aren't worth
dimes. My thoughts run to prose you see but never never into
poetry.

I wish you could meet your cousins in England. Someday we are
going to take a trip there and you will come along.

Love, Poppa

↬

August 6, 1945

Dear David,

I am sorry that I didn't hear about your decision to go to camp
until it was too late to write to Hinckle dinckle [*Hinckley*]. I remember when I was at camp (the Minneapolis Boy Scout Camp at Lake
Minnetonka) how I liked to get mail. Anyway I'm writing now and I
am going to write about camping.

I used to do a lot of camping. When I was 11 I went to a Jewish
camp run by some Minneapolis outfit. It was at Minnetonka across
the lake from the boy scout camp. It was pretty rough. My cousin
Ted Berman was in charge. He was pretty young to run a camp but
he ran it. We ate three meals a day most of the time. The program
consisted of swimming, eating, and sleeping.

The following year, let me see, that was 25 years ago, I went to the

Boy Scout camp. I didn't have a very good time. We drew lots to see what tent we were to sleep in and I drew Ellis Harris. Ellis was very big and pretty good company.

When I was thirteen I went again to the camp and this time I had a wonderful time. Two of my tent mates were Hymie and Nathan Berman. Our tent was called the best thirteen days out of fourteen. That year I went on a canoe trip to Northern Minnesota. Or was it that year? I know that after the canoe trip I went on a voyage on Lake Superior that I was very sea sick on and ended with my story where Bill saw me and said, "But poppa, how thin you are."

Now in the army I've had all I want of camping. As I wrote to Momma I never want to go on a picnic again. And I must whisper to you that the first picnic she suggests to go on with you and the other children, I'll grumble a bit outside, and inside I'll be tickled to death to go. Because it will always be a pleasure for me to go on picnics with my family. Remember how we used to go out to Lake Harriet and fry hamburgers? I guess I am getting to sound like Uncle Arnold now. He is always the one to reminisce.

David, I got me a brook trout pole and we are going fishing most every evening now. And I think before many weeks I'll catch a fish. So far we have just gone fishing. We haven't caught anything.

Enough for now. I'm looking forward to seeing you in not too many weeks. Be a good boy. Thanks for the letter, and write often.

Love, Poppa

⌐

August 8, 1945

Dearest Isabel,

It has been raining so much here that I haven't much chance to use my newly acquired fishing tackle. There are some wonderful trout streams in the neighborhood. Some of the men have brought home as many as thirty trout in one afternoon. So far for me two expeditions but not a nibble. If the weather clears this evening I'll probably go out again.

Everybody is buzzing about the new atomic bomb. I'd like to know the chemical reaction that results in the release of so much energy. And I wonder why it is called the atomic bomb. I could give my conjecture of the nature of the reaction but again that is an item to be censored. I might be right! The bomb should do its share in shortening the Japanese war. If we can produce them fast enough its effect will be that of multiplying the airforce by 1000.

It doesn't take much foresight now to predict that if we have another war every major city of both sides will be destroyed. And the destruction we have seen in Germany—so bad that many observers suggest abandoning many large cities here—is only moderate compared to the destructive possibilities of the new bomb. The Germans were able to aim projectiles accurately enough to strike their urban targets from a launching point over two hundred miles away. I do not doubt that projectiles could be sent from Europe to the United States though perhaps with no effective accuracy. It is not difficult to figure out a way to correct deviations of course in the trajectory of such a bomb. All in all if we are not to see the complete annihilation of modern civilization we must prevent further warfare.

The last letters you wrote told about getting David ready overnight for camp. I think it is a good thing for him. He is an independent boy, but he has never been away from you for more than a few days. Except the one time I took him on the trip to Minneapolis from Texas. Lovely trip. I don't understand what you mean when you say he is restless.

I love your stories of the children at the restaurants. I can just picture Sammy walking down the counter at the Forum. They always loved cafeterias but I'm not so sure that we wouldn't be smarter to confine our eating out to restaurants where the food is ordered off a menu instead of super counters.

Are you writing frequently? I don't want you to quit because my orders to go home may come anytime. I hope soon.

Love, Reuben

August 26, 1945

Dearest Isabel,

They keep talking about all the 85 pointers and up going home before Christmas but so far I have seen no orders. Don't think that I am pessimistic however. I still am sure of being home by Oct 31.

I got a very nicely printed letter from Betsy. She wrote about the VJ cellebration. I follow Betsy's spelling of cellebrated.

Love, Reuben

September 18, 1945

Dearest Reuben:

It seems to me you should be on your way home by now. The last letter I have from you is dated September 5. It is a little hard to write when I have no letter to answer.

David came home from school yesterday all thrilled and pink cheeked because he had played so well in the clarinet try out. He had been sitting in the last stand of the third clarinet section. Now he hoped to be put up to the second stand. Today he found he was in the seventh stand. But still it is an improvement.

Sylvia took David to children's services at the Temple. He looked very beautiful in his light brown wool suit.

Martha told Betsy that if she would practice an hour a day for thirty days she could play for Mr. MacPhail. Betsy arranged to do it for three twenty minute periods. Betsy is willing to practice but she would rather read books.

Last night Sam and Anna Rush came over with some ice cream. Sam sat down to read the paper. Peter was insulted because Sam was paying no attention to him. Finally Peter got a tomato from the ice box and squeezed the tomato on Sam's coat. This got quite a rise. A little later he tried it again. Then he put his leather jacket on Sam's head. Finally Sam wrapped Peter up very tightly in the jacket. Peter was angry. He said, "Sam Rush, I hate you. I do not want to see you again. I am lonesome for my poppa, not for you." Sam told him he wouldn't be angry when they went to Excelsior together. The next day Peter telephoned for and got two sacks of paper from Sam.

Love, Isabel

⌐

September 17, 1945

Dearest Isabel,

This is the letter you have been waiting for. My orders are not so dramatic as to say that I am to proceed without delay to my wife and children in Minneapolis. But they do say that I am to go to LeHavre, thence to England, thence home.

It's been a terrific day. First the personnel officer called me to ask whether I was familiar with the contents of General Order number 99. That was the order awarding me the Bronze star. Five minutes later he called again and asked me to join the colonel in a conference to decide what to do about the medical officers. When I got to the conference it seems that there were vacancies for a number of medical officers to go home and whom should be picked. "Me," I said, and me it was. So I dashed home, packed up, and tomorrow I leave by air for LeHavre. The rest of the journey will be tough—boats trains ships. No more quick air travel.

I celebrated my last afternoon here by taking up a Cub for my final fling at free pilot time. Before supper I got suitably drunk and now I am writing my last letter to you from Germany.

When will I be home? This is my expected itinerary: Leave Kaufbeuren and arrive LeHavre 18 Sept. Leave LeHavre 21 Sept and arrive Liverpool 25 September. Leave Liverpool 1 October and arrive N.Y. 8 October. Leave N.Y. 11 October for Minneapolis and arrive on the 12th. Add two weeks to that and I should safely estimate that I will be home before the end of the month.

I decided at the last minute to send most of my worldly goods by

Reuben Berman, about 1948

parcel post. So expect a foot locker and two boxes filled with nothing but useless clothes. I couldn't leave them. Who knows? I may need them again!

These are my plans including the first two weeks in November. First I want to get reacquainted with my family. I must be in San Francisco on 11 November to take the State Board Oral examination. Would you like to come to California with me? Could we get anyone to stay with the children the two weeks we would be away? Beyond that I have no plans. Further plans await our discussion together at home.

If I were flying I could be home within a week. But I don't care. I'm happy now. I'm going home.

I love you.

Reuben

Postlude

And What Became of Them

RUTH BERMAN

Reuben returned to medical practice in Minneapolis, having suc-
cumbed to the family's opposition to moving to Sacramento. He
gave up smoking cigars, considering it a bad example for the children. He and Isabel had a fifth child (their third son, Theodore, born
in 1948) and then a sixth (third daughter, Jean, in 1951). After Jean
started nursery school, Isabel resumed part-time work as a child psy-
chologist, acting as an examiner for the public schools.

The family got their long-awaited dog after the war, Colonel, a
mixture of (probably) Labrador and spaniel. Her successor was Pixie,
a cocker spaniel, and she was followed by a line of cats.

In 1948, expecting Teddy, the family sold the house on Holmes
Avenue near Lake Calhoun and moved to a larger house, located
across the park from Lake Nokomis. This remained the family house
for almost forty years, until 1985. Isabel then was using a wheelchair
because an operation to remove a meningioma the year before had
resulted in left-side paralysis, and she and Reuben bought a smaller
house on the western edge of town near St. Louis Park. She died of
cancer in 1989.

David, Sam, and Ted grew up to become physicians, and they and
their wives, Maggie, MaryEllen, and Cheryl, live in Minneapolis.
Sam served as a doctor in the navy during the Vietnam War and
again during the Gulf War. As an adult, he continued to be fascinated by airplanes. In college he earned a pilot's license and has been
flying regularly ever since. Betsy became a mathematician; she and
her husband, Bradley Appelbaum, live in Kansas City, Kansas. Ruth
lives in Minneapolis and is a word processor and writer. Jean has

worked in city planning and the florist business and is currently a full-time homemaker. She and her husband, David Sogin, live in Chicago.

Music has continued to be a strong family interest. David on the clarinet and Betsy on the flute are the most active. Reuben fell in love with the bass clef and switched from clarinet to the bassoon in retirement. The grandchildren have been leaning to strings more than winds.

The family continues to be close-knit, both the immediate family and the extended Bermans, in-laws, and in-laws' in-laws. In 1992, 170 members of the extended Berman family and kinfolk gathered for a party to celebrate one hundred years in America. The fiftieth anniversary of D-Day in 1994 prompted some of the grandchildren to ask Reuben about his wartime experiences, and that led back to the long-stored V-mail letters—and this book.

Epilogue

The Warrior

REUBEN BERMAN

⌒

"Reuben Berman, Captain USA-Med Res, Greetings" was the salutation on a letter I received in my office in the Medical Arts Building in downtown Minneapolis on the morning of July 1, 1941. The letter continued "you are to report to the CO, Kelly Field, Texas, August 1 1941" and was signed "Franklin D. Roosevelt." A moment later the phone rang. A patient yelled, "Whadya mean charging me ten bucks! What did you do for ten dollars?" My response was immediate and quite clear: "You'll pay the ten dollars, you son of a bitch, or I'll sue you!" The very instant I received that letter I resigned from private practice!

So we shipped a houseful of furniture, including an Everett upright piano, to San Antonio, and that is where we lived until the summer of 1942. Isabel, David, Betsy, Sammy, and I occupied a four-bedroom house at 442 Thelma Drive. Every day Isabel drove northeast to Randolph Field where she was employed as a statistician. And I headed southwest by car or bicycle to Kelly Field.

Both of us working and three small children at home meant hiring a crew of two: a cook doubling as first-floor maid and an upstairs maid. If you understand the southern division of labor you will know the staircase never got cleaned.

I was in charge of a medical processing unit that started Air Corps cadets on their flight-training program. With four or five doctors we examined two to three hundred candidates a day five days a week.

On December 7, 1941, I was fiddling with my radio trying to pick up the Sunday New York Philharmonic concert. Every station was carrying news. Finally I listened to the news. Many people can remember such a tiny detail when a momentous change occurs in their lives. It was war with Japan that day and against Germany a few days later.

In June 1942 I was transferred to Fort Knox, and my entourage—wife, children, household furniture, and piano—went to Louisville, Kentucky. I got my private license to fly single-engine airplanes at Bowman Field. I took a lesson or two a week and got in some flying time with the army at Godman Field, the small air station at Knox. I thought that since I was going to serve as a flight surgeon I should know something about flying.

At Godman one day the CO called me in to say one of his junior flying officers told him he had lost his ability to fly and what should we do about that. I volunteered to go up with him. We took off in a B-26, a twin-engine bomber known as the "widowmaker." He made a nice takeoff, and at one thousand feet he said, "Doctor, you have it." I flew cautiously around the patch, and after a few minutes I said, "OK, you land it now." "But I don't know how to fly an airplane," he responded. "You'll have to land it!" I knew enough to fly a good downwind-and-base approach, and there I was on final approach coming down at six hundred feet per minute. "Don't you think you are little high, maybe you should cut the power a bit," he said. "Isn't this a good time to raise the yoke," and so on. We made a fine landing—wheels down, my hands, his advice. That ended his flying career, and I suppose almost ended mine.

Ruth was born at Louisville Jewish Hospital on November 15, 1942. Isabel was in the hospital, our two maids had the home situation and three children well in hand, and about November 22 I flew on a training mission to MacDill Field, Tampa, Florida, in the morning, the plan being to fly back to Godman in the afternoon. But at MacDill, when the pilot tested his magnetos, one was not functioning. The mechanic said it would take a few minutes to check the wiring, and we would be on our way. It took a week to repair the wiring system. We stayed with the airplane, expecting it to be ready any minute.

Isabel came home by ambulance, was carried into the house, and promptly got up and took care of the mothering business. Ruth was premature and remained in the hospital a few weeks. I am sure Isabel never forgot that week, but as always she forgave.

Our third and last station in the U.S. was MacDill. We rented a house in St. Petersburg. So in all we rented three houses, and we could have bought them all for twenty thousand dollars. It was not my first mistake, nor the last.

On June 23, 1943, I sailed out of New York for England on the converted cruise ship *Mariposa*. We were not in convoy. Fast cruise ships could outrun the German submarines. We landed at Liverpool and were met in the rain by a brave, English brass band. I stopped briefly at High Wycombe to check in with the Eighth Air Force Bomber command and was assigned to the Second Air Division, stationed at Norwich. This is a bleak town in Norfolk on the North Sea. We were visited nightly by German raiders, who were aiming usually for London. Later came the awful V-1s, our introduction to turbine flying engines. A V-1 is a long tube like a submarine torpedo and is surmounted by an engine nacelle. It flies at an altitude of about five hundred feet. Things get interesting when the "chug chug" sound of the engine abruptly ceases. That's when you dive for shelter because the explosion is only seconds away.

That winter I was reassigned to an intelligence unit probably because I entered "reads, speaks, understands German" on my 201 file. The winter of 1943–44 I was stationed at a British Royal Air Force field south of Loch Neigh, about twenty miles (two hours by slow train) out of Belfast. It was a pleasant town; we had no inkling of the civil war to follow.

From spring of 1944 through D-Day and into 1945 I was stationed in and around London. We were targets for the amazing V-2 bomb. Unlike the primitive V-1s, these were ultra-high, ultra-fast weapons whose only warning was the bright flash of the explosion. They could not be heard before arrival because they traveled faster than sound; then came the sonic boom and a shower of debris. One flashed high over my head in London, and I took cover in the nearest metal shelter, which was a garbage can.

For a fortnight I was assigned to a German-language class in a mansion off Regent's Park. I made a classic gaffe in that course when the instructor said that German for officer was *beamte*. I raised my hand to explain that that word was the office; the officer was a *beamter*. I understand this created a sensation in London circles as the teacher I presumed to correct was the outstanding German interpreter in England.

Visitors to England should be aware that there are two kinds of Englishmen: those who tolerate us and those who hate us. The universal complaint about Americans was that we were oversexed, overpaid, and over here.

I found I had a cousin practicing medicine in London, Dr. Joe Naftalin, and I became a frequent guest at his flat near Regent's Park. Joe, his wife, Leonore, and I were a trio at various London night spots. And our friendship continues to this day. Several Jewish holidays found me a visitor to other members of the Naftalin family living in Glasgow, Scotland.

The ground war began for me in March 1945 when we landed in France. My assignment was to investigate Luftwaffe medical research installations in France and Germany. It was a peculiar task. I left my unit and followed General George S. Patton across France and into Germany, traveling in a liberated Opel car, just me and my driver, behind the divisions but ahead of corps headquarters. I think we were spending the night at Ulm when the BBC announced, "Munich has fallen." Munich was one of my assigned targets, and I was supposed to see what was going on there after the fall but before the looting, meaning the same day or the day after the capture. As we drove along the Autobahn, my driver said, "I hear cannon fire."

I explained that cannon fire was audible for hundreds of miles and did not mean a thing. An hour later, he said, "I hear machine guns," and shortly thereafter the spitting noise of rifle fire. We turned around and went back to Ulm. The BBC was wrong. Munich was putting up stiff resistance. Three days later we rolled into Munich. There I visited a German military hospital and found they were "experimenting" on American prisoners. One American with a fractured hip was treated with (horrors) a huge iron spike across the fracture. That was my introduction to hip nailing.

I went to Dachau a few kilometers north of Munich three weeks after it was liberated by American troops—the dead still piled like cordwood and thousands of emaciated prisoners, many of whom died in the next few days. I visited the barracks where a typical bunk had three tiers, three men to each tier, nine men total on each. The "shower room," which was a gas chamber, and the ovens I have seen with my own eyes, and no one needs to tell me they existed. My secret report to the army complete with pictures of this atrocity is on file at the Minnesota Historical Society.

Tegernsee is a small town thirty kilometers south of Munich. There Hitler planned his final resistance. It was also the site of a huge Luftwaffe medical plant that I was to visit. Driving down we passed convoys of trucks jammed with German prisoners. Typically there would be a German driver, an American corporal in the front vehicle, and a sergeant in the rear—two American soldiers guarding about a thousand Germans. In early May 1945 the German soldiers desperately wanted to surrender to an American, if possible, otherwise to British or French forces and for God's sake not to a Russian.

When I passed a sign reading "Division headquarters" along the road near the town, I should have stopped. I was now ahead of the fighting army. But there was my target—a huge wooden structure, and I walked into it. It was dark, the power was off, and I bumped into a person. "Excuse me," say I. "Bitte," says he! Then this conversation: "Sind sie Deutch?" "Ja." "Soldat?" "Jawohl!" "Kriegsgefangene?" (Prisoner of war). "Nein! Sie sind der erste Americaner." I ordered him to evacuate the building and line up outside. In a few moments I was facing two lieutenants followed by two ranks of twenty-seven enlisted men. Then came a major running out of the building to the front of the troops where he saluted me. I captured fifty-seven Germans in all. I spoke to them—in German. My fractured German was mostly Yiddish, but nobody laughed, and I am sure they understood me very well. Like everyone else I met, they knew nothing of Dachau, and of course none of them was a Nazi. In fact I did not meet a single (admitted) Nazi then or ever.

It was a silly act of bravado, but I was convinced there was no fight left in them. The result proved I was right logically although I could have been fatally wrong practically.

I was in the service five years and in the ETO half that time. When I returned home, I wanted to get a California license to practice medicine. I appeared before the licensing board in my uniform. They asked me one question: What did I know about typhus fever? I said I had seen some seven hundred cases in Dachau a few months before. That ended the examination, and I got the license I was destined never to use.

Genealogy

GENEALOGY

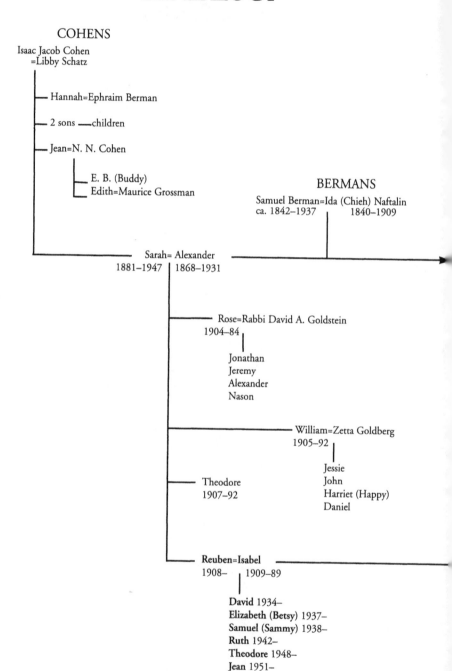

COHENS

Isaac Jacob Cohen
=Libby Schatz

— Hannah=Ephraim Berman

— 2 sons —children

— Jean=N. N. Cohen

— E. B. (Buddy)
— Edith=Maurice Grossman

BERMANS

Samuel Berman=Ida (Chieh) Naftalin
ca. 1842–1937   1840–1909

Sarah= Alexander
1881–1947 | 1868–1931

Rose=Rabbi David A. Goldstein
1904–84

Jonathan
Jeremy
Alexander
Nason

William=Zetta Goldberg
1905–92

Jessie
Theodore   John
1907–92   Harriet (Happy)
                  Daniel

Reuben=Isabel
1908– | 1909–89

David 1934–
Elizabeth (Betsy) 1937–
Samuel (Sammy) 1938–
Ruth 1942–
Theodore 1948–
Jean 1951–

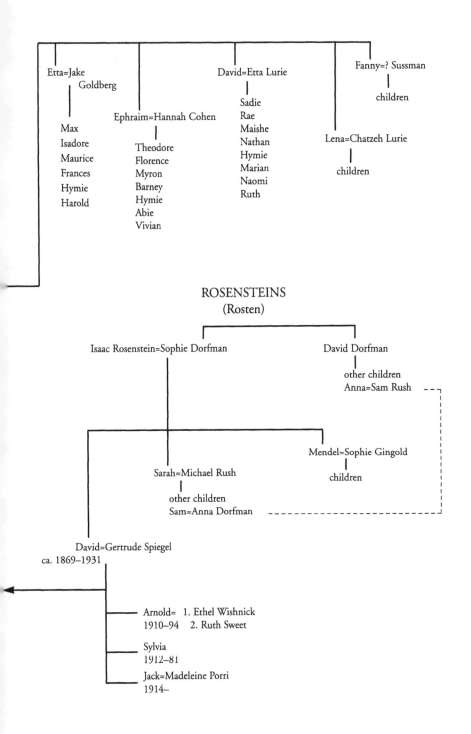

Etta=Jake
     Goldberg

David=Etta Lurie

Fanny=? Sussman

|

children

Max
Isadore
Maurice
Frances
Hymie
Harold

Ephraim=Hannah Cohen

|

Theodore
Florence
Myron
Barney
Hymie
Abie
Vivian

Sadie
Rae
Maishe
Nathan
Hymie
Marian
Naomi
Ruth

Lena=Chatzeh Lurie

|

children

ROSENSTEINS
(Rosten)

Isaac Rosenstein=Sophie Dorfman

David Dorfman

other children
Anna=Sam Rush

Sarah=Michael Rush

|

other children
Sam=Anna Dorfman

Mendel=Sophie Gingold

|

children

David=Gertrude Spiegel
ca. 1869–1931

Arnold= 1. Ethel Wishnick
1910–94   2. Ruth Sweet

Sylvia
1912–81

Jack=Madeleine Porri
1914–

www.ingramcontent.com/pod-product-compliance
Lightning Source LLC
Jackson TN
JSHW020014141224
75386JS00025B/525